The senses in early modern England, 1558–1660

Manchester University Press

The senses in early modern England, 1558–1660

edited by

SIMON SMITH, JACKIE WATSON

and AMY KENNY

Manchester University Press

Published by Manchester University Press
Altrincham Street, Manchester M1 7JA
www.manchesteruniversitypress.co.uk

British Library Cataloguing-in-Publication Data
A catalogue record for this book is available from the British Library

Library of Congress Cataloging-in-Publication Data applied for

ISBN 978 07190 9158 2 *hardback*

First published 2015

Typeset in Ehrhardt by
Koinonia, Manchester
Printed and bound in Great Britain by
TJ International Ltd, Padstow

Contents

Part III Aesthetic sensory experiences

Illustrations

Contributors

Hannah August holds a PhD from the London Shakespeare Centre at King's College London, and has taught at King's, at the universities of Otago and Victoria in New Zealand, and for Globe Education at Shakespeare's Globe. Her research interests include the history of reading and early modern drama in print and performance. She works as a writer, reviewer and researcher in Wellington, New Zealand.

Eleanor Decamp completed her DPhil in English Literature at the University of Oxford. Her thesis was runner up in the Shakespeare Association of America's J. Leeds Barroll Dissertation Prize 2013. She is preparing a monograph with Palgrave Macmillan on barber-surgery and early modern English Literature, and is co-editing and completing a chapter for a collection on medieval and early modern theories of blood. As joint coordinator of *The Blood Project*, a medical humanities venture, she co-convened an international conference at Oxford on the competing perceptions of blood between the fourteenth and seventeenth centuries, which included a production of *The Croxton Play of the Sacrament* (www.thebloodproject.net). Eleanor's interdisciplinary research interests include medicine and literature, early modern stagecraft, popular and material cultures in the period, and the London guilds.

Holly Dugan is Associate Professor of English at the George Washington University, Washington DC. Her research focuses on gender, sexuality and material culture in early modern England. She is the author of *The Ephemeral History of Perfume: Scent and Sense in Early Modern England* (Johns Hopkins University Press, 2011) and co-editor, with Lara Farina, of *The Intimate Senses*, a special issue of *Postmedieval*.

Natalie K. Eschenbaum holds a PhD in English from Emory University, Georgia, USA. She is Associate Professor of English at the University of Wisconsin – La Crosse, where she teaches writing, Shakespeare and the English Renaissance. Her current research focuses on expressions of sensation and the affect of disgust in seventeenth-century literature. She is co-editing (with Barbara Correll) *Disgust in Early Modern English Literature*, which includes a co-authored introduction and her essay, 'Desiring Disgust in Robert Herrick's Epigrams' (forthcoming from Ashgate).

Aurélie Griffin is Lecturer in English Literature at Université Jean Monnet, Saint-Etienne. She is the author of a dissertation entitled 'The Countess of Montgomeries Urania de Lady Mary Wroth: une poétique de la mélancolie', to be published by Classiques Garnier, and of several articles on Lady Mary Wroth and Sir Philip Sidney. In 2013, her dissertation was awarded premier prix de thèse de l'Institut du Genre, CNRS.

Farah Karim-Cooper is Head of Higher Education and Research at Globe Education, Shakespeare's Globe, and Visiting Research Fellow of King's College London. Recently, she led the research and co-managed the design and construction of the Sam Wanamaker Playhouse (the Globe's new indoor Jacobean theatre). She is author of *Cosmetics in Shakespearean and Renaissance Drama* (Edinburgh University Press, 2006); co-editor with Christie Carson of *Shakespeare's Globe: A Theatrical Experiment* (Cambridge University Press, 2008); co-editor with Tiffany Stern of *Shakespeare's Theatres and the Effects of Performance* (Arden/Bloomsbury, 2013); co-editor with Andrew Gurr of *Moving Shakespeare Indoors: Performance and Repertoire in the Jacobean Playhouse* (Cambridge University Press, 2014); and author of the forthcoming *The Hand on the Shakespearean Stage: Gesture, Touch and the Spectacle of Dismemberment* (Arden/Bloomsbury).

Amy Kenny holds a PhD in Early Modern Literature and Culture from the University of Sussex for her thesis on Shakespeare's representation of the family. She has dramaturged for 15 productions at Shakespeare's Globe and conducted over 80 interviews with actors and directors there on architecture, audiences and performance. She has lectured at King's College London, the University of Sussex, Shakespeare's Globe, the University of Concordia and Biola University, and has published on dramaturgy and women in early modern England. She is currently Lecturer at University of California, Riverside.

Lucy Munro is Lecturer in Shakespeare and Early Modern Drama at King's College London. She is the author of *Children of the Queen's Revels: A Jacobean Theatre Repertory* (Cambridge University Press, 2005) and *Archaic Style in English Literature, 1590–1674* (Cambridge University Press, 2013), and the editor of plays by Sharpham, Shakespeare and Wilkins, Brome and Fletcher. She is currently editing *The Witch of Edmonton* for Arden Early Modern Drama. Her previous research on topics connected with the senses has appeared in essays on music and sound for *The Oxford Handbook of Early Modern Theatre*, ed. Richard Dutton (Oxford University Press, 2009) and stage blood and body parts for *Shakespeare's Theatres and the Effects of Performance*, ed. Farah Karim-Cooper and Tiffany Stern (Arden/Bloomsbury, 2013).

Darren Royston is Artistic Director of Nonsuch History and Dance, and Tutor in Dance and Movement at the Royal Academy of Dramatic Art, London. He works as a choreographer and dance consultant, including with the National Theatre, Royal Shakespeare Company and Old Vic in the UK, and with Universidad Pablo de Olavide in Seville. He appeared as Dancing Master on the BBC4 dance history programme 'Dancing Cheek to Cheek' (2014). He is author of *Dramatic Dance: An Actor's Approach to Dance as a Dramatic Art* (Bloomsbury Methuen Drama, 2014).

Simon Smith is Leverhulme Early Career Fellow in the Faculty of English, University of Oxford and Junior Research Fellow of The Queen's College, Oxford. He has taught for the University of London at Birkbeck and at the Royal Central School of Speech and Drama. At Shakespeare's Globe he is Early Modern Music Research Associate, where he has provided historical music research for productions of plays by Shakespeare and his contemporaries. He has recently completed articles on early modern playhouse music for *Shakespeare Survey* and *Zeitsprünge*, and his monograph, *Musical Response in the Early Modern Playhouse, 1603–1625*, is in preparation.

Faye Tudor completed her PhD at the University of Strathclyde. Her research interests include mirroring in Renaissance literature and art, and the intersection of science, technology and literature in the early modern period. She has edited the journal *Ecloga*, presented at conferences in the UK, US and Canada, and has published on the topic of mirrors and vision in *Renaissance Theories of Vision*, edited by John Shannon Hendrix and Charles H. Carman (Ashgate, 2010).

Jackie Watson holds a PhD from Birkbeck, University of London, where she has also been an Associate Tutor. She has published on the early modern Inns of Court and is currently working on a collection focused on the Middle Temple in the 1590s. Further research interests include courtiership, homosociality, diplomatic and courtly letters and early modern playing space. She is an occasional reviewer for the *Times Literary Supplement* and Head of Sixth Form at a school in Oxford.

Susan Wiseman teaches Renaissance and seventeenth-century literature at Birkbeck, University of London. She is the author of *Writing Metamorphosis in the English Renaissance* (Cambridge University Press, 2014).

Note on the text

Quotations from pre-1700 texts preserve original spelling and punctuation, including u/v and i/j usage. All printed material pre-1700 is published in London, unless explicitly stated otherwise. Where the name of an early modern playing company and a date appear after the title of a play (e.g. *The Revenger's Tragedy* (King's Men, *c.* 1606)), these indicate the date and company of first performance.

Shakespearean references and quotations follow the most recent edition of The Oxford Shakespeare, including spelling and punctuation, unless otherwise stated (William Shakespeare, *The Complete Works*, gen. eds Stanley Wells and Gary Taylor, 2nd edn (Oxford: Clarendon Press, 2005)).

Acknowledgements

The editors of this book first began thinking together about the senses when organizing a conference on 'The Senses in Early Modern England', co-hosted by Shakespeare's Globe and the London Renaissance Seminar in October 2011. We are enormously grateful for the support of Shakespeare's Globe, the London Renaissance Seminar and the Department of English and Humanities at Birkbeck, University of London that made this event possible. The rich input from both speakers and audience members at the conference encouraged us to create this collection in the first place. Both this event, and Farah Karim-Cooper's conference on 'Shakespeare and the Senses' held at the Globe during the same season, brought us into contact with many of the scholars whose contributions we are so pleased to bring together in this volume.

As the project has progressed, we have had the pleasure of working with a slew of supportive and enthusiastic people. Matthew Frost at Manchester University Press has supported us through the editorial process with generosity and good humour. Our anonymous readers provided shrewd and erudite suggestions that vastly improved many aspects of the collection. Sue Wiseman at Birkbeck has been tremendously helpful right from the beginning; her encouragement and support in a number of capacities has been extraordinary. Finally, we would like to express our gratitude to all of the contributors to this volume. We feel very fortunate to have such a richness of perspectives on the senses represented in these chapters, and to have such engaging and inspiring material to include.

Introduction

Simon Smith, Jackie Watson and Amy Kenny

What can texts, performances and artworks tell us about the senses in early modern England? The sensory experiences of subjects living some four centuries ago are to some degree lost. We cannot hope to recreate the experiences of hearing, smelling and feeling the interior environment of a church at a service in the 1590s, or seeing, touching and tasting the River Thames on a boat journey in the 1640s. Today, we might encounter early modern culture through language, sight and touch, mediated by written texts, images, artefacts and architecture of the period. Early modern works of performative art such as theatre, music and dance are remade in new performances, generating new sensory encounters, but the sensory experiences of early modern performance are ephemeral, and long past.

Yet even while we cannot recreate early modern sensory experience, works of art from the period are often highly suggestive about the senses. Despite the ephemerality of sensation, artworks in forms as diverse as poetry, painting, music, drama, domestic objects and dance often preserve examinations of the senses, representations of sensory encounters, and even accounts of the sensory experiences that articulated everyday life for early modern subjects. This suggests a useful relationship of mutual elucidation between works of art and wider culture: not only can a clearer picture of early modern thinking about the senses clarify our understanding of particular artworks, but in turn, the ideas about sensory experience suggested in these artworks might illuminate wider early modern understandings of the senses. Our investigation aims at precisely this mutual illumination of early modern culture and works of art.

This collection's intention to explore both works of art and wider culture in early modern England is best illustrated by examining one specific artwork from several angles. Figure 1 offers an apt subject for this interrogation: a woodcut illustration depicting four figures seated in a relatively bare room, with a similarly economical landscape of rolling hills visible through a window in the background. Both smell and taste seem to be absent from this scene. Visual experience, however, is foregrounded substantially. The adult figures depicted on either side of the room look pointedly into one another's faces; the

1 Frontispiece illustration from *Tenor of the whole psalmes in foure partes* (1563)

child to the left of his mother looks across at his smaller brother with apparent suspicion; in turn, this smaller brother looks amusedly at his father, perhaps focusing his gaze on the father's hands. Touch is similarly emphasized: two children each hold an object in one hand – a book and a hobby-horse respectively – while seemingly clasping their mother with the other; meanwhile, the father touches his right thumb with his left forefinger. There is no clear manifestation of sound, or of hearing, to be seen.

It might surprise us, then, to learn that this image is a representation of domestic, devotional singing.[1] It appears in an early Elizabethan edition of psalm settings published as four part-books, 'set forth for the encrease of vertue: and abolishyng of other vayne and triflyng ballades'.[2] When encountering the image in this material context, facing a page of musical notation, one would presumably surmise that the book depicted in the hands of the larger child is a volume of music, perhaps representing the very book in which the image is printed. Moreover, the father's pointing to his thumb offers an additional representation of psalmody: he appears to be instructing the family to sing using the mnemonic system known as the 'Guidonian hand'.[3] Music is thus represented here in two forms: as the mnemonic touch of thumb on forefinger enacted by the father, and as the sight of printed notation in the book from which the child has (at least momentarily) turned his head. Yet music does not seem to appear in the form of sound. All four mouths are closed decorously, which if open might represent singing; if humming is taking place, this is not signalled to the viewer.

One immediate question relating to the senses might be why hearing is (apparently) not represented, with sight and touch instead used to indicate psalmody. Certainly, woodcut illustration is a medium that communicates most immediately through the visual (although the copies of this book held by the British Library are now remarkably pungent). Its mode of depiction is static, and very much representational, although we might perhaps think of this image as a composite representation, in which activities that take place variously during a session of domestic psalm singing are all depicted simultaneously. In short – and unsurprisingly – the illustration gives an extremely clear account of what domestic psalm singing might look like in the early modern period. What is far more challenging to communicate visually is what domestic psalm singing might sound like. Indeed, even if the figures had open mouths, we would need all the available contextual information in order to read this as a depiction of musical performance. Hearing is an experience in sound and in time, neither of which are particularly easy to represent pictorially. Significantly, then, by thinking about the (lack of) representation of hearing in this image, we arrive swiftly at a wider question about the senses and artistic expression: how does one represent an aural sensory experience in a visual medium, a visual experience in a linguistic medium, or a gustatory experience in a performative medium? This collection engages centrally with the challenges that various artistic media pose for the representation, exploration and consideration of the senses, challenges faced not only by early modern writers and artists, but also by scholars and historians today.

Turning from the practicalities of representation to the represented scene, we might next ask what a sensory approach can suggest about the particular context portrayed. Notably, the woodcut illustration appears to place clear emphasis on a particular set of sensory experiences that articulate the domestic intimacy of a family gathered around a psalm book or books. Through the senses of touch and sight, domestic psalm singing is represented in the image as private familial interaction, and these sensory exchanges are perhaps even more significant to the participants than musical performance itself. The family members communicate with one another in this collective household activity through physical contact, and through evocative visual interaction. There is a striking contrast between the barren representation of domestic space, and the vivacious evocation of emotion in the characters' carefully drawn gazes, in the interaction of their glances, and in their attendant facial expressions. For this early modern family imagined in ink and paper, psalmody is most importantly the *exchange* of sensory experiences, in looks, touches and (unrep-resented) musical sounds. This line of enquiry points towards the richness of sensory experience enacted by a particular cultural practice, a richness that could easily be overlooked when the musical component of psalmody draws attention inevitably towards sound and hearing. According to this woodcut illustration, perhaps more important than the music itself is the suggestion that the psalm singing facilitates a particular set of sensory interactions that reinforce domestic harmony, familial bonds and devotional sentiment.

We might even consider the role of this paratextual image in shaping the sensory experiences of real early modern subjects who purchased the part-books. Each volume has a title page and an imprint of the woodcut illustration, but no further prefatory material: no dedication to a patron; no address to a reader; no praise poems; no errata. Instead, the picture supplies the frame for the musical notation that follows, suggesting to purchasers how they might themselves use the volumes.[4] According to the image, the books do not just supply notation to be transformed into sound; those who purchase them can themselves also engage in the visual and tactile encounters represented in the image, with the attendant familial unity and pleasure that the scene suggests (only cynical viewers would find their eyes drawn to the landscape beyond the window, seeking amusements other than domestic psalm singing). The paratextual image does not just give an account of sensory experience in the particular context of psalmody, then; it offers this context of sensory encounter as a model or aspiration to early modern subjects who themselves intend to sing psalms domestically. The paratextual role of this image therefore suggests an important mutual relationship between artwork and wider early modern culture: not only does the image represent sensory encounters that might occur in domestic contexts, but in its role as a paratext, it encourages subjects to pursue similar sensations of their own. Not only could this text represent the sensory encounters encoded in an early modern cultural practice, it could also generate new sense experiences that follow its example. Here, artwork and wider culture are mutually constructive – even mutually constructing – in their configuration of sensory experience.

Throughout, this study seeks to illuminate both early modern works of art and the wider cultural moments in which they were produced and circulated. In so doing, our contributors consider a broad range of early modern texts, performances and other art forms including poetry, painting, music, drama, domestic objects and dance. The volume is divided into three sections, each focusing on a different question about the senses. The first section asks how individual senses appear in particular artworks, considering each of the five senses in turn. Why, for instance, is sound often portrayed as a problematic and invasive sensory stimulus in early modern drama? Can stage representations of visual self-fashioning help us excavate an early modern distrust of knowledge obtained through sight? In each case, questions about a single sense help elucidate early modern thinking about sensory experience more generally, these questions also generating fruitful readings of the particular artworks under consideration.

The second section asks how the senses were understood in particular early modern contexts explored in works of art, including contexts of night, of sexual pleasure, and of love melancholy. These investigations yield clear suggestions about early modern sensory configurations, as well as emphasizing the contingency of sensory experience. Once again, attention to the senses provides a distinctive route through the texts being interrogated, offering mutual illumination of cultural context and work of art.

The final section asks what sensory experiences might have been enacted when early modern subjects actually engaged with works of art, considering practical encounters with playhouse performance, painting and printed drama. The perspectives on sensory experience that emerge from the three sections together point towards a mutually elucidating relationship between the understandings of the senses suggested by early modern works of art, and sensory experiences in wider early modern culture.

This collection owes much to the wider critical field of sensory scholarship, responding to the extensive call for a historicized account of the senses in both literary and cultural studies in recent years. Scholars including Constance Classen, Alain Corbin, David Howes and Bruce R. Smith have argued in seminal works that sensory encounters are culturally specific, dependent upon the understandings of the senses current in a particular time and place.[5] It follows, therefore, that the sensory configurations of a particular cultural and historical moment must inform our later engagements with the art, life and wider culture of that moment. Making this case in relation to several diverse contexts, Constance Classen's pioneering work, *Worlds of Sense: Exploring the Senses in History and across Cultures*, has been seminal for scholarship within cultural studies, literary studies and other related disciplines. Beginning from the premise that the senses do not operate in fixed and universal ways, Classen argues that sensory experience itself is culturally contingent, exploring how different cultures configure the significance of the senses through contrasting formulations. Thus, while in contemporary Western culture sight is often considered the dominant sense and smell is perceived as marginal, Classen traces radically different attitudes to the relative importance of these two senses in the pre-modern West, reconstructing various significances of smell in late medieval and early modern culture that are now lost. As she notes, Shakespeare 'proclaims that "a rose by any other name would smell as sweet", not that it would *look* as fine'.[6]

Developing a similar line of enquiry with specific reference to early modern England, Holly Dugan's article on 'Shakespeare and the Senses' is a particularly influential recent contribution to the field in its interrogation of the shifting nature of bodily experience. Dugan traces divergent views of the senses from different cultural and historical perspectives, noting how some cultures even count six, seven or nine unique senses. Thus, both experience and understanding of the sensorium are culturally specific and deeply embodied, requiring scholars to take account of these shifting understandings when exploring historically distanced cultural contexts. Dugan asks, moreover, whether the body has adapted over time, or whether the shifts are merely in the theories and frameworks used to comprehend sensory experience. Dugan also asserts the significance of each individual's unique embodiment of sensory experience, arguing that 'individual bodies sense specific phenomena' divergently. In order to study the senses in context, then, we must also interrogate the 'shifting interface between individual cognition and shared material environments', remaining cautious about flattening individual sensory encounters into undifferentiated models of collective experience.[7]

In the same article, Dugan locates a separate, salient concern for sensory studies when she observes that cultural historians of the senses must engage with perceptions, experiences and bodily descriptions that are by nature ephemeral. If sensory experience cannot be preserved materially, how can scholars today interrogate early modern senses most productively? Here, Dugan acknowledges the challenges of researching ephemeral sensory encounters from a position of cultural and historical distance. Alain Corbin likewise addresses this concern when questioning the evidentiary value of written sensory configurations. He argues that while textual representations of the senses are often the most suggestive evidence available, we must remain aware of the limits of such discourse, taking care not to confuse what is articulated in language with what was actually experienced. He cautions other scholars not to fall into the 'trap which consists, for the historian, of confusing the reality of the employment of the senses and the picture of this employment decreed by observers'.[8]

A similarly significant issue is the relative level of scholarly attention that each sense is afforded. Since antiquity, writers have sought to organize the senses into hierarchies – of overall significance, of practical utility, or of epistemological value. Following Aristotle, sight and hearing generally prevail, whilst smell and taste are particularly prone to marginalization. These priorities are often broadly replicated in critical attention to the various senses: scholars have returned repeatedly to the visual above all, while the olfactory and gustatory are all too often overlooked. This is a particular concern for a study concerned with the senses in early modern England, a cultural context in which hierarchies of the senses were regularly challenged and destabilized as well as articulated; in which despite widespread emphasis on sight, the extreme 'ocularcentrism' of the twentieth and twenty-first centuries was not in place, and – as Classen reminds us in the passage quoted above – Shakespeare's rose could smell sweet rather than look fine. A study of early modern culture such as this volume must balance attention to the various senses, just as that culture explored and challenged the full sensorium.

One particularly effective means of countering this critical imbalance has been to offer studies focused explicitly on the senses less explored. The 'Sensory Formations' series edited by David Howes has been particularly significant in offering (among other volumes) 'readers' for each of the five traditional senses, including substantial volumes dedicated specifically to smell and to taste.[9] Likewise, Holly Dugan takes smell as a central topic of sensory interrogation as she investigates *The Ephemeral History of Perfume: Scent and Sense in Early Modern England*, using textual and material evidence to offer a complex and more equivocal picture of the early modern sensorium.[10]

An alternative means of challenging scholarly preoccupation with sight and sound has been to assert the importance of collective thinking about sensory experience, emphasizing the co-functionality of the senses in practice. David Howes's *Sensual Relations: Engaging the Senses in Culture and Social Theory* asserts that, as well as giving separate consideration to the five senses, scholars must consider their interrelations. As Howes observes, scholars have at times given the impression that each sense 'constituted a completely independent domain of experience, without exploring how the senses interact with each other in different combinations and hierarchies'.[11] Likewise, Michael Bull and Les Back's *The Auditory Culture Reader* takes a particular interest in sensory interrelationships, reminding us that 'it is difficult to separate out our senses' in practice.[12] Dealing as Bull and Back are with one of the senses more commonly explored, their explicit aim is to avoid 'supplant[ing] one "primary sense" with another', hoping instead that their volume can contribute to a scholarly 'democracy of the senses'.[13] The pertinence of these concerns to early modern studies is productively articulated by Alice Sanger and Siv Tove Kulbrandstad Walker in their recent edited collection concerned with early modern visual art. A survey of responses to artworks from 1300 to 1700, the volume inter-rogates the relationships between artwork and the consumer through Classical and Renaissance traditions of sensory thought, with a focus overwhelmingly upon visual art forms and exclusively outside England. The collection engages closely with questions of sensory hierarchy, exploring how the primacy of the visual interacts with viewers' other sensual experiences of art: 'in what ways, this volume asks, were the operations of visual culture inflected with meaning because of the value attached to hearing, smell, taste and touch?'[14] Sight was extremely important in early modern sensory configurations, but as Sanger and Walker acknowledge, so too were the other senses, requiring a critical approach to this period that is alert to a full range of senses.

Another question of perennial interest to scholars is that of the relationship between language and the senses. In Classen's seminal study introduced above, she explores the cultural contingency of sensory experience by demonstrating how language both reflects the sensual priorities of a given culture, and contributes to the continuing cultural replication of those priorities:

> The Ongee of the Andaman Islands in the South Pacific, for example, live in a world ordered by smell. [...] Therefore, when an Ongee wishes to refer to 'me', he or she points to his or her nose, the organ of smell. Likewise, when greeting a friend, an Ongee will ask 'How is your nose?'[15]

Studies of early modern culture have sustained Classen's line of enquiry with notable success; most recently, Katharine A. Craik and Tanya Pollard's *Shakespearean Sensations: Experiencing Literature in Early Modern England* directly addresses the issue of language and the senses by discussing how the vocabulary used to express and describe the sensorium and its perception of associated somatic reaction has shifted over time. As the editors point out, several of the period's phrases suggestive of literal reaction ('hot-headed' or 'cold-blooded', for example) have survived into the modern period as merely figurative; they remind us that '[u]nderstanding the period's psychophysiology requires recognizing that the boundaries between metaphorical and literal language were radically unstable'.[16] The contributors to their volume focus on written texts, and mainly on examples from Shakespeare, to explore textual depictions of the senses and their effects on an audience, examining the difference between 'affect' and 'emotion'. The volume explores early modern perceptions of changes in bodily state and in consciousness when reading a poem or going to the theatre, changes regarded as the results of the action of the five senses. The contributors root this understanding of the workings of the senses in its Classical background.

Particularly significant for scholars concerned with language and the senses is the recent translation of Michel Serres's *The Five Senses: A Philosophy of Mingled Bodies (I)*. First published in French in 1985, this seminal study explores the relationship between the body's senses and words, using sensory experience to challenge theoretical positions predicated on the primacy of language. Serres sets up bodily experience through the senses as fundamentally alternative to – even opposed to – language, a kind of knowing that is qualitatively and meaningfully different from language itself. As Steven Connor notes in his introduction to the English translation, 'Serres stakes on the senses the possibility of a return to the world, which means an escape from "the abominable verb to be", and the associated trap of linguistic identity'.[17] The new availability of this canonical text in translation is significant for Anglophone cultural and literary studies.

David Howes's influential edited collection, *Empire of the Senses: The Sensual Culture Reader*, appeared some 20 years after the original composition in French of Serres's seminal work. Howes can thus articulate the changed scholarly relationship since 1985 with both language and the body, resonating powerfully with Serres's aspirations in *The Five Senses*. As Howes explains, after 'the linguistic turn [in the second half of the twentieth century], [i]t has taken an ideological revolution to turn the tables and recover a full-bodied understanding of culture and experience'.[18] The volume is explicitly indebted to Serres as a harbinger of recent critical interest in the body, Howes acknowledging the significance of *The Five Senses* in his introduction and Steven Connor contributing a chapter concerned specifically with Serres's work.[19] With chapters from influential sensory scholars including Constance Classen, Alain Corbin, Carla Mazzio, Jim Drobnick, and Howes himself, the collection also makes a significant contribution to the strand of scholarship outlined above that both asserts and explores the cultural and historical contingency of sensory experience.

One distinctive feature of scholarship concerned with early modern sensory encounters is a consideration of the significance of Classical intellectual tradition to early modern understandings of the senses. As noted above, recent edited collections concerned both with visual art and with literary texts have offered detailed explorations of this significance.[20] Another study engaged with this topic is Lowell Gallagher and Shankar Raman's edited collection, *Knowing Shakespeare: Senses, Embodiment and Cognition*.[21] Focused on the Shakespearean text, this collection gives attention to the subject of the senses alongside both embodiment and cognition. Its central focus is on cognition in Shakespeare's canonical plays, examining the role of sensory experience and of the body in the acquisition of knowledge. The collection offers a broad-ranging account of Shakespeare's use of, and even participation in, contemporary intellectual debates about epistemology and the senses.

Our volume takes its cue from previous scholarship in its attempts to interrogate the literary, artistic and cultural output of early modern England. Perhaps most significantly, in focusing on a specific time and place we follow Classen's view that understandings of the senses, and sensory experience itself, are culturally and historically contingent; the collection thus explores the culturally specific role of the senses in textual and aesthetic encounters in England, often in London, between 1558 and 1660. A dual focus, though, on the early modern works of art under consideration, and the cultural moments of their production, allows us to explore further the critically important issue of ephemerality: how can sensory experience be represented in works of art, particularly if the artistic medium used does not communicate via the sense(s) in question? Contributors to this volume ask interpretative questions about how far the sensory encounters of early modern subjects themselves can be interrogated through such representations.

Equally, as in previous key studies of the senses, those writing here are concerned with the tension between sensory experience and linguistic description of that experience. Accepting that early modern sensory vocabulary in turn constructed ideas of sensory affect in the period, and that, moreover, there is a tension between language itself and the sensory experiences it aims to convey, several chapters evaluate how contemporary language reflected writers' engagement with the senses.

The substantial debt that we owe to previous work in this area is demonstrated both in chapters where our contributors develop existing scholarship, and in those where they take alternative directions, in both cases responding to the key concerns and insights of previous scholars. Perhaps most importantly, both the coverage and the methodologies of our volume intend to offer a 'democracy of the senses', rather than a sensory hierarchy, reflecting the early modern period's multiple and often entangled explorations of all five senses. By presenting chapters in our first section that each explore the representation of a single sense in artistic works, we aim for a balance between the five key senses. This balance is taken forward in the ensuing discussions of senses in context, and of the nature of early modern sensory engagements with works of art. The opening chapters raise key issues of the representation of senses such as taste and smell that can only be preserved indirectly, even as these contributors trace early modern representations of such sensory encounters as deeply powerful and affective.

Many of the essays in this volume draw upon previous scholarly attempts to trace theoretical backgrounds for early modern thinking about the senses and their actions on the individual. Contributors explore that relationship carefully, with several chapters demonstrating the contemporary importance of the ideas of classical writers such as Aristotle and Plato, Cicero and Lucretius. However, this volume does not take the epistemological value or status of the senses as a central topic of enquiry; neither does it intervene in the burgeoning field of scholarship that explores how Shakespeare (in particular) reflects or participates in intellectual debate around the senses and cognition. We choose instead to consider *how* sensory experience itself is represented in different media, and what this tells us about early modern culture.

A further departure from previous collections in this area lies in the range of artistic media covered in this volume. Having deliberately reduced geographical and historical parameters, we take care to examine a breadth of artistic forms, with research focusing on sensation in dramatic performance and in poetry matched by complementary work on the impact of musical performance, printed drama, theoretical writings, domestic objects, visual art and dance. As a result, although literary examples are still most frequent, we broaden the range of conclusions we can draw about early modern sensual engagement by drawing on cultural experiences, such as dance, which generate a number of simultaneous sensations. Further, the collection's dramatic and poetic material ranges deliberately wide, not least in order to avoid the tendency in some recent literary scholarship to lionize Shakespearean material.

The opening section of the collection, 'Tracing a Sense', follows Joachim-Ernst Berendt's call for 'a democracy of the senses' in preference to the various sensory hierarchies that have often shaped theory and criticism.[22] In doing so, we echo the early modern period's questioning and problematizing of received hierarchies of the senses, and its concomitant interest in the full gamut of sensory experience. The section offers one essay on each of the five senses, beginning and ending with two senses – taste and smell – that are often overlooked in studies of early modern culture. Beginning with an essay on taste by Lucy Munro, the volume's first example of the representation of an individual sense is one in which the perception of that sense – here in a variety of dramatic contexts – must be through a peculiar combination of imagination and second-hand sensation. In considering the personification of taste in the dramatic presentation of the glutton or epicure, and the role of the taster, the chapter begins the volume's project of characterizing sensual reception. By exploring the range of substances that are 'tasted' on stage, and their social and emblematic associations, Munro evaluates the stage's sensory language and the dramaturgical uses of taste through the work of a wide variety of playwrights, as well as assessing the place of taste in different dramatic genres.

The volume's movement away from scholarly hierarchizing continues in Jackie Watson's chapter on sight. Rather than showing vision as the chief and most valued of the senses, she instead explores the limitations early modern writers recognized in seeing, and the potential for deception which was consequent upon a reliance on appearance. With a particular focus on the representation of sight and appearance in stage portrayals of the courtier and those ambitious for courtly preferment, Watson argues that the playhouse itself challenged its audiences' reliance on the evidence of their own eyes, teaching early modern playgoers *how* to see and how to interpret the validity of the visual. Sharing Watson's interest in the sensory representation of court life, Darren Royston's essay on the importance of touch in poetic and dramatic depictions of dance addresses the moral value attached to fleshly contact. Royston explores the moral ambiguity of dance in early modern England through evidence presented by oppositional pamphleteers, courtly dance manuals and visual representations. In his examination of the poetic narrative of Sir John Davies's *Orchestra* and in dramatic examples from Shakespeare, he shows how dance relates to historically established rituals from the art of courtly love and proceeds to explore the complexity of touch in this context, even as the practical necessity of tactile contact was often elided in textual accounts of cosmic dance.

Eleanor Decamp's chapter on hearing opens in an unusual cultural domain, that of early modern barber shops. From an evocation of ear picking, she explores early modern perceptions of the vulnerability of the ear, proceeding to consider how barbery itself is represented acoustically, using Jonson's *Epicoene* as a key text in the assessment of the dramatic representation of the profession. Questioning how sound, especially for the anti-theatricalist, was perceived as frivolous, Decamp follows the three contributors before her in examining contemporary concerns surrounding a particular sense.

The final chapter in this section, as Munro's on taste, explores the difficulties of representing ephemeral early modern sensual experience. Taking twenty-first-century relationships with perfume and smell as an illuminating analogue, Holly Dugan's essay examines how early modern visual media sought to represent the qualities of particular scents in abstract ways. Through her examination of pomanders, Dugan considers the conjunction of aesthetic detail and utilitarian value in such objects as she examines how a synaesthetic approach to the history of olfaction might contribute to sensory history.

The second section explores early modern artistic accounts of the senses collectively, in three particular contexts. Natalie Eschenbaum's essay investigates Robert Herrick's accounts in *Hesperides* (1648) of how the senses function during sexual pleasure and contact. Eschenbaum argues that Herrick's fluid depictions of sensation respond (in a small way) to the tradition of poetic sensoria and (in a substantial way) to the early modern debate about how and why the five (or six) senses worked as they did. For Eschenbaum, this debate explains why Herrick configures sensation as a full body, materialist and Epicurean experience. Her attention to Herrick's problematizing of received sensory configurations continues the volume's attempts to move away from scholarly hierarchizing, even as it demonstrates the purchase of our approach on early modern culture.

The section continues to explore sensory experiences in context as Susan Wiseman interrogates textual accounts of the senses at night in writings from the English Renaissance. Focusing on poetry by Donne and Chapman, this essay questions how far textual accounts of night and the senses might be connected to larger, culturally and socially significant shifts in encounters – sensory, social and intellectual – with night, light and shadow in early modern England. In the final essay in this section, Griffin explores Mary Wroth's accounts of the senses in the context of early modern love melancholy, this being the topic of a rich and often anxious discourse in the period. Griffin explores how the sensory debates that elsewhere motivate Herrick's writing alternatively inspire Wroth's creative, and sometimes conflicting, conceptions of melancholic love. The essay argues that the melancholic subject's senses – sight in particular – were repeatedly described as unreliable, and therefore he or she was considered to be susceptible to illusion. Griffin explores how Mary Wroth responded to contemporary theoretical conceptions of the senses by suggesting that melancholic love can both trouble and heighten the senses. Following the example of her uncle Philip Sidney, Mary Wroth both represented the ways in which melancholy was believed to affect the senses, and exploited the connection between melancholy and creativity, locating her writing in contemporary debates surrounding the 'disease'.

The essays in this section offer a picture of early modern thought in which sensory encounters are unstable, suggesting ways in which the senses are influenced by the contexts in which they are experienced: at night, in states of sexual excitement, or even when melancholic. Where earlier chapters focused on representations of the five senses in turn, these essays argue for the collective volatility of the sensorium. Those writing in this section suggest that attention to specific contexts for sensory experience is vital to our understanding of early modern engagements with the sensorium in literature, art, theatre and culture.

If the second section looks outward most notably – from works of art to wider early modern culture – then in contrast, the third and final section directs attention most directly towards works of art themselves. Here, Simon Smith, Faye Tudor and Hannah August consider the significance of the senses for early modern subjects attending a play, regarding a painting, and reading a printed volume. In examining the sensory processes that might be enacted when encountering texts, artworks and performances in early modern England, this section shifts focus from how artistic producers might have thought about the senses to the sensory experiences early modern subjects may have faced as they encountered works of art.

In the first chapter, Smith considers playhouse musical performance, taking the example of Shakespeare's *Antony and Cleopatra*. Beginning with the observation that early modern sources often present musical experience as a fundamentally multi-sensory phenomenon, he argues that early modern culture placed particular significance on visual engagement with musical performance. Playhouses were in fact unusual in their habitual placement of musicians out of the audience's sight, with precise and distinct responses anticipated when unseen music sounded. Smith argues that in *Antony and Cleopatra*, certain responses are invited – through hidden music – at moments of particular dramatic significance, making the sensory experience of this music integral to the dramaturgy of Shakespeare's play in early modern performance. This interrogation of sensory experience contributes to wider critical debates about the nature of the playhouse as a cultural space, and indeed about the place of music in dramatic performance. It also seeks to complicate the notion of musical experience as a solely aural phenomenon in early modern culture; rather, subjects encountering the particular early modern performance medium of playhouse musical performance did so through a range of sensory engagements, involving sight in particular as well as hearing.

Tudor's chapter is also concerned with looking, but in the rather more familiar context of painting. This chapter explores the visual experience of the viewer and the viewed, as these experiences were manifested when early modern subjects encountered a painted work of art. The concerns of painters themselves with the act of looking are central to this investigation; taking the self-reflexive gaze into a mirror as a rubric through which to examine self-portraits by female artists such as Sofonisba Anguissola, Tudor argues for a distinctively early modern configuration of viewing, tracing the significance of this configuration for encounters with a painting through a wide range of texts, including writings by Edmund Spenser and James Shirley. These specific understandings of visual engagement with paintings yield significant suggestions about the sensory configurations of early aesthetic encounters.

August concludes our volume with a return to early modern drama; however, where other contributions focus on playhouse performance, this chapter considers the widespread early modern consumption of comedy in print. Drawing evidence from dramatic paratexts, manuscript commonplace books and other early modern non-dramatic writings, this chapter interrogates the sensory quality of the pleasure that printed comedies may have provided early modern readers. It argues that the sense of sight, when deployed by imaginative readers, could provide a dual pleasure that was conceived as both aesthetic and erotic, and that comedies that 'tickled the senses' in performance were just as capable of doing so in print. Recalling earlier chapters by Munro and Dugan, August pursues early modern accounts of sensory experience that marshal both immediate sensory stimuli and an imagination of the senses towards a distinctive mode of sensory encounter with printed drama.

This section offers a view of early modern encounters with artworks that above all emphasizes the importance of the senses in articulating these encounters. The chapters make a common assertion, too, that those involved with the production and consumption of artworks were themselves often fascinated by the sensory experiences that their work would facilitate for audiences and consumers; indeed, each contribution argues for early modern attempts to comprehend the complicated sensory encounters encoded in aesthetic experiences. Moreover, ideas explored in earlier sections – about the importance of particular contexts for sensory encounters, and the challenges of negotiating and representing particular sensory experiences – reappear in these discussions. Here, they take on slightly different contours, now yielding alternative insights through attention not to artistic production, but rather to consumption.

We began with a problem for sensory studies, in the form of 'lost' early modern sensory encounters: a church service in the 1590s; a boat trip on the Thames in the 1640s. We end, however, with an assertion of what is possible: despite the ephemerality of sensation itself, we can nonetheless make significant propositions about early modern culture by considering the senses through works of art. The questions pursued in this collection yield a range of suggestions about the place and nature of the senses in early modern art, life and thought. By asking how individual senses appear in works of art, how particular contexts for sensory experience are described and represented, and how artworks might themselves have generated particular sensory encounters, we hope to add new contours to the critical picture of the senses in early modern England.

Notes

1 David Lindley considers this image within a larger discussion of psalm singing in *Shakespeare and Music* (London: Thomson, 2006), pp. 65–68. An earlier consideration of the image appears in Lelan Ryken, *Worldly Saints: the Puritans as they really were* (Grand Rapids, MI: Zondervan, 1986), p. 72.

2 *The Whole Psalmes in Foure Partes* (1563), A1r.

3 This memory technique, named for Guido of Arezzo, uses the joints of the hand as an aid in teaching solmization. Numerous images depicting the 'Guidonian hand' survive from the early modern period. See Susan Forscher Weiss, 'The Singing Hand', in *Writing on Hands: Memory and Knowledge in Early Modern Europe*, ed. by Claire Richter Sherman (Carlisle, PA: Trout Gallery & Folger Shakespeare Library, 2000), pp. 35–45 (p. 37); Lindley, p. 67.

4 It is relatively unusual to find an image framing musical notation in place of an address to the reader or a dedication. Thomas Coryate's playful venture into travel writing, *Coryats Crudities* (1611), includes a song that praises his achievements through favourable and extended comparison to 'a Porcupen' (E6v), thus framing a written text with a musical paratext. Whilst sharing our 1563 psalter's interest in non-linguistic textual framing, the song to Coryate perhaps operates on a level of irony not found in volumes of devotional music published with the stated aim of 'abolishyng […] other vayne and triflyng ballades' (A1r).

5 See Constance Classen, *Worlds of Sense: Exploring the Senses in History and Across Cultures* (London: Routledge, 1993); Alain Corbin, *Time, Desire and Horror: Towards a History of the Senses*, trans. by Jean Birrell (Cambridge: Polity Press, 1995); David Howes, *Sensual Relations: Engaging the Senses in Culture and Social Theory* (Ann Arbor: University of Michigan Press, 2003), Bruce R. Smith, *The Acoustic World of Early Modern England: Attending to the O-Factor* (Chicago: University of Chicago Press, 1999); 'Sensory Formations' series (Oxford: Berg, 2003–09).

6 Classen, p. 25.

7 Holly Dugan, 'Shakespeare and the Senses', *Literature Compass*, 6 (2009), 726–40 (p. 727).

8 Corbin, p. 187.

9 *The Smell Culture Reader*, ed. by Jim Drobnick, Sensory Formations (Oxford: Berg, 2006); *The Taste Culture Reader: Experiencing Food and Drink*, ed. by Carolyn Korsmeyer, Sensory Formations (Oxford: Berg, 2005).

10 Holly Dugan, *The Ephemeral History of Perfume: Scent and Sense in Early Modern England* (Baltimore, MD: Johns Hopkins University Press, 2011).

11 Howes, p. xi.

12 *The Auditory Culture Reader*, ed. by Michael Bull and Les Back (Oxford: Berg, 2003), p. 3.

13 Bull and Back, p. 2. Bull and Back adopt this extremely helpful concept of 'a democracy of the senses' from Joachim-Ernst Berendt's *The Third Ear: On Listening to the World*, trans. by Tim Nevill (Shaftesbury: Element, 1988), p. 32.

14 *Sense and the Senses in Early Modern Art and Cultural Practice*, ed. by Alice Sanger and Siv Tove Kulbrandstad Walker (Farnham: Ashgate, 2012), p. 2.

15 Classen, p. 1.

16 *Shakespearean Sensations: Experiencing Literature in Early Modern England*, ed. by Katharine A. Craik and Tanya Pollard (Cambridge: Cambridge University Press, 2013), p. 7.

17 Steven Connor, 'Introduction', in Michel Serres, *The Five Senses: A Philosophy of Mingled Bodies (I)*, trans. by Margaret Sankey and Peter Cowley (London: Continuum, 2008), pp. 1–16 (p. 9).

18 *Empire of the Senses: The Sensual Culture Reader*, ed. by David Howes, Sensory Formations (Oxford: Berg, 2005), pp. 1–17 (p. 1).

19 Howes (ed.), p. 1; Steven Connor, 'Michel Serres' Five Senses', in *Empire of the Senses*, ed. by Howes, pp. 318–34.

20 *Art and Cultural Practice*, ed. by Sanger and Walker, pp. 6–10; *Shakespearean Sensations*, ed. by Craik and Pollard, pp. 9–11.

21 *Knowing Shakespeare: Senses, Embodiment and Cognition*, ed. by Lowell Gallagher and Shankar Raman (Basingstoke: Palgrave, 2010).

22 Berendt, p. 32.

Part I

Tracing a sense

1

Staging taste

Lucy Munro

Thomas Randolph's *The Muses' Looking Glass*, first performed by the Children of the Revels around 1630, features a character called Acolastus, a semi-allegorical caricature of a '*voluptuous Epicure, that out of an immoderate, and untam'd desire seekes after all pleasures promiscuously, without respect of honest or lawfull*'. Perhaps unsurprisingly, Acolastus is obsessed with taste, and he delivers a paean to his favourite sensory experience:

> Foole was he that wish'd but a cranes short neck.
> Give me one, nature, long as is a Cable,
> Or sounding line, and all the way a palate
> To tast my meate the longer. I would have
> My senses feast together; Nature envied us
> In giving single pleasures; let me have
> My eares, eyes, palate, nose, and touch, at once
> Injoy their happinesse[.][1]

Acolastus's desire to prolong and intensify the sensation of taste is evoked in his declaration that to have a neck like a crane – the desire of the glutton, Philoxenus, cited in Aristotle's *Eudemian Ethics* – displayed a sad lack of ambition. Taste is, for Acolastus, the pinnacle of all other senses, which will 'feast together'. He desires to experience all of the senses simultaneously, in a heady, synesthetic experience, and his description conjures in sensuous detail the intensity of its sensation. In performance, moreover, Randolph's words would combine with the performance of the actor, who perhaps draws out the vowels in 'one … long … sounding … longer' or uses gesture to suggest the glutton's ecstatic frustration.

Taking Acolastus's transcendent fantasy as its starting point, this essay explores the ways in which taste was staged in early modern plays, situating it in the context of broader debates about the nature and status of this sensory experience. Recent studies of taste in early modern drama have tended to focus on its metaphorical use – usually via its connection with food, appetite and consumption – or on its material connection with the substances that are tasted. Jeff Masten, for example, provides a wonderfully illuminating account of the linguistic, material and dramatic uses of sweetness; Peter Stallybrass explores the physicality of the image of consumption in Thomas Middleton's *The Revenger's Tragedy* (King's Men, *c.* 1606); Stanley Cavell analyses the ways in which food figures in Shakespeare's *Coriolanus* (King's Men, *c.* 1609); and Karen Britland untangles some of the connections between women and wine in early modern drama.[2]

While it draws on these approaches, this essay is a response to Farah Karim-Cooper's provocative recent analysis of touch and – to a lesser extent – taste in the early modern playhouse.[3] In particular, it explores the fundamental paradox of taste's simultaneously bodily and immaterial dramatic status, focusing on the specifics of the way in which taste was literally and metaphorically 'staged'. My focus is on the precise moments at which characters are required to taste something – foodstuffs, drink, other characters' lips – and the ways in which these moments supplement, reinforce or, potentially, challenge a discourse of taste that is deployed elsewhere in the plays and in early modern culture. The first section, 'Tasting', explores the divided reputation that this sense had in early modern England, drawing on visual, medical and moral traditions. The remainder of the essay then looks in detail at taste in the playhouse. Section two, 'Material tasting', examines the ways in which the physical action of tasting was presented on stage, concluding in a short analysis of Thomas Dekker and Philip Massinger's *The Virgin Martyr*; the third section, 'Immaterial tasting' looks at figurative and semi-figurative uses of taste in early modern plays, finishing with an account of Shakespeare's *Troilus and Cressida*. Finally, section four, 'Material and immaterial tasting', brings the elements together in an analysis of Middleton's taste-infused tragedy *Women Beware Women*. Throughout, I explore something that we might term a theatrical aesthetics of taste, one that draws on the raw physicality of the action of tasting, on the metaphorical notion of tasting as exploring or testing, and on emerging notions of aesthetic taste.

Tasting

Although comic, Acolastus's speech encapsulates and depends upon some of the most important preconceptions about taste that circulated in early modern England. Taste was frequently seen as one of the lower bodily or material senses. Aristotle in *De Sensu* famously notes that 'the sense of smell comes midway between the tactile senses (touch and taste) and those that operate through a medium (sight and hearing)'.[4] Whereas senses such as touch and taste involve direct physical contact, sight and hearing are seen as working through the 'mediums' of air and water. As Helkiah Crooke relates, '*Aristotle* and almost all Philosophers' ranked sight as the highest sense, followed by hearing, smell, taste and touch, although 'Physitians & Anatomists' often argued for a reverse order: touch, taste, smell, hearing and sight.[5] From this perspective, touch was the highest sense precisely because it was the most material, solid and reliable, and it was sometimes viewed as being synonymous with the experience of life itself.[6]

As Acolastus seems to recognize, taste is also intertwined with the other senses. It interacts with smell, as odour and taste both relate to flavour or savour (*OED* flavour, n. 1–2; savour, n. 1–2, 3), and it shares with touch its dependence on corporeal experience. Indeed, the earliest uses of the word 'taste' in English appear to mean touch (*OED* n.[1] 1, v. 1): taste emerges from touch, and shares many of its conceptual and experiential uses and problems. Taste is, in addition, similar to touch – and unlike the other senses – in terms of the range of functions associated with its primary organ, the tongue, which plays a role in eating, kissing, pulling faces, and so on.

Taste's divided reputation is clear in early modern texts. Crooke quotes extensively from Julius Casserius Placentinus, who places touch first in his hierarchy of the senses and argues that taste, placed second, is 'not only commodious [...] but also necessarie vnto the conseruation of the *Indiuiduum*' because it is 'the chiefe Sense in discerning of Sapors [tastes or flavours]' and therefore it has a crucial role in protecting the rest of the body:

> without it we cannot discerne of Sapours, nor iudge betwixt hurtfull things and healthfull, neyther betweene that which is pleasant and vnpleasant, but become inferiour not onely to brute beasts but also to plants, which do not confusedly and without choyce, attract any Aliment but that which is most agreeable to their Nature, and so conuert it into their owne substance. (pp. 649–50)

Yet the powerful hold that taste held over the body and its desires also made it open to abuse. It was associated strongly in Christian thought with the Fall from the Garden of Eden. Richard Brathwaite begins his essay on taste with the comment 'THis *Sence* makes mee weeppe ere I speake of her; sith hence came our greefe, hence our miserie: when I represent her before my eyes, my eyes become blinded with weeping, remembring my grandame *Eue*, how soone she was induced to *taste* that shee ought not'.[7] Similarly, in his *Essays* (1600–01), William Cornwallis declares that 'The trap of our first parents, was licourishnesse: and all our calamities are licourishnesse, not induring wholesomnesse without sweetnesse'.[8] Taste might be not simply crude, but dangerous to the spiritual health.

In *A Good Companion for a Christian* (1632), John Norden discusses in detail the spiritual benefits and bodily hazards associated with taste, commenting:

> take heed thou pleasest not thy taste too much, for if thou giue way vnto it, it will ouermaster thee, and exact from thee, that will make thee a poore man, bee thy meanes to feed it neuer so great [...] at length it will grow strong and ouermatch thee, and make thee seruile and slauish vnto it, and in the end deuoure thee.[9]

Bodily taste should be carefully moderated, and spiritual taste equally carefully cultivated; Norden argues that 'the temperate man, the man knowing and fearing God, findeth in himselfe a taste of another and of a more high nature a *spirituall appetite*, and hungreth and thristeth as much for heauenly and permanent, as doth the *corporall appetite*, for vanishing and perishing food' (G12ᵛ–H1ʳ). Brathwaite similarly extracts a moral lesson from the fleeting sensation of a particular taste, comparing it to 'the frailty and breuity of all earthly pleasures' and writing, 'Whatsoeuer ministers singular'st content vnto our *appetite*, is no longer satisfieing then in the *palate*; for after going into the stomach, that content is done' (p. 46).

Supremely unaware of the spiritual dimensions of taste, Acolastus nonetheless embodies the warnings of moralists about its bodily temptation. This aspect of taste is developed in detail in early modern visual representations of the senses, in which a number of features recur.[10] Some seventeenth-century Dutch images of taste portray a pancake woman surrounded by peasants who eat hungrily, as in Cornelis Dusart's 'De Smaek' (*c.* 1693), while a print by Crispijn de Passe the Elder (*c.* 1590–1637) shows a man and a woman, the man clutching a leg of mutton.[11] The woman, who is noticeably more richly dressed, holds a drinking vessel, and a monkey sits on her shoulder. Women also represent taste in other prints. In three images published in England in the 1620s and 30s, taste is a fashionably dressed woman smoking a pipe. In George Glover's engraving (*c.* 1625–35), a glass of sack sits beside her on a table, while in those of Johan Bara (*c.* 1623–35) and an anonymous artist (*c.* 1630–40) she holds it in her free hand.[12] Bara and the anonymous artist also include a monkey who is greedily eating. In each print the image is combined with text. A caption on Glover's engraving comments, 'To none of our Viragoes shee'l giue place, | For Healthing Sacke, and Smoaking with a Grace', Bara's makes the lesson more explicit, commenting 'Tis Not proper for This Sex and Kind', and the third comments more broadly:

> Som with the Smoaking Pype and quaffing Cupp,
> Whole Lordships oft have swallow'd and blowne vpp:
> Their names, fames, goods, strengths, healths, & lives still wasting
> In practicing the Apish Art of Tasting.

Taste is here represented as a woman who breaks social taboos: she wears quasi-masculine clothing of the kind criticized in the satirical pamphlet *Hic Mulier, or The Man-Woman* (1620), smokes tobacco and, it is suggested, drinks the sack that was often associated with male carousing. Further, although the caption to the 1630s print suggests that the monkey represents the imitative aspect of tasting that was prominent in convivial drunkenness and smoking, it also had connections with lust. The connection between taste and lust features in other prints. Like de Passe's engraving, many images of taste portray men and women together in postures that suggest sexual interest. An early eighteenth-century French print by Pierre Aveline shows couples eating and kissing, while a late

Philocothonista,
OR, THE
DRVNKARD,
Opened, Diſſected, and Anatomized.

LONDON,

Printed by *Robert Raworth*; and are to be ſold at his houſe
neere the *White-Hart* Taverne in *Smithfield.* 1635.

2 Frontispiece illustration from Thomas Heywood, *Philocothonista,
or, the Drvnkard, Opened, Dissected, and Anatomized* (1635)

sixteenth-century print by Jan Saenredam, based on an image by Hendrick Goltzius, shows a woman feeding a man a piece of fruit while he caresses her breast, a chained monkey looking on from the wall behind them.[13]

While monkeys represent the capacity of taste to entice, and its connections with lustful actions such as kissing, elsewhere animals are used to emphasize the bestial associations of taste with drunkenness. The title page of *Philoco-thonista, or The Drunkard Opened, Dissected, and Anatomized* (1635) (Figure 2) shows a collection of bird- and beast-headed men drinking and, in one case, regurgitating the substances that taste leads them to over-consume. An ox-headed man tastes tobacco, ram- and crane-headed men drink from cups, a pig-headed creature vomits, and bear- and ass-headed creatures pick a fight in the background; the only wholly human figure is that of the maidservant who apparently enables this bad behaviour.

Taken together, these verbal and visual responses to taste suggest its dominant associations in the early modern period. Linked with bodily pleasure and fleshly desire, taste both enabled the Fall and forcibly reminded commentators of it, facilitating lesser sins that mirrored the great Christian act of transgression; simultaneously, however, taste protected the body and allowed for discrimination. All of these features made it ripe for exploitation within the playhouse.

Material tasting

Randolph's depiction of Acolastus and these pictorial representations of taste all suggest taste's dependence on the other senses for its visual and dramatic 'life'. Experiences of tasting were, of course, available in the playhouse in both literal and metaphorical terms: nuts and other foodstuffs were sold and consumed;[14] playgoers might 'taste' each other's lips when they kissed, either in friendly or sexual contexts; and the experience of watching a play was itself a form of 'tasting', through the term's association with experiencing, sampling, testing or judging (*OED* n. 2, 6–7; v. 2–3). But a spectator always experienced a play's representation of tasting at a remove. Even when two people taste the same substance their experience may be markedly different, and except in very limited or carefully designed contexts spectators cannot literally taste what a character or actor appears to taste. Taste was necessarily proxied, therefore, by the other senses. A playgoer might watch a character taste something, might hear their description of that taste, might even smell a foodstuff if the playhouse was small or the audience were pressed close to the stage. Taste on stage is second-hand and strangely disembodied, despite its status as one of the most corporeal and fleshy of senses.

Acolastus embodies one way in which taste appears on the early modern stage: in the form of an allegorical figure. Similar characters appear in Thomas Nabbes's *Microcosmus* (Queen Henrietta Maria's Men, 1637), in the Masque of the Five Senses in Shakespeare and Middleton's *Timon of Athens* (King's Men, *c.* 1607), and in Thomas Tomkis's Cambridge University play *Lingua* (published 1607), in which Gustus appears with Appetitus, his 'hungry Parasite'.[15] In addition, the figure of gluttony features, with the other Deadly Sins, in Marlowe's *Doctor Faustus* (Strange's Men, 1589–92). Plays also introduce the figure of the taster, the court officer whose duty it was to protect a ruler from poison: such characters appear in *The Troublesome Reign of King John* (Queen Elizabeth's Men, 1588); Robert Greene's *Alphonsus, King of Aragon* (?Queen Elizabeth's Men, *c.* 1590), Henry Chettle's *Tragedy of Hoffman* (Admiral's Men, 1603); and Barnabe Barnes's *The Devil's Charter* (King's Men, 1606).

Elsewhere, acts of tasting appeared in less formal but nonetheless richly symbolic contexts, the physical gestures of the actors being supplemented with dialogue. Often characters inform spectators about the flavours they taste, be they pleasant or unpleasant, in ways that are tailored to the dramatic context. 'The taste is perfect, and most delicate' comments Arnoldo of a banquet presented to him in Fletcher and Massinger's *The Custom of the Country* (King's Men, *c.* 1620), his pleasure suggesting his vulnerability to Hyppolita's carefully staged seduction.[16] In contrast, Mulligrub in John Marston's *The Dutch Courtesan* (Children of the Queen's Revels, 1605–06) enjoys the taste of a cooked salmon that he thinks has been delivered to him by mistake. 'Some vinegar, quick! Some good luck yet. Faith, I never tasted salmon relished better. O, when a man feeds at other men's cost!', he cries, only to comment 'Pah! how this salmon stinks!' when he realizes that he has been gulled.[17] Here, taste is clearly subjective, affected by the circumstances in which a foodstuff is consumed.

A yet clearer example of the way in which dialogue shapes the perception of taste appears in *How a Man May Tell a Good Wife from a Bad* (Worcester's Men, *c.* 1601), in which the abused Mistress Arthur describes the pledge offered to her by her erring husband:

> The welcom'st pledge that yet I euer tooke:
> Were this wine poyson, or did taste like gall,
> The honey sweet condition of your draught,
> Would make it drinke like Nectar[.][18]

Taste may deceive, but dialogue can create the impression of pleasant flavours for the audience, an effect that is achieved partly through references to familiar taste-sensations such as the 'honey' and 'sweet' of *How a Man May Tell a Good Wife from a Bad*, or to specific substances such as the vinegar that will accentuate the taste of the salmon in *The Dutch Courtesan*. Richard Brome and Thomas Heywood's *The Late Lancashire Witches* (King's Men, 1634), in contrast, creates through dialogue the paradoxical impression of food that does not taste of anything. The witches have stolen from the wedding feast of Lawrence and Parnell, and while they enjoy the food the boy they have kidnapped complains, 'Meat, lie there, for thou hast no taste, and drink, there, for thou hast no relish, for in neither of them is there either salt or savour.'[19] The witches' feast is unnatural, and their treatment of the boy impedes his ability to taste the rich food properly.

I will pause here on one of the most intriguing presentations of the literal act of taste on the early modern stage, in Dekker and Massinger's *The Virgin Martyr*, performed by the Revels Company at the Red Bull playhouse in 1620. The play focuses on the mission and martyrdom of St Dorothy, or Dorothea as she is named here, and its climax focuses on the conversion of her main tormentor, Theophilus. Theophilus is brought a basket of fruit and flowers by Angelo, a mysterious boy – in reality an angel – who accompanied Dorothea in earlier scenes. As Jane Hwang Degenhardt points out, Dekker and Massinger draw closely on established, Catholic tradition in which:

> On her way to her own execution Dorothy's unwavering faith is mocked by a scribe called Theophilus, who asks her to send some roses and apples from the garden of her spouse, Christ. Shortly after Dorothy's execution, Theophilus is visited by a fair, curly haired child dressed in a purple garment, from whom he receives the very basket of roses and apples that he had requested. Theophilus is immediately converted to Christianity and goes on to help convert most of the city before he too is martyred under the pagan prefect.[20]

One of the ways in which the dramatists adapt this narrative is in heightening its visual and theatrical impact; they achieve their effect by manipulating references to the senses and, especially, taste, and by carefully staging the act of tasting.

Theophilus's initial response to the basket exploits the relationship between actors, props and dramatic dialogue. 'Tis a tempting fruit', he says, 'And the most bright cheek'd child I euer view'd, | Sweete smelling goodly fruit, what flowers are these?'[21] The reference to Angelo is almost an aside, presented between the two responses to the contents of the basket, yet Theophilus's allusion to the 'bright cheek'd child' suggests that he responds to a complete sensory experience, one that entices and tempts him, even though at this point he is not sure what this temptation might involve. When he succumbs and eats some of the fruit, the audience see him eat it, and hear the response of the devil, Harpax, who has accompanied Theophilus in the guise of his servant. Theophilus addresses the absent Angelo, but the response to his words and actions comes not from the angel but from the devil:

<pre>
                          be thou a spirit
      Sent from that Witch to mock me, I am sure
      This is essentiall, and how ere it growes,
      Will taste it.   *Eates.*
        Harpax. Ha, ha, ha, ha.   Harpax *within.*
</pre>

Theophilus. So good, ile haue some now sure.
Harpax. Ha, ha, ha, ha, great lickorish foole.
(5.1.78–83)

The dialogue emphasizes the corporeal reality of the fruit, and the staging presents Theophilus performing the act of tasting on the main stage while Harpax mocks him from within.[22] Furthermore, the devil's description of Theophilus as a 'great lickorish foole' underlines the scene's emphasis on the sensual experience of eating and tasting.

Theophilus eats again, and Harpax is provoked into entering the stage, appearing for the first time in his true form:

Theophilus. Agen, what dainty rellish on my tongue
This fruit hath left, some Angell hath me fed,
If so toothfull, I will be banqueted.   *Eates another.*

Enter Harpax *in a fearefull shape, fire flashing out of the study.*

Harpax. Hold.
Theophilus.   Not for *Cæsar.*
(5.1.120–23)

Although the appearance of Harpax must have been a notable *coup de théâtre*, taste appears to outstrip sight: Theophilus's experience of tasting the 'dainty' and 'toothfull' fruit, which he compares to the elite sensory event of the banquet, is so intense that he barely seems to register Harpax's '*fearefull*' new appearance. Moreover, the power of the fruit's taste is emphasized in Theophilus's response to Harpax, and his newly rebellious stance in relation to both spiritual and temporal authority.

The scene climaxes as Harpax intensifies his attempt to stop Theophilus from eating:

Harpax. [...] cast thou downe
That Basket with the things in't, and fetch vp
What thou hast swallowed, and then take a drinke
Which I shall giue thee, and I'me gon.
     Theophilus. My Fruit!
Does this offend thee? see.
     Harpax. Spet it to'th earth,
And tread vpon it, or ile peece-meale teare thee.
     Theophilus. Art thou with this affrighted? see, heares more.   *Flowers.*
     Harpax. Fling them away, ile take thee else & hang thee
In a contorted Chaine of Isicles
I'th frigid Zone: downe with them.
     Theophilus. At the botome,
One thing I found not yet, see.   *A crosse of Flowers.*
     Harpax Oh, I'me tortur'd.
(5.1.129–39)

The raw physicality of the scene is underlined in the devil's attempt to make Theophilus vomit up what he has eaten. Theophilus's refusal to submit, and his desire to continue tasting the fruit is further emphasized on the word 'see', at which point he apparently eats again. The line also suggests, in addition, the role that sight increasingly plays here, and at the climax the 'higher' sense takes over with the appearance of the '*crosse of Flowers*' from the bottom of the basket.

The sequence parodies the Fall, which, as we have seen, was closely associated with the sense of taste; Harpax's description of Theophilus as a 'great lickorish foole' even echoes Cornwallis's language. Eve's guilty act of eating the apple on Satan's suggestion is mirrored by Theophilus's compulsive consumption of Angelo's gift. Enticed by the appearance of the fruit and, thereafter, its taste, Theophilus is overwhelmed by the sensory experience. The sequence oscillates between the 'low' sense of taste – here recuperated as a tool of salvation through a paradoxical form of virtuous gluttony – and the 'high' sense of sight that eventually caps Theophilus's conversion and his divinely inspired rejection of Harpax.

Immaterial tasting

Theophilus's taste-assisted conversion in *The Virgin Martyr* suggests both the complex associations of taste in the playhouse and the opportunities that the physical representation of tasting offered to dramatists. Similar processes are at work in early modern drama's deployment of semi-figurative and metaphorical uses of taste. Many Jacobean and, especially, Caroline playwrights employed a discourse of taste in order to shape spectators' responses, drawing on an emergent model of aesthetic taste that is more often seen as a characteristic of eighteenth-century culture.[23] Plays thus often present themselves as dishes that are 'tasted' by spectators. '*PLays are like Feasts*', declares the epilogue to John Suckling's *Aglaura* (King's Men, 1638), declaring that '*everie Act should bee | Another Course, and still varietie*',[24] while the prologue to Ben Jonson's *Epicoene* (Children of the Queen's Revels, 1609–10) claims that 'Our wishes, like to those make public feasts, | Are not to please the cook's tastes, but the guests'.[25] Probably encouraged by the fact that many of his scenes are set in a venue for eating and drinking, in his prologue to *The Demoiselle, or The New Ordinary* (Queen Henrietta Maria's Men, *c.* 1638) Brome takes this stance further, saying:

> Readers and audients make good plays or books;
> 'Tis appetite makes dishes, 'tis not cooks.
> But let me tell you, though you have the power
> To kill or save, they're tyrants that devour
> And princes that preserve.[26]

Here, the ability of the audience to taste, in the sense of to test or try, and to come to the right opinion about what they taste, is figured through the ability to judge culinary flavours accurately. The *Demoiselle* prologue is apparently optimistic about its ability to shape the taste of the spectators, but others were less so. The prologue to James Shirley's *St Patrick for Ireland*, performed at the Werburgh Street playhouse in Dublin around 1639, appears to despair of ever being able to diagnose accurately the audience's taste: '*WE know not what will take, your pallats are* | *Various, and many of them sick I feare:* | *We can but serve up what our Poets dresse.*'[27] Such prologues and epilogues helped to shape and broaden an existing playhouse discourse of taste, linking the representation of taste on the stage with the processes through which those plays were received and 'tasted' by playgoers.

Within plays, the language of taste often inflects the treatment of kissing and, in particular, kissing on the lips. Some writers refer to the tastes of specific drinks or foodstuffs. Mercury in the Folio version of Jonson's *Cynthia's Revels* (Children of the Chapel, 1600), parodying courtly modes of courtship, cries, 'He that had the grace to print a kiss on these lips should taste wine and rose-leaves.'[28] References to sweetness are ubiquitous, and they frequently take on a high degree of irony, especially when stage action and dialogue combine. In Middleton's *The Revenger's Tragedy* (King's Men, *c.* 1606), Spurio comments as he kisses his stepmother, the Duchess, 'Had not that kiss a taste of sin, 'twere sweet.'[29] The 'sweetness' of a forbidden kiss is invoked elsewhere. In Massinger's *The Roman Actor* (King's Men, 1626), for instance, the idea that a kiss tastes like nectar is invoked twice in relation to Domitia, initially Lamia's wife, who is coveted by the tyrannical emperor Domitian. Parthenius tells the unwilling Lamia, 'She's Caesar's choice. It is sufficient honour | You were his taster in this heavenly nectar, | But now must quit the office', and Domitian reinforces the insult when he kisses Domitia shortly afterwards to underline his possession of her, commenting, 'There's no drop | Of melting nectar I taste from her lip | But yields a touch of immortality.'[30] The language of taste here conveys both sexual allure and the abuse of the royal prerogative.

Images of tasting as the expression of sexual appetite are further removed from stage action and become more purely metaphorical.[31] Gazetto in Dekker's *Match Me in London* (Queen Anna's Men, *c.* 1611–13) describes lecherous men as being 'like Mice amongst many Cheeses, they taste euery one, but feed vpon the best'.[32] Women's desire is also figured through taste. Emilia in *Othello* (King's Men, *c.* 1604) draws on the conventional references to specific flavours that we saw in physical representations of taste on the stage, telling Desdemona:

> Let husbands know
> Their wives have sense like them. They see, and smell,
> And have their palates both for sweet and sour,
> As husbands have.
> (4.3.92–95)

Here, the progression from sight to smell to taste appears to map a descent from the higher to the lower senses, as the case that Emilia makes for women's agency becomes increasingly sexualized. In other plays, the idea that sexual desire is a form of appetite, dependent on the achieved or anticipated 'taste' of the lover, becomes more unsettling. In the first scene of Shakespeare and Wilkins's *Pericles* (King's Men, *c.* 1607), the hero is determined to solve Antiochus's riddle and thus win his daughter, crying:

> You gods that made me man, and sway in love,
> That have inflamed desire in my breast
> To taste the fruit of yon celestial tree
> Or die in the adventure, be my helps[.]
> (1.62–65)

Pericles's image is relatively conventional in the context of courtship, but the presentation of sexual desire as appetite becomes increasingly disturbing as the scene progresses. The incestuous relationship between Antiochus and his daughter – of which the audience are forewarned – is made clear to Pericles through images of consumption. The opening of the daughter's riddle reads, 'I am no viper, yet I feed | On mother's flesh which did me breed' (1.107–8), and the shocked Pericles tells Antiochus that his daughter is 'an eater of her mother's flesh, | By the defiling of her parents' bed' and the father and daughter 'both like serpents are, who though they feed | On sweetest flowers, yet they poison breed' (1.173–76). Such images both reinforce and complicate the references to taste uttered by characters when they kiss, and the repeated allusions to serpents recall again the links between taste and the Fall.[33]

A full range of the figurative uses of taste are brought into play in Shakespeare's *Troilus and Cressida* (Chamberlain's Men, *c.* 1602–03). As Britland notes, conviviality plays an important role in this play, occurring 'in a space between battles', during which a 'metaphorical feasting on strange flesh generates a notion of a community creating its martial identity through the expulsion of an alternative conceived as luxurious, effeminising and dangerous'.[34] The play's uses of the idea of taste run alongside this multivalent 'feasting', both complementing and complicating its political, martial and gendered positions. In the early scenes references to taste figure strongly in discussions of the quarrel between the Trojans and Greeks, and the presentation of political advice. Nestor, for example, repeatedly refers to taste, declaring to the assembled Greek lords, 'For here the Trojans taste our dear'st repute | With their fin'st palate' (1.3.331–32), and commenting of Ulysses's plan to set Ajax against Achilles, 'I begin to relish thy advice, | And I will give a taste of it forthwith | To Agamemnon' (1.3.380–82). Here, taste figures in a generally positive manner – Nestor likes the taste of Ulysses's advice, and his diagnosis of the political dispute depends on his ability to judge the Trojans' own ability to discriminate. 'Bad' political advice is also figured through taste. Troilus's inability to take Cassandra seriously is evoked in his resistance to the idea that her warning might 'distaste' their cause:

> Her brainsick raptures
> Cannot distaste the goodness of a quarrel
> Which hath our several honours all engaged
> To make it gracious.
> (2.2.121–24)

Similarly, the political danger that Achilles's refusal to cooperate poses for the Greeks is suggested by Agamemnon in his resonant description of way in which the warrior no longer 'tastes' the same to him:

> Yet all his virtues,
> Not virtuously of his own part beheld,
> Do in our eyes begin to lose their gloss,
> Yea, and like fair fruit in an unwholesome dish
> Are like to rot untasted.
> (2.3.116–20)

The play thus begins to associate correct and decorous acts of tasting with male martial valour, and to associate 'distasting' with effeminate behaviour or female characters.

These associations, established in the early scenes of the play, develop and modulate as the action progresses. As Troilus waits for his encounter with Cressida he invokes the sensation of taste:

> I am giddy. Expectation whirls me round.
> Th'imaginary relish is so sweet
> That it enchants my sense. What will it be
> When that the wat'ry palates taste indeed
> Love's thrice-repurèd nectar?
> (3.2.16–20)

Troilus here uses the intensity of taste as a sensory experience to evoke his sexual anticipation and frustration. And the image is still on his mind when Cressida casts doubt on the performance and faith of lovers: 'Praise us as we are tasted; allow us as we prove' (3.2.87–88), he tells her, punning on the use of taste to mean 'test'. Yet the taste metaphor cannot stand well against this kind of pressure. When Cressida is forced to leave Troilus she cries:

> Why tell you me of moderation?
> The grief is fine, full, perfect that I taste,
> And violenteth in a sense as strong
> As that which causeth it. How can I moderate it?
> If I could temporize with my affection
> Or brew it to a weak and colder palate,
> The like allayment could I give my grief.
> (4.5.2–8)

Again, the immediacy of tasting as an experience is evoked, and the capacity to overpower mental and bodily decorum noted by Norden and others. Troilus is not on stage when Cressida says these words, but he nonetheless picks up her metaphor, saying that Time 'scants us with a single famished kiss, | Distasted with the salt of broken tears' (4.5.46–47). The idea of kissing as tasting is not articulated in the following sequence during which Cressida is kissed by each of the Greek lords in turn, yet it reverberates through it, and through the action that follows. Taste, like the dispute itself, is increasingly associated with sexuality – we recall Thersites's declarations that 'All the argument is a whore and a cuckold' (2.3.71) and 'Lechery, lechery, still wars and lechery! Nothing else holds fashion' (5.2.196–97). Notably, in this context, Diomedes's scepticism about Helen's worth is encapsulated in the taste metaphor that sets up his critique, as he tells Paris that the Trojans are 'as well to keep her that defend her, | Not palating the taste of her dishonour, | With such a costly loss of wealth and friends' (4.1.60–62). Although politicians may attempt to control its uses, and to regulate it, taste is overpowering and uncontrollable, the domain of fevered appetites and famished kisses.

Material and immaterial tasting

I close this chapter with Middleton's *Women Beware Women*, performed by the King's Men, probably in the early 1620s. This play brings together some of the tactics through which dramatists and actors 'staged' taste – literal and figurative, visual and verbal – that I have surveyed so far. Middleton's skilful handling of sustained lines of imagery has been well-known since the important work of M.C. Bradbrook and Christopher Ricks, both of whom pick up on the play's food imagery. Bradbrook counts a total of 22 passages in which food imagery is crucial, and notes the presence of 'continual direct references to feasting', while Margot Heinemann comments on its 'reiterated metaphors from cooking and house-keeping'.[35] Yet the specific ways in which taste blurs the boundaries between what is said and what is staged mean that this brand of sensory imagery cannot be wholly subsumed within *Women Beware Women*'s broader language of food.

Images of tasting are first introduced by Livia when she and Fabritio discuss the problem of arranged marriages and society's refusal to allow women to choose their own husbands. Invoking a sexual double-standard, Livia declares that the husband:

> tastes of many sundry dishes
> That we poor wretches never lay our lips to,
> As obedience, forsooth, subjection, duty, and such kickshaws
> All of our making, but served in to them;
> And if we lick a finger then sometimes,
> We are not to blame; your best cooks use it.[36]

In Livia's cynical view of the relationship between men and women, women in their sexual capacity are presented as 'dishes' served up to men, while marital infidelity is 'lick[ing] a finger'. Like Shakespeare in *Troilus and Cressida*, Middleton draws here on the unruliness of taste.

Perhaps unsurprisingly, the image of taste then recurs in the opening of Livia's exchange with Isabella, in which the older woman attempts to persuade the younger to respond positively to her uncle Hippolito's sexual desire for her. She tells her, 'If you can make shift here to taste your happiness, | Or pick out aught that likes you, much good do you. | You see your cheer; I'll make you no set dinner' (2.1.121–23). Isabella, who was not present at the earlier debate, fails to understand the metaphor fully, and responds, 'And, trust me, I may starve for all the good | I can find yet in this. Sweet aunt, deal plainlier' (ll. 124–25). There is a heavy irony to Middleton's use of the rhetoric of taste: not only was it intertwined with sexual behaviours and assumptions – as we have seen in the preceding discussion – but it was often used in reference to bawds and whores.[37] Livia is thus Isabella's 'aunt' – a slang word for a bawd – in more ways than one, and the exchange with her niece slips into established patterns of stage dialogue.

The ironies intensify as Livia's cheerful amorality and materialism – together with her use of the taste metaphor – are assimilated by Isabella after her aunt has convinced her that she is not her father's daughter. When Isabella apologizes to Hippolito for rejecting him she deploys the sexual associations of taste, food and appetite, telling him:

When we invite our best friends to a feast,
'Tis not all sweetmeats that we set before them;
There's somewhat sharp and salt, both to whet appetite
And make 'em taste their wine well. So methinks
After a friendly sharp and savoury chiding,
A kiss tastes wondrous well, and full o'th' grape.
                                        [*She kisses him*]
How think'st thou: does't not?
(ll. 198–204)

Isabella apparently kisses Hippolito as she describes the kiss, and her metaphor draws on the range of flavours evoked in dramatic contexts, moving from the 'sharp and salt' rejection to the kiss that tastes of wine. Middleton brings together visual and verbal representations of tasting – the audience hear about the taste of the kiss even as they watch the actors 'taste' each other's lips. Intensifying the implications of taste within the play, Isabella also uses this line of imagery in the following Act, when she discusses the Ward and his desire to inspect her before marriage, saying:

the comfort is
He's but a cater's place on't, and provides
All for another's table. Yet how curious
The ass is! – like some nice professor on't
That buys up all the daintiest food i'th' markets,
And seldom licks his lips after a taste on't.
(3.3.37–42)

The Ward is figured here as the expert professional caterer, purchasing rich foodstuffs and their pleasurable tastes for another's ultimate benefit.

Although the majority of the images of taste feature in the sub-plot, their applicability to the main plot, in which the Duke forces his sexual attentions on to the newly married Bianca, is evident. Indeed, it is underlined in Livia's comment after the 'seduction' which she facilitates – again acting in the role of the bawd who caters to the 'taste' of her clients – 'Sin tastes at the first draught like wormwood-water, | But, drunk again, 'tis nectar ever after' (2.2.475–76). These lines close the second Act, suggesting Middleton's structural uses of the image of taste. Furthermore, as Helen Wilcox points out, the centrepiece of *Women Beware Women* is the banquet that takes place in Act 3, and 'this mouth-watering but disturbing moment in the play symbolizes the unworthy desires of those many characters who long to taste "sweetmeats" and, as the play proceeds, "grow so greedy" (3.1.268, 3.2.77)'.[38]

The ironies of Middleton's use of images of taste become, however, fully apparent only at the end of the play. Although Ricks finds this sequence 'pitifully unconvincing' it in fact represents the culmination of the dramatist's careful combination of visual and verbal representations of taste.[39] In the opening lines of the wedding masque, Hymen presents a cup to Bianca, and Ganymede and Hebe offer 'nectar' to the Duke and Cardinal:

> *Hymen.* To thee, fair bride, Hymen offers up
> Of nuptial joys this the celestial cup.
> Taste it, and thou shalt ever find
> Love in thy bed, peace in thy mind.
>   *Bianca.* We'll taste you sure; 'twere pity to disgrace
> So pretty a beginning.
>   [*She drinks*]
>   *Duke.*   'Twas spoke nobly.
>   *Ganymede.* Two cups of nectar have we begged from Jove.
> Hebe, give that to innocence, I this to love.
>   [*He gives the Duke a cup, and Hebe gives the Lord Cardinal a cup*]
> (5.1.88–95.1)

This ceremonial 'tasting' is apparently part of a socially sanctioned process, yet the play's earlier uses of taste, and its association with illicit and coercive sexuality, endow the moment with added ambiguity and significance. Moreover, the presentation of 'nectar' here echoes in a potentially disturbing fashion Livia's reference to the way in which accustomed sexual sinning 'tastes' like nectar.

Perhaps unsurprisingly, therefore, one of the cups of nectar has been poisoned by Bianca and is intended for the Cardinal who has opposed her marriage. However, Ganymede and Hebe manage to give it to the wrong man: the Duke. Again, ironies gather around the image of taste – the Duke's desire to 'taste' Bianca sexually eventually results in his tasting the poison. When Hippolito, the Duke's opposite number in the sub-plot, dies, the applicability of the taste metaphor is made explicit:

> Lust and forgetfulness has been amongst us,
> And we are brought to nothing.
> [...]
> > Leantio's death
> Has brought all this upon us – now I taste it –
> And made us lay plots to confound each other.
> (ll. 184–85, 187–89)

'Taste' here means to touch, feel or experience, but it also registers the physical impact of death upon Hippolito's and, in performance, the actor's body.

Bianca's death, which caps the sequence, is presented as a literal and figurative tasting. She drinks from the same cup as the Duke, and declares,

> Pride, greatness, honours, beauty, youth, ambition,
> You must all down together, there's no help for't.
> Yet this my gladness is, that I remove
> Tasting the same death in a cup of love.
> (ll. 259–62)

Bianca's final action, tasting the poison that she meant for the Cardinal, and her last words, which underscore that gesture, connect together all of the acts of sexual betrayal that have been encapsulated and enabled by the action and metaphor of taste. Taste thus shapes the verbal texture, staging and dramaturgical structure of Middleton's tragedy.

Conclusion

In Shakespeare's *The Taming of the Shrew* (Chamberlain's Men, *c.* 1590–02), Katherine calls Grumio – who is starving her on Petruccio's orders – a 'false, deluding slave | That feed'st me with the very name of meat' (4.3.31–32). In doing so she describes a strategy crucial to the staging of taste, and one that was central to its power on the early modern stage. Because taste can never be fully shared, spectators are always 'fed' a substitute experience. They see Theophilus eat the fruit, and perhaps smell it too; they hear Troilus complain that kisses taste salty when they are mingled with tears. As we have seen, the potent associations of taste with both physical excess and spiritual endeavour, with cultivated appreciation and violent dislike, made it amenable to a wide range of dramatic uses, across innumerable styles and many genres. Like Acolastas, the embodiment of the sense with which I began this essay, taste can be simultaneously bodily and ecstatic, able to evoke both bestial desire and spiritual gluttony. This potent combination of materiality and ineffability lends it both imaginative and dramaturgical power, as generations of early modern playwrights were acutely aware.

Notes

1 *Poems with The Mvses Looking-Glasse: and Amyntas* (Oxford, 1638), p. 27 (the play has separate pagination).

2 See Masten, 'Toward a Queer Address: The Taste of Letters and Early Modern Male Friendship', *GLQ: A Journal of Lesbian and Gay Studies*, 10 (2004), 367–84; Stallybrass, 'Reading the Body: *The Revenger's Tragedy* and the Jacobean Theater of Consumption', *Renaissance Drama*, 18 (1987), 121–48; Cavell, '"Who Does the Wolf Love?": Reading *Coriolanus*', *Representations*, 3 (1983), 1–20; Britland, 'Circe's Cup: Wine and Women in Early Modern Drama', in *A Pleasing Sinne: Drink and Conviviality in Seventeenth-Century England*, ed. by Adam Smyth (Woodbridge: Brewer, 2004), pp. 109–25. For useful overviews of the field see Patricia Cahill, 'Take Five: Renaissance Literature and the Study of the Senses', *Literature Compass*, 6 (2009), 1014–30; Holly Dugan, 'Shakespeare and the Senses', *Literature Compass*, 6 (2009), 726–40; Joan Fitzpatrick, 'Reading Early Modern Food: A Review Article', *Literature Compass*, 8 (2011), 118–29; David Goldstein, 'Shakespeare and Food: A Review Essay', *Literature Compass*, 6 (2009), 153–74.

3 'Touch and Taste in Shakespeare's Theatres', in *Shakespeare's Theatres and the Effects of Performance*, ed. by Farah Karim-Cooper and Tiffany Stern (London: Arden Shakespeare, 2013), pp. 214–36.

4 *Parva Naturalia*, revised text with introduction and commentary by David Ross (Oxford: Clarendon Press, 1955), p. 212 (ch. 5, 445a 4).

5 *Mikrokosmographia: A Description of the Body of Man* (1615), p. 661. On hierarchies of the senses see also Louise Vinge, *The Five Senses: Studies in a Literary Tradition* (Lund: Gleerup, 1975).

6 For further discussion see Elizabeth Harvey, 'Introduction: The "Sense of All Senses"', in *Sensible Flesh: On Touch in Early Modern Culture* (Philadelphia: University of Pennsylvania Press, 2003), pp. 1–21.

7 *Essaies Vpon the Fiue Senses with a Pithie One Vpon Detraction* (1620), p. 45.

8 William Cornwallis, *Essayes* (1600–01), 2B8v.

9 *A Good Companion for a Christian Directing Him in the Way to God* (1632), G1v-G2r.

10 All of the images discussed in this paragraph and the one following are available on the British Museum's Collection Online. See www.britishmuseum.org/research/collection_online/search.aspx. On visual representations of the senses see also Carl Nordenfalk, 'The Five Senses in Late Medieval and Renaissance Art', *Journal of the Warburg and Courtauld Institutes*, 28 (1985), 1–22.

11 See British Museum S.3810 and 1873,0809.721.

12 See British Museum 1870,0514.1121, 1870,0514.1126 and 1997,0928.25.

13 See British Museum 1875,0508.14 and 1874,0711.1864.

14 See Karim-Cooper, 'Touch and Taste', p. 234.

15 *Lingua: Or the Combat of the Tongue, And the Five Senses for Superiority* (1607), C4r.

16 *The Custom of the Country*, ed. by Cyrus Hoy, in *The Dramatic Works in the Beaumont and Fletcher Canon*, general editor Fredson Bowers, 10 vols (Cambridge: Cambridge University Press, 1966–96), VIII, 3.2.53.

17 *The Dutch Courtesan*, ed. by David Crane (London: A&C Black, 1997), 3.3.74–76, 93.

18 *A Pleasant Conceited Comedie, Wherein is Shewed, How a Man may Chuse a Good Wife From a Bad* (1602), G3v.

19 *The Late Lancashire Witches*, ed. by Helen Ostovich, in *Richard Brome Online*, general editor Richard Cave (Royal Holloway, University of London/Humanities Research Institute, Sheffield University, 2010), www.hrionline.ac.uk/brome, 4.1; speech 597 (this edition numbers speeches rather than lines).

20 'Catholic Martyrdom in Dekker and Massinger's *The Virgin Martir* and the Early Modern Threat of "Turning Turk"', *ELH*, 73 (2006), 83–117 (p. 87). For an illuminating account of the uses of spectacle in this play see also Holly Crawford Pickett, 'Dramatic Nostalgia and Spectacular Conversion in Dekker and Massinger's *The Virgin Martyr*', *Studies in English Literature*, 49 (2009), 437–62.

21 *The Virgin Martyr*, in *The Dramatic Works of Thomas Dekker*, ed. by Fredson Bowers, 4 vols (Cambridge: Cambridge University Press, 1953–61), III, 5.1.56–58.

22 On this technique see Mariko Ichikawa, '"*Maluolio within*": Acting on the Threshold Between Onstage and Offstage Spaces', *Medieval and Renaissance Drama in England*, 18 (2005), 123–45 (pp. 124–25).

23 For further discussion of this issue see Karim-Cooper, 'Touch and Taste', pp. 231–34; on the history of aesthetic taste see Denise Gigante, *Taste: A Literary History* (New Haven, CT: Yale University Press, 2005), esp. pp. 3–18.

24 *Aglaura* (1638), p. 50.

25 *Epicene*, ed. by David Bevington, in *The Cambridge Edition of the Plays of Ben Jonson*, general editors David Bevington, Martin Butler and Ian Donaldson, 6 vols (Cambridge: Cambridge University Press, 2012), III, Prologue, ll. 8–9.

26 *The Demoiselle*, ed. by Lucy Munro, in *Richard Brome Online*, Prologue (speech 2).

27 *St Patrick for Ireland. The First Part* (1640), A2r.

28 *Cynthia's Revels: Revised Scenes from the 1616 Folio*, ed. by Eric Rasmussen and Matthew Steggle, in *Cambridge Ben Jonson*, V, 5.4.442–43.

29 *The Revenger's Tragedy*, ed. by MacDonald P. Jackson, in *Thomas Middleton: The Collected Works*, general editors Gary Taylor and John Lavagnino (Oxford: Oxford University Press, 2007), 3.5.204.

30 *The Roman Actor*, ed. by Martin White (Manchester: Manchester University Press, 2007), 1.2.62–64, 2.1.197–99.

31 On sexual 'tasting' see Gordon Williams, *A Dictionary of Sexual Language and Imagery in Shakespearean and Stuart Literature*, 3 vols (London: Athlone, 1994), III, 1367–68.

32 *Dramatic Works of Dekker*, III, 4.1.87–88.

33 For more detailed discussion of food images in *Pericles* see Doreen DelVecchio and
    Antony Hammond, eds, *Pericles* (Cambridge: Cambridge University Press, 1998),
    pp. 49–51.
34 Britland, pp. 109, 110.
35 Bradbrook, *Themes and Conventions of Elizabethan Tragedy*, 2nd edn (Cambridge:
    Cambridge University Press, 1980), p. 229; Heinemann, *Puritanism and Theatre:
    Thomas Middleton and Opposition Drama Under the Early Stuarts* (Cambridge:
    Cambridge University Press, 1980), p. 188. See also Ricks, 'Wordplay in Middle-
    ton's *Women Beware Women*', *Review of English Studies*, 12 (1961), 238–50. For a
    suggestive reading of the uses of the senses in the play, which looks briefly at taste,
    see Helen Wilcox, 'New Directions: *Women Beware Women* and the Arts of Looking
    and Listening', in *Women Beware Women: A Critical Guide*, ed. by Andrew Hiscock
    (London: Continuum, 2011), pp. 121–38. Other useful accounts include J.A. Cole,
    'Sunday Dinner and Thursday Suppers: Social and Moral Contexts of the Food
    Imagery in *Women Beware Women*', in *Jacobean Drama Studies: Jacobean Miscellany
    4*, ed. by James Hogg (Salzburg: Institut für Anglistik und Amerikanistik, Univer-
    sität Salzburg, 1984), pp. 86–98; Ann C. Christensen, 'Settling House in Middle-
    ton's *Women Beware Women*', *Comparative Drama* 29 (1995–6), 493–506.
36 *Women, Beware Women*, ed. by John Jowett, in *Middleton: Collected Works*, 1.2.40–
    45.
37 See Williams, III, 1367–68.
38 Wilcox, p. 121.
39 Ricks, p. 246.

2

'Dove-like looks' and 'serpents eyes': staging visual clues and early modern aspiration

Jackie Watson

The traditional sensual hierarchy, in the tradition of Aristotle, gave primacy to the sense of sight.[1] However, there is much evidence to suggest that the judgements of many late Elizabethans were more ambivalent. In this chapter I shall ask how far an early modern playgoer could trust the evidence of his or her own eyes. Sight was, at the same time, the most perfect of senses and the potential entry route for evil. It was the means by which men and women fell in love, and the means by which they established a false appearance. It was both highly valorized and deeply distrusted. Nowhere was it more so than at court, where men depended, for preferment and even survival, on the images they projected to others, but where their manipulation of one another was often interpreted as morally dubious. In their depictions of the performative nature of court life and the achievement of early modern ambition, late Elizabethan plays were engaged in this debate, and stage and court developed analogous modes of image projection. Here, I shall explore conflicting philosophical and early scientific attitudes to visual clues, before examining the moral judgements of seeing in late Elizabethan drama. Examples from these plays show appearance as a practical means of fulfilling courtly aspiration, but also suggest the moral concern surrounding such ambitions. These issues were of personal interest to the ambitious, playgoing young gentlemen of the Inns of Court. Finally, suggesting the irony of such a debate in a medium which itself relies so much upon appearance and deception, I shall conclude by considering the ways in which writers for the 'new technology' of the playhouse were engaged in guiding their audiences both in how to see, and how to interpret the validity of the visual.

Classical writers opened a debate on the operation of the eyes and the process of visual perception, which emerged as two contrasting theories. The 'emission theory' maintained that seeing was the result of rays being emitted from the eyes and falling upon an object in the outside world, with Euclid's *Optica* examining the idea that sight was enabled by beams from the eyes, and Ptolemy's *Optics* beginning to explore the properties of light which enabled vision. Contrasting 'intromission' theories were championed by Galen and Aristotle.

Their speculative ideas on the entry into the eye of something representative of the object viewed was subsequently found by experimental scientists to be nearer the truth. In *De Oratore* Cicero shows himself to be in sympathy with earlier writers in his preoccupation with seeing, and the popularity of this text in the education of Tudor England makes examination of his ideas important. He notes, 'the keenest of all our senses is the sense of sight', and in his allusion to the 'memory palace' of the lyric poet, Simonides of Ceos, he proposes a method of memory and subsequent rhetorical deployment which he shares with another major influence on Renaissance education, Quintilian's *Institutio Oratoria*. In developing this idea, Cicero demonstrates how sight enables the memory to be effectively deployed:

> perceptions received by the ears or by reflection can be most easily retained in the mind if they are also conveyed to our minds by the mediation of the eyes, [...] things not seen and not lying in the field of visual discernment are earmarked by a sort of image and shape so that we keep hold of as it were by an act of sight things that we can scarcely embrace by an act of thought.[2]

Cicero implies that there is a direct link between the eyes and the mind. Through whatever channel the images reach the eye, input progressing to the mind through that means is the most easily assimilated and the most long lasting, and the mind is able to embrace ideas through seeing that it can barely conceptualize. There is no sense here of deception. The implication is that sight conveys truth, and the action of the eyes leads the brain to perceive what exists.

The French physician André du Laurens followed this classical lead. Du Laurens connects his work firmly with the classical tradition and claims to convey 'the common judgement of all the Philosophers' in his conclusion that sight is 'the most noble, perfect and admirable' of the senses.[3] Despite his argument that the body could continue to exist with only taste and touch, his hierarchy continues in the Aristotelian mode and fixes hearing, and especially sight, as superior: those senses are allied to the mind. His explanation of sight's perfection is in religious terms. He lists four reasons for sight's supremacy, the first three of which clearly link seeing with virtue and bring this sense closer to God. The fourth has a moral quality of its own; sight is perfect 'in respect of the certaintie of his action' (p. 13). This belief in the veracity of visual perception, and its ability to convey truth to the mind, is developed further, and du Laurens establishes his reasons for 'the certaintie of [its] function':

> For it is out of all doubt that this is the most infallible sence, and that which least deceiveth: according to that which men are wont to say [...] that they see it with their owne eyes. And the proverbe used amongst men of olde time, is most true, that it is better to have a witnes which hath seene the thing, then ten which speake but by hearsay. (p. 17)

His faith in sight's veracity is shared by Robert Burton, who remarks in *The Anatomy of Melancholy*: 'Of [the] fiue Senses, Sight is held to bee most pretious, and the best, and that by reason of his obiect, it sees all the body at once, by it wee learne, & discerne all things, a sense most excellent for vse.'[4]

Du Laurens is also aware of the classical debate surrounding emission and intromission:

> Some [classical writers] would have that there should issue out of the eye bright beames or a certaine light which should reach unto the obiect, and thereby cause us to see it: other some would have it, that the obiect commeth unto the eye, and that nothing goeth out of the eye: the first doe hold that we see by emission or having something going forth of the eye, the latter by reception or receiving of the obiect into the eye. (p. 37)

Explaining the points of conflict, and outlining the reasons on both sides of the debate, du Laurens admits that emission is 'the most common receiued opinion', and begins his list of the arguments on the side of the 'manie learned clerkes', including Plato and Pythagoras, who support this view, presenting the evidence provided by the Basilisk and continuing: 'Women hauing their natural courses, infect the looking-glasses vpon which they cast their eyes. Some report, that if a Woolfe doe first see a man, that then such a man will become hoarse' (p. 38).[5]

On the 'intromission' side of the debate, the arguments supported by Aristotle 'and an infinite number of others', according to du Laurens, are based on the crystalline nature of the eye, and its being composed of water, rather than Plato's proposal of the eye being composed of fire and capable of emitting beams. Thus, as water is made to receive not to emit, the eye, he argues, sees by receiving:

> euery action therefore of the sences is accomplished by recieuing, and not by sending forth of any thing, which is an action; as for example the eare heareth by receiuing of sounds; smelling, by receiuing of odours; taste, by receiuing of tastes; and feeling, by receiuing of such qualities as may be felt: and then why should the eye by debarred of this receite? (p. 41)

In conclusion, du Laurens positions himself on the intromission side of the debate by way of a clear analogy: 'we see by receiving in, and not sending forth of anything [...] the eye is like unto the looking glasse, and this receiveth all such shapes as are brought unto it, without sending anything of it owne unto the object' (p. 41).

That this debate was perceived in the latter part of the sixteenth century as important, and that it was not regarded as a decided matter, is shown by Henry Wotton's choice of the subject in 1588 for his final university disputation. His three lectures on the eye, at the culmination of his studies at Queen's College, Oxford, were followed by a disputation on the 'Optique question, *Whether we see by the emission of the Beams from within, or the Reception of the Species from without*'.[6] Wotton, who was later to join the Middle Temple, was apparently persuasive in his arguments and impressed the much-admired academic Albericus Gentilis.

Much early modern discussion of the operation of sight emphasizes the link between the eye and the brain, rather as du Laurens does in his *Discourse*. A further connection is commonly made between the eye and the heart, the centre of emotional 'truth'. This link is perceived to be equally self-evident. Evidence of the ubiquity of this belief is shown in the Middle Temple's *Prince D'Amour* revels of 1597/8 where the subjects of the 'worthy Prince' are said to 'express their mindes by looks and touches, the most significant utterance of amorous Passions'.[7] There is humour, and suggestive innuendo, in the revels, but the equation here of the emission of looks with the utterance of love relies upon a general acceptance of the connection between love and seeing.[8] Du Laurens continues his account of the power of sight with the question 'how many soules have lost their libertie through the sight of the eyes?' Referring to theories of emission and intromission in this context, he explains that the link can be seen in two ways. The 'blind archer', Cupid:

> men say [...] doth enter into our hearts by this doore, and [...] loue is shaped by the glittering glimces which issue out of the eyes, or rather by certaine subtile and thin spirits, which passe from the heart to the eye through a straite and narrow way very secretly, and having deceived this porter, doe place love within. (p. 12)

Although du Laurens is still extolling the virtues of the visual, and argues throughout that the eye is superior to other sensual receptors in the body, in this account he has suggested the potential for even the 'most noble, perfect and admirable' of the senses to be an entry for the passion which overcomes reason. He has thus also introduced the idea of visual deception.

In the play in which Shakespeare makes the largest number of references to eyes, *A Midsummer Night's Dream*, written only a few years before the publication of Surphlet's translation of du Laurens, the playwright enters into the debate about the uncertain relationship of sight with the centres of feeling. This confusion is shown from the start, as Helena sets the play's debate about the nature and action of love into a multi-sensual context:

> O happy fair!
> Your eyes are lodestars, and your tongue's sweet air
> More tuneable than lark to shepherd's ear [...]
> Sickness is catching. O, were favour so!
> Your words I catch, fair Hermia; ere I go,
> My ear should catch your voice, my eye your eye,
> My tongue should catch your tongue's sweet melody.
> (1.1.182–89)

Shortly after this plaint from Helena, Hermia's address to Lysander, just before she exits to prepare for their flight to the woods, plays on the synaesthetic nature of love, telling him that 'we must starve our sight | From lovers' food, till morrow deep midnight' (ll. 222–23). Yet, despite the sensuousness sustained throughout the play, there is no doubt that the most influential sense is that of sight, shown clearly in the recurrent use of 'love-in-idleness', deceiving the visual perception of Titania as well as the human lovers. Hermia's 'lodestars', admired by Helena, suggest the Platonic vision of eyes composed of fire, emitting beams, and the conflicting ideas of emission and intromission are a preoccupation of the play as a whole. In her soliloquy at the end of the opening scene Shakespeare has Helena lament that Demetrius did not fall in love 'ere [he] looked on Hermia's eyne' (l. 242), showing her uncertainty as to whose eyes were the actors and whose the receivers. She is clearly confused, as du Laurens admits is common, as to whether the action of his looking caused the love to flow from him, or whether beholding Hermia's eyes allowed him to perceive something in the beauty of those eyes that she was emitting. Just prior to these lines, she has concluded, ironically, that 'Love looks not with the eyes, but with the mind, | And therefore is winged Cupid painted blind' (ll. 234–35). Her image of 'Cupid painted blind' brings us back to du Laurens's 'blind archer' who placed love within by deceiving 'this porter', the eye. Helena's confusion over the source of love and Oberon's ability to influence the reception of viewed images through the action of Puck, added to the 'deception' referred to by even the admiring du Laurens and show a common awareness of the moral problems of sight.

Much distrust of sight was the effect of contemporary theological writing. Luther famously argued that Christian faith was not to be grasped by human sight, and Erasmus's illustration of the limitations of human free will, analogous to the limitations of sight, shows a clear belief in the inadequacy of the senses:

> A human eye that is quite sound sees nothing in the dark, a blind one sees nothing in the light; thus the will though free can do nothing if grace withdraws from it, and yet when the light is infused, he who has sound eyes can shut off the sight of the object so as not to see, can avert his eyes, so that he ceases to see what he previously saw[.][9]

Doubts concerning the reliability of the senses, particularly vision, lay behind the arguments of many of those opposing the playhouses. The battle of antitheatrical tracts around 1580, for which Stephen Gosson's *The Schoole of Abuse* (1579) proved the catalyst, demonstrated a consistent attack on the arts' engagement with the senses of their audiences.[10] Gosson in later life became a Church of England clergyman, but he knew that of which he spoke, having dabbled with play writing during his early life in London. Anthony Munday, in support of Gosson, also wrote and acted for the theatre he apparently condemned. Though the purpose of his anonymously published 1580 polemic was to attack the watching of plays, and not all kinds of visual perception, the means of achieving the former equally condemned the latter. In stridently moral terms, he reveals a fear of sensual experiences and their connection with the mind and the heart: a link that, as we have seen, philosophers and early scientists took to be close. Plays, Munday argues, lead to sin through the action on playgoers' eyes:

> Are not our eies [at the playhouse] carried awaie with the pride of vanitie? [...] Are not our hartes through the pleasure of the flesh; the delight of the eie; and the fond motions of the mind, withdrawen from the seruice of the Lord, & meditation of his goodness?[11]

Although the experience is clearly a multi-sensory one, Munday supports others' opinions that the power of sight is above that of all the other senses and ironically this makes it an area of particular vulnerability, providing as it does access to the heart, the mind and the soul. He declaims, 'There commeth much evil in at the eares, but more at the eies, by these two open windowes death breaketh into the soule'. Munday justifies the potential harm of vision, with reference to the memory palace (which he associates with Petrarch rather than with Simonides of Ceos, Cicero or Quintilian):

> Nothing entereth in more effectualie into the memorie, than that which commeth by seeing; things heard do lightlie passe awaie, but the tokens of that which wee haue seene, saith Petrarch, sticke fast in vs whether we wil or no [...] Alack what violence carieth vs awaie, to be merie an hower, and always after to be sad; to see that at one time, which a thousande times after wee shal rue that euer we sawe it! (pp. 95–96)[12]

Gosson, with a similarly anti-theatrical purpose in his second tract, *Playes Confuted in Five Actions* (1582), claims that 'the longer we gaze, the more we crave'.[13] In the work of both men, the action of seeing is inherently luxurious and sinful and allows death to enter man's spiritual core. The vulnerability of the eyes, and the potential for love, or evil, to enter therein is further demonstrated in *Twelfth Night* where Shakespeare develops a plot to untangle what appears initially to be another chain of unreturned affections. This time, rather than the magical effects of the juice of 'love-in-idleness' applied to the eyes, Olivia exemplifies the common belief that sight of one's beloved renders one helpless to resist. Comparing falling in love to succumbing to plague, she exclaims that she feels Cesario's 'perfections | With an invisible and a subtle stealth | To creep in at mine eyes' (1.5.286–88). The combination of images of bodily invasion, secrecy and disease suggests common ground with those who believed the eyes to be an entry point for evil. As with the actions of a miasma, the individual body – the soul and the mind, as well as the heart – are penetrated, corrupted, deformed by the material entering at the 'open windowes' of the eyes.

As we saw earlier, eyes rendered one vulnerable to deception as well as to love. Munday makes his dread of visual deception clear in his comparison of sin and misleading appearance:

> It were il painting the Diuel like an Angel, he must be portraied forth as he is, that he maie the better be knowen. Sinne hath alwaies a faire cloake to couer his filthie bodie. And therefore he is to be turned out of his case into his naked skin, that his nastie filthie bodie, and stinking corruption being perceaued, he might come into the hatred and horror of men. (p. 44)

This argument takes for granted that moral judgement is naturally based on appearance and revealed by dress. In other parts of the tract, it is viewed behaviour which establishes the virtue, or lack of it, in the playgoing public: 'For who can see man or woman resort to an house which is notoriouslie wicked, but will judge them to be of the crewe of the wicked and vngodlie?' (p. 55). There is a causal connection between what a man sees and the judgement he makes. Rather than questioning whether people should trust the judgement of their eyes, however, Munday argues that because of this natural link people should work hard to appear as they wish to be judged. If they are innocent, they should not look or behave as if they were sinful.

The audience's perception of appearance and reality on stage, for instance their apprehension of Viola's transformation into Cesario, shows this judgement in practice. This is an example of a key area of objection to playgoing. Gosson's *Playes Confuted* is the first of the anti-theatrical tracts to cite *Deuteronomy*'s sanction against cross-dressing, though he is not the first to find this aspect of early modern theatre morally reprehensible. Analogous with Munday's description of the devil's deceptive clothing, a boy actor in women's dress was open to an accusation of sin through taking on a false appearance. Known to Gosson from sermons attended while he was a student at Corpus Christi College, Oxford, John Rainolds, a leading voice in late Elizabethan Protestantism, also wrote strongly against boys in female costume on the stage. His strength of feeling perhaps derived from his acting of the role of Hippolyta in *Palamon and Arcite* in his own student days at the college.[14] An epistolary exchange between Rainolds and William Gager, much of which was published in 1599, was the means of their debate on theatrical morality, and in response to Gager's rather disingenuous defence of cross-dressing (that one who only adopted female clothing for an hour or two could not be said to 'wear' it) Rainolds tells an anecdote which stresses the importance of visual perception to the theatre-going audience:

> For how many hundreds are there of eye-witnesses, that your *Euryclea, Melantho, Penelope, Phaedra, Nais*, others, did weare wemens raiment? Howe many did obserue, and with mislike haue mentioned, that *Penelopes* maides did not only weare it, but also sate in it among true wemen in deed [...]? neither were more

knowne to them to bee men, then *Achilles* was at firste to *Deidamia*; vntill they
suspected it, seeing them entreated by the wooers to rise and dance vpon the
stage. I wish there had not bene so bad a token to convince you; nor so many
beholders to testifie thereof: though I am glad withal that they had such mislike
of the thing testified.[15]

What Rainolds describes here is the belief of the female playgoers in the evidence
of their own eyes. The actors who appear in the garb of Penelope's maids sit
amongst them, dressed as women amongst women, and taken as such without
question. The visual clues lie in their dress, probably their pre-pubescent
complexions and perhaps learned feminine gestures. But there is no doubting
their ability to deceive the eyes of spectators, as elsewhere we are told, of a good
actor, that 'what we see him personate, wee thinke truly done before vs'.[16] John
Manningham, at the Inns of Court and ambitious for success, may well have
been such a spectator. His well-known summary of the 1601/2 performance of
Twelfth Night at Middle Temple is as follows:

A good practice in it to make the steward believe his lady-widow was in love with
him, by counterfeiting a letter as from his lady, in general terms telling him what
she liked best in him and prescribing his gesture in smiling, his apparel etc. and
then, when he came to practice, making him believe they took him to be mad.[17]

Henk K. Gras, exploring the importance of Manningham's diary entry,
proposes that the young Innsman was entirely convinced of Olivia's being a
woman and a widow, reliant both on the visual clues of the actor and his appearance. Gras suggests that Manningham 'notices the characters as if they were
living beings and more in terms of what they did than of what they said, more
in terms of what they looked like, than of what they were'. Suggesting that the
most likely reason for Manningham's assumption that Olivia is a widow would
be the black costume the actor would have worn to signify her mourning for her
brother, Gras concludes, 'Manningham takes Olivia to be a lady, not particularly responding to the fact that a boy played the part. Since he commented
on a performance, not on a literary text,' just like the playgoers taken in by
Penelope's maids 'the theatrical illusion of reality worked for him'.[18]

Manningham's focus appears to be not on the Olivia/Cesario/Orsino plot,
but, as we can see, on that of the steward, Malvolio. *Twelfth Night* demonstrates
the importance of appearance to those, like Manningham and his peers, who
desired patronage and preferment. Malvolio is an example of such a man, keen
to rise through his career. In his case it was through marriage with a social
superior, as, indeed, it was for John Manningham himself. Malvolio recognizes
that to do this he must first 'look the part', and the humour of the letter scene
begins with Maria's description of the Steward 'yonder i' the sun practising
behaviour to his own shadow this half-hour' (2.5.15–16). The comic effect of
the scene, of course, is reliant upon observation, and demonstrates further an

aspiring man's need to appear to be not only what he wished to be judged by others, but also what he wished to *become*. Contemporary 'courtier literature', like anti-theatrical tract writing, reveals simultaneously a belief that appearance reflected reality, and the potential for visual deception.

Writings about the appearance and behaviour of men in power, which sometimes explicitly and sometimes inadvertently advised those who wished to be in power, seem to have seen visual clues reflecting moral worth directly.[19] Giovanni della Casa, whose *Galateo* was translated by Robert Peterson of Lincoln's Inn in 1576, explores this correlation between visual clues and the reality which underlies them. The book is subtitled 'A treatise of the ma[n]ners and behauiours, it behoueth a man to vse and eschewe, in his familiar conuersation. A worke very necessary & profitable for all Gentlemen, or other'. In it, della Casa explicitly advises his gentlemen, and aspirant gentlemen, on the expectations of sophisticated courtiership. Implicitly casting doubt on the self-sufficient value of virtue, men need to behave appropriately, he comments, as 'Without [gracefulness] even goodness has no beauty and beauty has no charm [...]'. The implication is again that there is a connection between goodness and beauty which it is the courtier's responsibility to make explicit by his behaviour. Della Casa goes on to establish this correlation between appearance and moral value more firmly, noting how self-evident it is that 'all forms of vice are in themselves obnoxious, for vice is ugly'.[20] The courtier's appearance of social ease, giving the visual clues of being comfortable in his rank, knowing how to dress, act and so on, creates in the observer a belief in his worth.

Late Elizabethan drama is rich in examples of those who, like Malvolio, desired to rise by appearing to be sophisticated: to be what Michelle O'Callaghan terms the *urbanissimus homo*. She outlines 'the change in behaviour and "ways of seeing" during the Renaissance, occasioned by the dissemination of civility from forms of aristocratic distinction to codes of conduct for the expanding "gentle" classes'.[21] That is, young men who had benefited from the increased access to education, at the universities and the Inns of Court, and who aspired to use this learning to gain preferment, needed to learn to *appear* as their predecessors, mainly of more elite, aristocratic origins, had *been*. As in the construction of theatrical performance, this action was conscious and 'codes of conduct', such as *Galateo* and many others like it, encouraged men to build up a deception which could, in time, become a new reality. As Harold Brooks comments in his introduction to *A Midsummer Night's Dream*, 'Identity [...] rests in great measure upon perception, upon how we appear to others and to ourselves.'[22] The 'ourselves' here suggests that the barrier between reality and appearance is rather a permeable one; that what is originally a posture, masking a man's lack of real courtly sophistication, by repetition becomes the thing it apes. The eyes begin by deceiving, but in time what was false becomes true. Observers may conclude, 'Cultivation of the surface shapes concern over what, if anything, lies below, and the notion of identity comes to seem increasingly precarious.'[23] Virtue and truth risk losing their existential reality.

This process was not a hidden one and many were conscious of the processes involved in the social mobility which surrounded them. Such rising men became the victims of satirical stage portrayals. Just as Gosson and Munday were able to write more effectively about the threats posed by theatrical performance because of their having been part of the playing world, many of those who wrote the most effective satires of aspirant young men were from that same background and environment. One might consider Templar playwright John Marston's Balurdo, the persistent, if not very bright, young man of ambition in the *Antonio* plays, who shows his desire to succeed at court by carrying around 'tables' where he can jot down his thoughts, in a parody perhaps of Hamlet.[24] Henk K. Gras suggests that this was by no means unusual, and that '"note-taking" is thought to have been written practice, both at plays and at sermons'.[25] Certainly Jonson comments on 'narrow-eyed decipherers with their writing tables' in *Every Man Out of his Humour* and, as we might expect of Marston, at this point still a legal student, the depiction of Balurdo is closely based on the appearance and behaviour of real young men of his acquaintance.[26] Rather than the debate upon the value of existence we see in *Hamlet*, Balurdo's thoughts are considerably more limited, and practical. Marston demonstrates his understanding that the aspirant courtier needs to appear more sophisticated than he is in visually comic *tours de forces* such as the dumb-show which opens Act 3, Scene 2 of *Antonio and Mellida*:

> Enter *Balurdo*, backward; *Dildo* following him with a looking glasse in one hand, & a candle in the other hand: *Flavia* following him backward, with a looking glasse in one hand, and a candle in the other. *Rossaline* following her. *Balurdo* and *Rossaline* stand setting of faces[.][27]

The focus is on conscious visual deception, with the looking glasses demonstrating the vanity that accompanies such aspirations. The character Balurdo is a means by which Marston satirizes those who try to learn their trade and to rise by means of their appearance, delivered before a Paul's playhouse audience with many of those present trying to 'achieve greatness' through the adoption of courtly behaviour. The assumption that audience members went to the theatre to learn as they were watching the actors what visual clues to project to those watching them is parallel to Munday's belief that watching infidelity on stage will lead the spectators to engage in similarly sinful behaviour:

> some hauing noted the ensamples how maidens restrained from the marriage of those whome their frends haue misliked, haue learned a policie to preuent their parents by stealing them awaie; some seeing by ensample of the stage plaier one carried with too much liking of an other mans wife, hauing noted by what practise she hath bene assailed and ouertaken, haue not failed to put the like in effect in earnest, that was afore showen in iest. (pp. 97–98)

While Balurdo's fascination with clothing and imagery of textiles reveals the importance of visual appearance for those aspirant young men whom the playwright knew and who formed one of his most important audience segments, Marston aims to shape their response to this phenomenon through his characterization of Balurdo.[28] The boy actor playing the role at the Paul's playhouse announces in the opening metatheatrical Induction that he is to play 'the part of all the world [...] the fool' (Induction, 29–31) and it is in sensual terms that Balurdo's foolishness is framed from the beginning. His opening words in *Antonio and Mellida* reveal his lack of 'sense' in the confusion of 'Oh, I smell a sound' (1.1.44). This is not the overpowering synaesthesia of love seen in *A Midsummer Night's Dream*, but the confusion of one uncontrolled in both his sensory perception, and the clues he gives to others. There is no doubt that, as Catzo tells his fellow servant, Dildo, who works for Balurdo, 'thy master' is an 'Idiot' (2.1.24).

The actor playing Balurdo also tells us of his social status, as 'a wealthy mountebanking Burgomasco's heir of Venice' (32), and the would-be courtier's wealth allows him to base his courtly aspiration on the costly appearance he believes will impress potential patrons or a mistress. Reassuring Rossaline that she may have had his 'thought for a penny', he cannot help swearing in passing 'by this crimson satin that cost eleven shillings, thirteen pence, three pence halfpenny a yard' (2.1.74–77), and a little later returning to the subject, noting approvingly that 'my silk stocking hath a good gloss and I thank my planets my leg is not altogether unpropitiously shap'd' (100–01). In focusing so intently on his dress and appearance, Balurdo is following the advice of texts such as *Galateo*, where della Casa tells his reader, 'Your apparell must be shaped according to the fashion of the time, and your calling [...] Euery man may applie those fashions, that be in common vse, ye moste to his owne aduantage, that he can', then spends some time discussing flattering fabrics and fashions for specific body shapes.[29] The potential for superficiality and vanity to be the results of the process of courtly advancement is implied by Marston, and may be a warning, or even a reprimand, to the aspirant members of the Inns of Court he knew so well and whose attitudes would be affected by what they observed on stage. As one recent scholar has noted, 'The more glittering the surface the more doubt it created about the nature and quality of what might be "below" it'; Balurdo's demonstration of the courtier's fixation with transmitting the appropriate visual signals makes him '[t]he figure of fashion, who stages his own persona as a carefully manufactured display of collected fragments, [and who] becomes a focus of interest and anxiety'.[30]

Balurdo is mocked by his on-stage audience, the malcontent Feliche, as Malvolio was by Sir Toby and his associates. For his Paul's playhouse audience Marston satirizes the shallowness of a court so driven by considerations of appearance. The visual clues that a fool such as Balurdo attempts to give to those observing him are attempts to conceal his lack of worth. One cannot help but recall the deception and manipulation of playgoers' sight described by Gosson, Munday and Rainolds. Marston, though not opposing the theatre, shares with those who argued its immorality many of their beliefs about its affective power.

Playwrights thus did not merely reflect what they saw in society. But as well as the satirical depiction of foolish courtiers, some did more to suggest disapproval of that societal shift which made reality uncertain, and mixed vice and virtue in a potentially dangerous fashion. Pettie's 1581 translation of Guazzo's *Civil Conversation* notes:

> That he which is evill and taken to bee good, may doe muche mischiefe. Notwithstanding, I put these same in the number of the tollerable: for though it trouble your conscience to come in their companie, yet you give no occasion of mislike to the worlde, for that they are not reputed evill[.][31]

The recognition of evil, while at the same time deciding to classify it as 'tollerable', is a demonstration of the pragmatic moral attitude that many commentators feared. Guazzo's Count Annibale, later in the same text, argues for a version of the sumptuary laws, that the ruler should restrict those who are not gentry, 'forcing them to weare such apparel as may bee at least different from Gentlemen' as 'under such a maske there may be much falshood wrought'. Princes, also, 'ought not to suffer the honour and degree of gentrie to be disgraced by the presumption of malapert clownes'.[32] The inappropriate assumption of a false place in society by della Casa's 'and other' is one issue identified here, and is perhaps seen as a greater problem than those who are evil but who, by their manipulation of visual clues, are not taken to be so. Yet the potential for deceptive appearance to equate with falsehood and evil intent is demonstrated by the whole succession of villainous stage figures of this period who manipulate the noble and the good by their 'mischiefe'. From Shakespeare's Iago, Edmund and Don John, to Marston's Piero, or Jonson's Sejanus, those writing for the stage deliver a clear sense in histories and tragedies of the threat of visual deception. And it is impossible for a modern student of this theatre not to see irony in their seeming disapproval of the mechanism of deception, for upon what, if not that, did theatre itself rely? Marston and others of his profession, such as Gosson, who had worked for the theatre, and Munday, who was to do so again, were conscious of the dubious morality of theatrical presentation, of the ambiguity of visual clues in society itself and of the way that stage performances used those clues to manipulate their audiences.

The practicalities of sixteenth-century social mobility, and the demands it made on people's need to 'see' differently as well as to judge sight itself in a new way, had for the theatre an unexpected effect: one which allowed contemporary dramatists to work with their audience to develop a new way of interpreting

action in the playhouse. It is clear that many commentators on the new Elizabethan theatrical experience felt that audience behaviour would be directly
affected by what was seen on stage, as we saw Munday argue earlier.[33] There is
a direct causal link envisaged between the stage example and the real lives of
the playgoers, yet while watching a play in the theatre itself, the relationship
between playgoers and what they saw was perhaps in nature somewhere *between*
their reaction to fact and that to fiction. During the performance, audiences
undoubtedly perceived the action as to some degree mimetic but, accustomed
in life to developing a new *modus operandi* in terms of visual clues, they found
themselves called upon to use those strategies in the theatre.[34] There was a
connection between stage representation and reality: the interaction between
the two was complex, but it is my proposal that there was a closer link than,
perhaps, in much theatre today, and, among this social group, a kind of circu-
larity. Plays of the late Elizabethan period represented rising courtiers working
to suit their appearance to the career they desired, and those plays were being
watched, and in some cases written too, by the men of the Inns of Court, many
learning their trade as rising courtiers and reading the literature which advised
them how to appear.

I conclude this chapter with an example from the work quoted in my title.
This is a play unusual in its depiction of an ambitious man who succeeds
through increased Tudor social mobility without being a villain. Written by
the intriguing W.S., and performed by the Lord Chamberlain's Men, the
play has much to say to its initial audience about the visual.[35] It may have
had a particularly powerful effect on that segment of the audience who were
themselves ambitious for courtly preferment. *Thomas, Lord Cromwell* shows
the famous Henrician reformer coming from his roots in a London smithy, and,
through intellect, education and generous behaviour towards others, becoming
the King's highest courtier. His rise provokes opposition from those repre-
sentatives of the established elite that such a man challenges. Chief amongst
those is Bishop Stephen Gardiner, whose desire to defeat Cromwell's ambitions
leads him to build a false case against the Lord Chancellor. In his opposition
to the honest Cromwell, Gardiner lies and deceives, showing all the signs of a
typical stage villain; he is a man who, as Guazzo warned us, 'is evill and taken
to bee good' and by this he 'may doe muche mischiefe'. Yet the ambivalent
moral attitude of Guazzo also warned us that the world does not always punish
wrongdoers and champion the cause of the right. *Thomas, Lord Cromwell* stages
the existence of such evil men unpunished in the world, 'for that they are not
reputed evill'. In the less than perfect world in which theatre audiences live, 'wee
ought to satisfie rather others than our selves, and to give place to the common
custome', so Gardiner's plots succeed, and he manages to bring his opponent
down through his slander.[36] Almost the last words addressed to Cromwell are
the churchman's jubilant summation, 'Your Dove-like looks were view'd with

serpents eyes.'[37] Suggestive of the split between reality and appearance at the court where Thomas has been conspicuously successful, the strange accusation also shows the ambivalence surrounding the visual sense. It appears to evoke the ancient debate on emission and intromission theories of sight, asking how much meaning lies in the eyes of the man viewing, and how much in the looks seen. Gardiner intends to cloud his opponent's virtue, suggesting what appears to be a dove is actually a serpent, but his words suggest the potential for visual clues to put in doubt, at least on stage, the existential reality of moral concepts and of virtues; Gardiner's real achievement in his ambiguous utterance is, as Cromwell responds, that we think of Gardiner himself, the man of God, as the real serpent.

Finally, this discussion illustrates how the playwright guides audience members on the cultivation of response through the manipulation of visual clues. A segment of that audience, such as the men from the Inns of Court who were themselves treading the paths of courtly ambition, could well have seen in *Thomas, Lord Cromwell* the enactment of a process with which they would engage in their own lives. A man whose beginnings were lowly, whose intellect, appearance and behaviour enabled him to rise, is at his downfall represented in terms of problematic visual clues. Rising courtiers, as other members of W.S.'s audience, became, in this way, increasingly adept at recognizing the ambiguities and potential deceptions of things they 'saw' on the late Elizabethan stage.[38]

Notes

1 Aristotle, *De anima* (*On the Soul*), trans., intro. and notes H. Lawson-Tancred (Harmondsworth: Penguin, 1986), bk. II, chap. 7–11, pp. 173–86.

2 *De Oratore*, trans. E.W. Sutton, Loeb Classical Library (London: Heinemann, 1967), 2.87.357.

3 *A Discourse of the Preservation of the Sight: of Melancholike diseases; of Rheumes, and of Old age. Composed by M. Andreas Laurentius, ordinarie Physition to the King, and publike professor of Phisicke in the Universitie of Mompelier. Translated out of French into English, according to the last Edition, by Richard Surphlet, Practitioner in Phisicke* (1599), pp. 12–13. Further references cited in the text.

4 *The Anatomy of Melancholy* (1621), Cr: Part 1, Section 1, Member 2, Subsection 6.

5 The Basilisk was a mythological creature whose looks could kill; cf. *Winter's Tale* (1.2.388–90) where Polixenes shows his despair to Camillo: 'Make me not sighted like the basilisk. | I have looked on thousands who have sped the better | By my regard, but killed none so', or *2 Henry VI* (3.2.51–53) where the king cries out to Suffolk, 'Look not upon me, for thine eyes are wounding – | Yet do not go away. Come, basilisk, | And kill the innocent gazer with thy sight.'

6 Isaac Walton, *The Lives of Dr. John Donne, Sir Henry Wotton, Mr. Richard Hooker, and Mr. George Herbert* (1670), p. 12.

7 Benjamin Rudyerd, *Le Prince D'Amour* (1660), pp. 4–5. For more on the connection between Inns of Court revels, drama and aspiring courtiership, see my article,

"'He writes, he railes, he jests, he courts, what not,/ And all from out his huge long scraped stock/ Of well penn'd playes": learning the performance of courtiership at the early modern Inns of Court', in *Spectatorship at the Elizabethan Court*, eds Susanne Scholz and Daniel Dornhofer, special issue of *Zeitspruenge. Forschungen zur Fruehen Neuzeit*, 17 (2013), 63–83.

8   For further discussion of the connection between sight and love, see Aurelie Griffin's essay in this volume.

9   'On the Freedom of the Will', translated by E. Gordon Rupp, in *Luther and Erasmus: Free Will and Salvation* (Philadelphia: The Westminster Press, 1969), p. 91.

10 For further discussion of the sensory engagement antitheatricalists associated with theatregoing see Hannah August's Chapter 11, in this volume.

11 *A second and third blast of retrait from plaies and Theaters* (1580), p. 64. All further references are cited in the text.

12 For further examination of the role of the mind, as well as the eyes, in visual decep-tion see Stuart Clark's *Vanities of the Eye: Vision in Early Modern European Culture* (Oxford: Oxford University Press, 2007): 'visual experiences were constructed out of mental expectations as well as data transmitted by the crystalline lens' (p. 60). This clearly has relevance for my later comments here on Manningham.

13 *Playes Confuted in Five Actions* (1582), F6r (4th Action).

14 According to Mordechai Feingold, in his entry on Rainolds for the *ODNB*, 'judging by the vehemence with which he criticized stage plays a quarter of a century later, this experience left an indelible impression on him'.

15 *Th'Overthrow of Stage-Playes, by the Way of Controversie betwixt D. Gager and D. Rainoldes* (Middelburg: Richard Schilders, 1599), p. 102.

16 'An Excellent Actor' from Thomas Overbury, *Characters* (1616), M2v.

17 *Diary of John Manningham of the Middle Temple and of Bradbourne, Kent, Barrister-at-Law, 1602-3*, ed. John Bruce, Esq. (London: J.B. Nichols and Sons, 1868), p. 18.

18 'Direct Evidence and Audience Response to *Twelfth Night*: The Case of John Manningham of the Middle Temple', *Shakespeare Studies*, 21 (1995), 109–154 (p. 112).

19 For further discussion of the purposes, both those declared and those undeclared, of courtier literature, see Frank Whigham, *Ambition and Privilege: The Social Tropes of Elizabethan Courtesy Theory* (Berkeley, CA: University of California Press, 1984).

20 Giovanni della Casa, *Galateo*, translated by Robert Peterson of Lincoln's Inn (1576), p. 106.

21 Michelle O'Callaghan, *The English Wits: Literature and Sociability in Early Modern England* (Cambridge: Cambridge University Press, 2007), p. 27.

22 Harold Brooks (ed.), *A Midsummer Night's Dream*, The Arden Shakespeare Second Series (London: Methuen, 1979), p. cxxxvii.

23 Janette Dillon, *Drama, Court and City, 1595-1610: Drama and Social Space in London* (Cambridge: Cambridge University Press, 2000), p. 65.

24 Tables, 'A small portable tablet for writing upon, esp. for notes or memoranda' (*OED*, 2b.), were commonplace amongst the educated; cf. *Hamlet*, 'O villain, villain, smiling, damnèd villain! | My tables, | My tables – meet it is I set it down | That one may smile and smile and be a villain' (1.5.106–09).

25 'Direct Evidence and Audience Response', p. 114.

26 *The Works of Ben Jonson*, ed. by Herford and Simpson (Oxford: Clarendon Press, 1925–52), III, 2.6.171.

27 *Antonio and Mellida*, ed. by G.K. Hunter (London: Edward Arnold, 1965); all further quotations are from this edition and are cited in the text.

28 See Charles Whitney's *Early Responses to Renaissance Drama* (Cambridge: Cambridge University Press, 2006), which proposes the term 'segments' for different portions of an audience, each of which has its own background and interests, and thus a different relationship with the performance.

29 della Casa, pp. 108–09.

30 Dillon, p. 64.

31 *La Civile Conversation of M. Steeven Guazzo*, trans. by George Pettie (books 1–3, 1581) in *The Tudor Translations*, 2 vols (London: Constable, 1925), I, 62.

32 *La Civile Conversation*, I, 196–97.

33 *A second and third blast*, pp. 97–98.

34 See Laurie Maguire's comments on mimesis and representation in, 'Audience-Actor Boundaries and *Othello*', *Proceedings of the British Academy – 181, 2010–11 Lectures* (Oxford: Oxford University Press for the British Academy, 2012), p. 131. In this lecture she suggests that audiences of early modern drama were being directed and educated in their responses to the work being presented on stage by regular textual guidance.

35 The seventeenth-century attribution of the play to Shakespeare is now generally doubted, and the author is still unknown; first published in 1602, critics also dispute the time of writing, dating the play most often from the final years of Elizabeth's reign.

36 *La Civile Conversation*, I, 62.

37 *The True Chronicle Historie of the whole life and death of Thomas Lord Cromwell* (1602), F3v.

38 This chapter comes out of a paper presented at the Birkbeck Senses PhD Forum in October 2011. I should like to thank all those present who gave comments and asked questions, and especially Katherine Duncan-Jones for her helpful advice.

3

'Filthie groping and uncleane handlings': an examination of touching moments in dance of court and courtship

Darren Royston

Accost, Sir Andrew, accost [...]
front her, board her, woo her, assail her!
(Sir Toby Belch to Sir Andrew Aguecheek, upon meeting Maria;
Twelfth Night, 1.3.46–54)

When a person becomes aware of having physical, bodily contact with an external object, then the sense of touch creates a variety of specific feelings and sensations. When someone is physically linked to another person, a private communication channel can be established based on different ways of touching which are interpreted as different emotional responses. These responses or sensations may be hidden from others not engaged in the act, even if the touching can be clearly seen. However, as Constance Classen points out, such sensual interaction is 'not just a private act. It is a fundamental medium for the expression, experience and contestation of social values and hierarchies. The culture of touch involves all of culture.'[1] Using this definition of touch, this chapter will consider what level of contact occurred during the activity of dancing in social situations in early modern England and will examine how the private sensations produced were then recorded and commented upon in different written, visual and theatrical forms. Sometimes the purpose of such records was for practical instruction, and I will consider the importance given to the tactile in developing a communication skill which had to be mastered by those courtiers wanting to excel in courtly dance. From this practical understanding of the dance technique based on touching between partners, this chapter will consider the representation of such courtly dance in artistic works of different media using examples of paintings, poetry and drama. Courtly dance was also referred to outside of the court environment in which it was performed, and examples from the plays of Shakespeare will demonstrate how physical contact occurring in dance gains dramatic effects in the public playhouse, with the effect depending on the characters and the situations in which they find themselves. In particular this chapter considers how specific images, technical words and gestural actions can signal particular touch qualities even if the viewer, reader or audience member is not physically involved with the activity themselves. The most extensive written material commenting on the touching of partners in dance is actually by those wishing the activity to be prohibited. It is with these writers that we will begin this investigation, for they describe clear categories of physical touching determined by the types of people involved and the specific places where these touching moments occur.

Unclean handling

In early modern England the social activity of dancing was fiercely criticized because of the opportunity it afforded for partners to come into close proximity with, and physically touch, someone of the opposite sex: 'what clipping, what culling, what kissing and bussing, what smouching & slabbering one of another, what filthie groping and vncleane handling is not practiced euery wher in these dauncings?'[2] These words, spoken by the puritanical character of Philoponus in *The Anatomy of Abuses*, may indeed be the viewpoint of the puritan writer Philip Stubbes whose published work was a vitriolic attack on the manners, customs, amusements and fashions of the period. One chapter entitled 'The horrible Vice of pestiferous dauncing, used in Ailgna' is the report of a fictional traveller who has witnessed how social dance has become a totally immoral activity. Such 'beastlie slabberings, bussings & smouchings and other filthie gestures & misdemeanors therin accustomed' (N8ᵛ) must, he insists, inevitably lead to promiscuous behaviour between men and women. It would be as impossible to avoid such behaviour as it would be 'for a naked Man to lye in the middest of a hote burning fire, and not to consume' (N8ᵛ). Ailgna is none other than England, and the activities being criticized are current, prolific and morally dangerous. Within this conceit Stubbes has Philoponus use very sensual words to describe the activity of dancing and to warn his fellow 'brother' Spudeus of what would inevitably happen if he danced with a woman.

Other pamphlets at this time warn against the same situation, some even more directly. John Northbrooke produced a treatise in 1579 criticizing dicing, dancing and the performance of plays. It is dancing which he terms the 'vilest vice' because this activity allows physical contact between men and women: 'Maidens and matrones are groped and handled with vnchaste hands, and kissed & dishonestly embraced'.[3] Dancing schools are here seen as 'houses of bauldrie' as they teach young women how to hold onto men's arms so that they can 'hop the higher' (fol. 64ᵛ). In 1582, Christopher Fetherston produced *A Dialogue against light, lewd and lascivious dancing* in the hope of preventing those who obtain their 'wicked purposes' and then 'entise others to naughtines'.[4] The main criticism shared by these moral writers is that the purpose of dancing is sexual and made entirely explicit through the act of touching. Northbrooke comments that 'the things, which nature hath hidden, & modestlie couered, are then oftentimes by meanes of lasciuiousnesse made naked' (fol. 66ᵛ) and Stubbes's Philoponos confesses he has seen 'the very deed and action it selfe [...] purtrayed and shewed foorth in their bawdye gestures of one to another' (M8ᵛ), which will 'stir vp carnall appetites and fleshlie motions' (N3ʳ⁻ᵛ). Even if he does not wish to offend 'chast eares' (M8ᵛ) by actually naming the sexual act that these gestures simulate and stimulate, the full-bodied language conveys the salaciousness of the physical behaviour.

Likewise, the 1581 *Treatise of Dances* contained in the Archbishop of Canterbury's Lambeth Palace Library puts forward the view that dance can only lead to one thing: whoredom.[5] Dances are 'nothing els but impudent, shameles, and dissolute gestures, by which the lust of the flesh is awaked, stirred vp, and inflamed, as wel in men as in wome[n]' (A5ʳ). This 'lust of the flesh' is then put into action when men and women 'mingle mangle' (B1ᵛ), a phrase emphasizing the physical connection when 'the lusty and fyne man should holde a young damosel, or a woman by the hand' (B7ʳ). Following this he may 'remoue himselfe, whirle about, & shake his legges alofte' (B7ʳ) while presenting 'wordes, amorous deuises, or deuises of loue' which convey 'wanton communications or speeches or markes onely knowen to the Ladye, or Gentlewoman' (B7ᵛ). The opportunity to speak privately while dancing is one of the most dangerous aspects, and this is initiated by the intimacy provided by the touching of hands, thus bringing the bodies closer together. These puritanical texts appear to propose a link between the practice of early modern dance and an overt display of sexual desire.

However, such writers do not place all activities named 'dance' in this 'unclean handling' category. Stubbes's dialogue between Philoponus and Spudeus is a lengthy discussion, considering many specific occasions when different types of dancing would occur, and even Philoponus does not think that all dancing is an abuse. He remarks that, 'as concerning daucing, I wold not haue thee (good Reader) to think that I condemne the exercyse it self altogether' (¶6ᵛ). He makes it clear that 'though I conde[m]ne all filthie, luxurious and uncleane daucing, yet I condemne not al kind of daucing generally (N8ʳ). He is able to discern between dances that are morally acceptable and those that are not. The level of touching that occurs in dance could be one of the main distinguishing factors in categorizing different forms of dance in the early modern period, contributing to whether the dance form would be morally acceptable. Poetic and dramatic references to specific dance types may also imply precise physical sensations of different types of dancing. These were real sensations experienced by those dancing. An observer standing outside of the dance may not have felt this sensation, so may only imagine what things might have been occurring during the dance. Without feeling the touch themselves it remains pure conjecture, and the image may have deceived the viewer. Here I would refer you to the idea of visual deception in courtly behaviour and theatrical performance as discussed in Chapter 2 by Jackie Watson.

Chaste concord

To puritan moralists the image of holding hands in dance may have signified illicit fornication, but there are examples where the same dancing image is used as a symbol of chaste concord. Partners holding hands and touching during dance was a well-established symbol to signify harmony between either groups of people or indeed a man and a woman. The ultimate religious blessing for a couple was the union in marriage where their hands would be joined in a Christian ceremony. Dancing was part of the courtship ritual frequently used by the European royal and ducal courts to establish unions between different dynasties.[6] Even Stubbes's puritan figure of Philoponus agrees that this type of dance may be considered 'both a recreation for the minde, & also an exercyse for the body, very holsome, and not only that, but also, a meane wherby loue is acquired' (M8[r]).

The champion of this form of wholesome dance is Sir Thomas Elyot, who uses this example of a dancing couple in his treatise *The Book of the Governor*, written in 1531 and dedicated to King Henry VIII. An entire chapter is devoted to putting forward arguments to support the inclusion of dance in the humanist education of noble men, from the age of seven until 20. Even though Elyot mentions those who have attacked dancing, such as Saint Augustine who criticized the connection of dance to paganism and saw it as part of the worship of gods such as Venus and Bacchus, he argues that it is the 'interlaced ditties of wanton love or ribaldry' accompanying such dancing which should be avoided, and not the practical activity as such.[7]

Elyot proposes that dancing can be part of moral instruction, teaching a man about the virtue of Prudence, and the associated skill of governing oneself by reason. He entitles Chapter XXII, '*How dancing may be an introduction unto the first moral virtue, called prudence*' (p. 78). Central to this is the perfect symbol of a couple dancing holding hands: 'In every dance, of a most ancient custom, there danceth together a man and a woman, holding each other by the hand or the arm, which betokeneth concord' (p. 77). The balance between a man and a woman would be a combination of the different qualities perceived as masculine and feminine, being stereotypically considered as 'fierce' for the man and 'mild' for the woman: 'Wherefore, when we behold a man and a woman dancing together, let us support there to be a concord of all the said qualities being joined together' (p. 78). The physical action of linking by hands demonstrates how two people are now joined and seen to be operating as one, and for this activity to be honest, virtuous and modest, the dance would begin by making 'a reverent inclination of curtsey' to the female partner, while showing 'due honour to God, which is the root of Prudence' (p. 79). Only after this moment displaying reverence should the hands of the couple be joined.

Alongside this connection to the Christian God there is also a reference to the neo-Platonic idea of cosmic dance:

> The interpreters of Plato do think that the wonderful and incomprehensible order of the celestial bodies, I mean stars and planets, and their motions harmonical, gave to them [...] a form of imitation of a semblable motion, which they called dancing or saltation; wherefore the more near they approached to that temperance and subtle modulation of the said superior bodies, the more perfect and commendable is their dancing. (p. 73)

Although practically the dance would comprise human bodies physically touching by joining their hands, the poetic image avoids being visceral. There is no mention of what happens when hands touch in dance. The union remains spiritual and ethereal in quality.

Elyot is not writing an instruction manual for practical dancing, rather he uses dance to discuss the ideas of leadership and self-control. However, to understand the dance metaphor requires the reader to have detailed knowledge of the terminology for the specific dance form he refers to: the *Basse Dance*.

Basse Dance or base dance: practical techniques

The *Basse Dance* was one of the principal courtly dances in early Tudor England and practical instruction for it has survived in written form. An abridged translation of the standard fifteenth-century French treatise was printed on the final leaf of a volume of papers published by Robert Coplande in 1521, entitled 'The manner of dancing of *basses dances* after the use of France and other places'.[8] A year previously, the English nobles had danced with the French court at the Field of the Cloth of Gold, where King Henry VIII of England met King François I of France. The chronicler Edward Hall reports how dancing brought the two courts together, and remarks on the behaviour of the French king:

> Before he started to dance the French king went from one end of the room to the other, carrying his hat in his hand and kissing all the ladies on both sides – except for four or five that were too old and ugly. He then returned to the queen [Queen Katharine of England] and spoke with her for a while before spending the rest of the day dancing.[9]

Courtiers throughout Europe would need to share knowledge of certain dance forms, to be able to partner people of other nations at formal and social occasions. The French *Basse Dance* repertoire comprised different choreographies, each with variable combinations of basic step units, following specific structural metrical rules which Coplande's commentary explains. It assumes that the reader will know this was a dance for a couple, requiring men and women to dance side by side, with hands joined. In such a dance it was the male partner's responsibility to lead the lady positioned to his right with his right hand around the room. Through the handhold she would need to receive the information of the pace being taken, and the direction in which to step, in addition to the step–sequence being performed.[10]

Coplande's text does not discuss the use of hands, nor the female partner at all. Information needs to be gathered from other sources to begin to understand how partners could communicate during courtly dance, and then to consider how the same dance could have contrasting interpretations: as a virtuous display of 'chaste concord' or as immoral 'filthy gropings'. French dance instruction manuals of the sixteenth century were addressed to the male partner, and offer practical advice on how to implement such a technique through the sense of touch.[11]

The *Basse Dance* was still considered the most virtuous dance in the late sixteenth century, appearing in *Orchesographie* of 1589 and the republished 1596 version.[12] The title page of this manual states the aim to teach the 'honête' form of dances so that 'all manner of persons may easily acquire and practice the honourable exercise of dancing'.[13] The dialogue is between a young student of law, named Capriol, who returns to his former teacher, Monsieur Arbeau, to ask advice on how to improve his skill in dancing. He thinks that he needs this skill to be able to impress the young ladies, believing that the whole reputation of an eligible young man depends on it (p. 11). Arbeau had a reputation for being a good dancer in his youth, and willingly agrees to share his knowledge of social dances 'in the hope that such honourable dances are reinstated and replace the lascivious, shameless ones introduced in their stead to the regret of wise lords and ladies and matrons of sound and chaste judgement' (p. 59). The teacher informs his pupil that 'a mistress is won by the good temper and grace' displayed while dancing (p. 12), and instructs him in the first instance on how to show reverence and offer his right hand to the lady. Then, the lady 'being sensible and well brought up' will give her left hand, stand up and join him to dance (p. 52).

Arbeau states that the principal purpose of all dancing is to woo a female partner: 'For dancing is practised to reveal whether lovers are in good health and sound of limb, after which they are permitted to kiss their mistresses in order that they may touch and savour one another' (p. 12). Touching can join with the sense of taste and smell to ascertain if their dancing partners 'are shapely or emit an unpleasant odour as of bad meat' (p. 12). From this activity of kissing and caressing, the aim is to form a respectful social union through marriage, and Arbeau concludes that 'from this standpoint, quite apart from the many other advantages to be derived from dancing, it becomes an essential in a well–ordered society' (p. 12). Although he notes that the *Basse Dance* had been danced 30 or 40 years previously, Arbeau hopes that 'such honourable dances are reinstated' and this dance is the first to be described in detail (pp. 59–76).

Arbeau acknowledges that he had learnt from his teacher, Antonius Arena, who penned a similar dance treatise *Ad Suos Compagnos* in 1528 when the *Basse Dance* was in fashion.[14] Many further editions of this text remained in circulation throughout the sixteenth century.[15] Preceding an extensive list of *Basse Dance* choreographies, written in the same form as the English translation by Coplande, is a poetic elegy advising his student friends on how to use the activity of dance to impress the ladies. Written in macaronic Latin with colloquial student slang, these tongue-in-cheek instructions suggest that even in the sedate *Basse Dance* the touch between the man and the woman can communicate sexual intention. He implies that holding hands is the most important element, for the man must first remove his gloves to allow the caressing of the hand.[16] Issues of leadership are considered, such as the man placing the lady close enough to him so he can set the pace, to be able to prevent her moving ahead too hastily or being left trailing behind. While dancing side by side, the man would communicate his desire through 'tender messages' (p. 165). For this reason, being able to see the eyes of his partner during dance was important, so Arena insists that there should be torches when dancing at night (p. 165). Respect for the lady must be made by only using moderate force when leading with the hand, so as not to give her any cause for complaint (p. 157). In practice, this involves subtle changes of muscle tension in the leading hand, to create an unspoken understanding between the dancing partners: different instructions are interpreted from the intensity of the grip, the manipulation of the fingers, the direction given by pressure from the hand, and flow signals to stop and start motion. Similar practical techniques of using the hand to guide the lady are also noted by Arbeau, for example when considering how a couple could turn together to face a different direction in the room, requiring the lady to follow the lead of the man's hand, which he calls a *conversion*.[17] Throughout both these manuals it is evident that an intimate communication between the man and woman is being encouraged, aided by the close proximity of the moving bodies and the touch of bare hands: an *artis secreta* or secret art that would be hard to perceive from the outside. Maybe it was the secrecy of this communication that fuelled the fears of those believing that immoral practice was being initiated? Maybe the female would have no choice but to follow the male's lead if she agreed to join the dance? Maybe the male partner could take advantage of this moment of touch?

Following discussion of the *Basse Dance*, both instructors consider other dances that offer even more extreme physical contact. Arena encourages 'kissing dances' to make further contact with the ladies, reminding his friends not to eat onions so that their breath remains sweet while giving prolonged kisses during these dances.[18] Arbeau includes instructions for one such kissing dance, the *gavotte branle*, which allows kissing between all partners in the dance. He remarks on the care needed by the man when leading a lady in lively dances such as the *tordion* so that he does not cause 'needless discomfort and jolting' to the lady.[19] This will lead him to mention 'wanton and wayward dances' including the most 'lascivious' of such dances he will identify as *lavoltas*. Despite this reproachful mention, Arbeau will give full instructions for this specific dance later in the manual, explaining its very particular technique for physically handling the female partner when she is lifted and turned in the air.[20]

Lascivious *lavoltas*

'Volta' means literally 'to turn', so to begin with, Arbeau instructs the man how to make his turn, without mentioning where the lady would be placed. This instruction follows on from extremely detailed explanations of various steps for the *tordion* and *galliard*, and this new dance links to the same rhythm and vigour of the intricate jumping and turning steps. The young pupil, Capriol, is quick to question how he could possibly execute such leaps and turns if he held the lady with only the normal handhold: she would be so far away from him. His teacher then explains that having taken her hand during the reverence and led her around the room, he must now bring his partner as close to him as possible, lifting her with one arm 'grasping and holding her firmly by the waist' with his hand on her hip (pp. 120–21). The closeness of the bodies in this dance is an image used to imply secret physical intimacy, such as in the Elegy *Callirée* by Amadis Jamyn (1575) where a couple touch 'flanc contre flanc' and Venus, while dancing with Mars, exposes her thighs.[21]

While holding the lady around her waist, Arbeau describes the lifting technique needed to combine with his turning-jump: with one leg lifted behind the lady, pushing her forward with his thigh, the opposing hand is placed at the front of her body, lifting her up by pushing towards her. Three points of contact with the lady's body are needed: an arm around her waist, a knee under her posterior, and one hand pushing against her bodice. It is this third point of contact that appeared to be the most salacious. Arbeau specifically refers to this place as 'under her busk'.[22]

The word busk may refer to the corset worn by the lady, and sometimes specifically the wooden piece running vertically at the front. This was a reinforcement to which the corset was fastened, and consequently acted almost like another spine running down the front of the dress to the triangular point of the bodice, technically called the 'stomacher'. The man's hand grabbing in this area may justify why the dance was considered scandalous, being viewed as a simulation of a sexual act.

The busk is mentioned with overt sexual connotations in *A Glass Wherein is the Pride of Vainglorious Women* (1595) during a criticism of foreign additions to female fashion.[23] This 'bawdy busk' is something that men must attempt to break through to become intimate with the lady. In his 1591 translation of *Orlando Furioso*, Sir John Harington uses this dance specifically to imagine

Mercury's rape of the nymph Chloris: once caught in his net he teaches her 'to daunce *la volta*'.[24] In practice, however, the lady would need to be in complete agreement to allow the turn to occur by freely jumping high herself. From the outside, however, the dance could appear as a display of indiscreet manhandling.

Despite Arbeau's stated intention to eradicate such dances, the technical description given to his pupil is detailed enough for precise practical dance reconstruction in historical costume replication even today.[25] Following such precise practical descriptions, the tutor steps away from the moral debate:

> Ie vous laisse a considerer si c'est chose bien seante a une jeune fille de faire grands pas et overtures de jambes.

> ['I leave it to you to judge whether it is a becoming thing for a young girl to take such long strides and separate her legs.'] (p. 121)

Whether the dance is enjoyed by the individual will of course depend on the felt sensation.

The dance sensation

Arbeau also captures the feeling of the dance, mentioning the likelihood that the lifting and turning would give a dizzy sensation to the lady in the air as well as to the man making the moves: 'However brave a face she shows, she will feel her brain reeling and her head full of dizzy whirlings; and you yourself will be no better off' (p. 121). When performing such a dance, both partners need to synchronize their rhythm, ensuring that the bending and jumping match the musical structure, and that each turn places the lady three-quarters around the circle, so that after four turning-lifts the couple remain facing the front position ready to recommence a further travelling section. The hold of the lady needs to be secure, and she will need to use one hand to hold down her farthingale skirt, as it is likely to rise as the body is lifted. When the dance is being executed correctly at a lively pace there is little time to sense where the hands are being placed on the body. The touch of the man's hand would hardly penetrate the many layers of corset, bodice and skirts. Even the active leg, thigh and hand of the man helping the lady to be lifted are sensed as a combined assertion, rather than individual elements. Dancers joined together will still be able to see each other's faces and enjoy the shared experience of dancing as one entwined couple.

The visual appearance

An outside observer may notice other elements that the dancing couple would not be so aware of. A couple dancing the *lavolta* takes central position in a painting of a court scene, dated around 1574, that now hangs in Penshurst Place.[26] A consort of viols plays music as a lady is lifted mid-air by a jumping

man. Her legs are identified by red stockings, showing her legs apart, with the
man's lifted foot visible, indicating that the thigh of his leg is pushing her from
behind. The man's right hand is shown pushing into the lady's skirt between
her open legs: the artist appears to have interpreted the 'under the busk'
location as the lady's genital area.

Striking similarities are found between this painting and another anonymous painting found in France, identified as being at the Court of Henri III in
France. Although art historians are reluctant to identity the figures as particular
members of the royal household, the dance of *lavolta* is strongly associated with
the King's sister, Marguerite de Valois.[27] Marguerite's memoirs inform us that
she knew of the origins of *volte de Provence* as a dance performed expertly by a
group of ladies. She mentions the many balls she attended herself: dancing solo,
joining with her brother or coupling with other noble gentlemen, but changing
partners frequently. This would be one of the rare dances to allow a female
dancer to display some virtuosity in rhythmic capering.[28] Dancing *lavoltas* with
many different male partners seems to match her reputation for having many
lovers, both before and during her marriage.[29]

De Valois's courtly dancing was apparently worthy of gossip over in England.
In 1580, Lady Cobham writes a letter home to report how the French king
dances each dance with a different partner, before dancing the *lavoltas* 'very
lustily' and another visiting courtier, Richard Cook, confirms this custom.
He describes the set order of dances at King Henri III's court including the
fifth dance where: 'the violins sound *Lavolta* in the which the King taketh his
greatest pleasure, [the King] will always dance the same [*lavoltas*] with the
Q[ueen] Mother's maids of honour'.[30]

Did the dance scene in England resemble that of France, with couples
touching in such an openly sexual way, or are the visual depictions being used
as warnings against the practice of the dance? It is unlikely that the many-
partnered Queen Marguerite dancing *lavoltas* would be a model for the chaste
Queen Elizabeth. In fact in one of the English madrigals in *The Triumph of
Oriana*, dedicated to Queen Elizabeth, shepherds and nymphs are wantonly
dancing '*Lavoltos* in a dairy-tapstred valley' until the 'bright majesty' Oriana
arrives as 'A crowne grac't Virgin whom all people honor' to immediately stop
such dancing.[31]

The two paintings depict not only the dance of *lavoltas* but also visualize
physical touching being made by observers of the dance. Around the central
dancing couple are other couples also engaged in intimate physical contact.
Arms are hidden behind bodies, and hands are secretly joined, hidden from
view of the other courtiers. The use of hands in bowing and plucking of the
musical instruments is also emphasized. Fingers are fiddling everywhere in this
painting. 'Unclean handling' is not only occurring in the dance, but by all those
involved at the court seen to be sharing these touching moments.

Early modern poetry and drama suggests that such lascivious touching dances did occur in England, however. In Shakespeare's history of *Henry V* the Duke of Bourbon suggests that English dancing schools could teach the French the '*lavoltas* high' as they flee the battlefield (3.5.33). Although practical dance manuals in English for this period have not been found, the members of the Inns of Court noted dances related to the Revels: occasions when the young men could meet women and woo them for pleasure. By the time John Ramsey is admitted into the Middle Temple on 23 March 1605, the '*French lavolta*' is included.[32] His brief description mentions the holding of hands and use of the arms and legs to lift his partner, although the dance needs to be learnt 'by demonstration'. It concludes with the customary 'honor and ende' to restore dignity to the occasion. It was at such an occasion at Inner Temple in 1561 that Queen Elizabeth was said to have first admired the dancing of Christopher Hatton, later knighting him and elevating him to the position of Lord Chancellor. Such young suitors would attempt to woo their Queen, hoping that a touch of the hands during dance may lead to a ceremonial touch of the sword: if they lifted the Queen in the *lavoltas* would they then rise in the court too?[33]

Declining to dance

Whether through sedate gliding in the *Basse Dance* or vigorous leaping in the *lavoltas*, many dances could contribute to the wooing of a lady. What the manuals do not comment upon, however, is how to deal with a situation where a lady refuses to take hands and dance. This exact situation is the theme of the poem *Orchestra* written by Sir John Davies when he was a student at the Middle Temple. Although the work is subtitled 'a Poeme of Dauncing', the narrative is concerned with a lady who actually refuses to accept a man's invitation to dance. The lady in question is Queen Penelope, arguably the most chaste queen from classical literature, and the male courtier figure is the most devious of the suitors in Homer's story, named Antinous.[34]

In the classical tale, Antinous attempts to convince Penelope that she should not wait for Ulysses to return, and asks her to consider taking him as her new husband. The Elizabethan poet imagines a scene where the queen is asked to dance. The Queen is, however, seriously concerned that dance is nothing but a frenzied immoral activity, and Antinous must therefore put forward many arguments to convince her that dancing with him would actually be a decent and honourable activity, leading to love rather than lust.

For the male suitor to achieve his objective he must obtain a real physical commitment from the female partner, so that they can touch and begin dancing together. Contrary to the classical depiction of Antinous, in *Orchestra* this suitor is described as having 'faire maners' (stanza 11), and he first addresses Penelope as a goddess who could move as a celestial being, thus connecting to the idea of the dancing cosmos. Antinous's request to be her 'mouer' is a request to lead her around as a male partner would lead a female (stanza 13). The queen rejects this idea immediately. If Antinous were following the guidance from the dance manuals and the ideas from the art of courtly love, his words would be accompanied by the reverence with an offer of his hand to begin the dance.[35] As this process fails, the suitor can only present his many arguments as a verbal 'moot' speech based on the poetic conceit that Love created many different types of dance forms appropriate for different people and occasions, even considering the whole natural world to be following a dance-like motion. Throughout many variations on the same theme, Penelope steadfastly refuses to become involved with the activity she can only uphold as 'frantick iollitie' (stanza 26). When she does respond in words, she entirely dismisses the idea that Love has anything to do with this situation.

The catalogue of dance forms, used as examples in Antinous's argument to positively support the act of dancing, are actual dances from the Elizabethan court, which the contemporary readership would have entirely understood in physical terms. However, certain elements of these dance forms have been modified in their poetic rendition, so that dance is presented as being part of a courtly love tradition, and any violent 'skippings and leapings' are refined. The idea of kissing in dance is attached to the flowers who touch each other when they move in the wind waving 'their tender bodies here and there' (stanza 55), and the vine around the elm tree is seen to be 'imbrac[ing]' during a dance (stanza 56), while the streams run to the sea as nymphs holding hands in 'rounds' and 'winding heys' (stanzas 63–64). From these poetic visualizations of examples from nature, the suitor moves closer and closer to the civilized world of his present day. The rhythms of dances are categorized, speaking of the meter and musical structures which connect these supposedly ancient dances with popular equivalents that would be easily identified by members of the Elizabethan court: such as the 'fiue paces' of the *cinquepas* (*sink-a-pace*), the 'gallant' and 'liuely' *galliard*, and the 'currant trauases' [i.e. traverses] of the *coranto* (stanzas 67–69). Within this context the poet introduces the dance of *lavoltas* (stanza 70):

> Yet is there one, the most delightfull kind
> A lofty iumping, or a leaping round,
> When arme in arme two Dauncers are entwind
> And whirle themselues with strickt embracements bound,
> And still their feet an Anapest do sound:
> An Anapest is all theyr musicks song,
> Whose first two feet are short, & third is long.

Reading this poetic description alongside the dance instructions allows us to imagine how the contemporary reader would have understood the physical actions being referred to, although Antinous disguises this 'most lascivious' dance as 'delightfull'. The rhythm of the feet is emphasized, synchronizing with harmonious music, while equality between the two people is implied by the couple formation made with arms 'entwind'. In the next stanza the 'wayward dance' is metamorphosed into the twins of Castor and Pollux, mythological figures who are apotheosized into astrological formations:

> As the victorious twinns of *Læda* and *Ioue*
> That taught the Spartans dauncing on the sands,
> Of swift *Eurotas*, daunce in Heau'n aboue,
> Knit and vnited with eternall hands;
> Among the starres their double Image stands,
> Where both are carried with an equall pace,
> Together iumping in their turning race.
> (stanza 71)

Here the hands are eternally united in the dance in a celestial formation. His next stanza is more salacious, however, as he refers to the image of Venus and Mars discovered in an 'entangled' position dancing *lavoltas*:

> This is the net wherein the Sunn's bright eye
> *Venus* and *Mars* entangled did behold,
> For in thys Daunce, their armes they so imply
> As each doth seeme the other to enfold.
> What if lewd wits another tale haue told,
> Of iealous *Vulcan*, and of yron chaines?
> Yet this true sence that forged lye containes.
> (stanza 72)

In the classical myth, jealous Vulcan discovers that his wife Venus is 'entangled' with Mars and catches them in his net for all to see their adultery. The story of Venus and Mars is a central part in Ovid's erotic text *Ars Amatoria* and the tale of transformation of the twins is a reference to Zeus raping Leda in Ovid's *Metamorphosis*. Eroticism and sexual relationships are still connected to this dance through such classical allusions. The suitor would love an opportunity to dance *lavoltas* with his lady, but these violent and passionate desires have to be poeticized in an attempt to woo a lady who is resisting any form of physical engagement.

Orchestra demonstrates a real practical understanding of dance and the techniques involved. Information from the poem can develop ideas from the French treatises, including reference to leading by touch where the idea of dance representing concord, in the manner of Elyot, is presented as a constant negotiation happening through the physical activity of touch. Stanza 111 insists that the lady must follow the man's lead:

> For whether forth or back, or round he goe
> As the man doth, so must the woman doe[.]

However the stanza following considers 'enterchange' of place where the woman will get the 'vpper hand' during the dance, before returning to the usual position.

Embrace

Of all the dances catalogued in Antinous's wooing rhyme, *lavoltas* allow most closeness for the touching couple as they 'whirle themselues with strickt embracements bound'. The term 'to embrace' is used specifically in the commonplace memory cribs of choreographed sequences from the Inns of Court.[36] As a dance instruction the idea of embrace may appear morally acceptable, as a symbol of harmony, but it also could be the beginning of something more sexual. One early modern dance in particular uses the action of embrace repeatedly for this reason. It is an *almain* appearing in all the Inns of Court manuscripts dated from 1565 onwards with identical choreography and similarly sounding names: *Cycllya Alemayne*, *sicillia Almaine*, *Madam Sosilia pavin*, *Cecilia 7 Measure Sicilia Almaine*. One can speculate whether the dance was named after a certain lady Cecilia, or as a dance from Sicily, or both or neither, although the connection to Princess Cecilia of Sweden and her visit to the Elizabethan court does seem plausible.[37] This royal celebrity arrived in England in 1565 along with rumours that a few years before at her sister's wedding she had been caught with a man in her bedchamber. Princess Cecilia remained in England for a full year and was in attendance at the court, wooing Queen Elizabeth on the part of her half-brother, King Erik XIV. Such a scandalous story of men climbing into her bedroom window, along with the idea of this being a tale set in Sicily, allows us to make connections to the plot and setting of Shakespeare's *Much Ado About Nothing*. This play includes a theatrical use of touch in dance to discuss the courtly systems of social negotiation.

In *Much Ado*, social dance is used to make potential new marriage matches when Don Pedro, the Prince of Aragon arrives at the house of Leonato, the governor of Messina, Sicily. As Leonato's niece Beatrice tells his daughter Hero, 'the fault will be in the music, cousin, if you be not wooed in good time' (2.1.62–63). Beatrice then continues by demonstrating a practical understanding of the different categories of dance, listing their appropriate place for performance. A *Scotch jig* is the style of wooing as the man impresses with his solo capering; a *Measure* for the wedding would be similar to a *Basse Dance*, with sedate steps as the couple stand side by side touching hands. In the *cinquepas* the man would move away from the lady to present his *galliard* combinations, with an opportunity to impress not only his lady beside him but also others around, although Beatrice's image of sinking into a grave refers to the dangers of tripping backwards and collapsing on to the floor by being too ambitious.

For the partnering implied in the text for the actual dance scene (2.1.77–144), an *almain* dance such as *Cecilia* would be suitable for use on stage as couples circle the room, enabling the dialogue of those nearest the front of the stage to speak their lines. This dialogue could either be spoken as the couples begin to join hands ready to dance, leaving the stage space for the audience to imagine the dance, or a dance could have been staged at this part of the play, and the dialogue spoken over the dance proper. The dance scene in the play is complicated further by the men appearing masked. The comedy of the dialogue is based on the fact that the ladies can immediately 'see through' the disguises and the physical touch confirms this. The serving maid Ursula knows it is Signor Antonio from his 'dry hand up and down' (l. 108). Benedick and Beatrice have in some way been left behind in the actual dancing, as Beatrice ends their sparring with the insistence that they must 'follow the leaders' (l. 141) and if they go astray she will leave them 'at the next turning' (ll. 143–44) which would match the frequent choreographic device in the *almain* of turning around each other.[38] Don Pedro has used the opportunity in couple dancing for private conversation, advising Hero to 'speak low if you speak love' (l. 90). The 'much ado' that develops is created because what is seen to be physical contact is not as it appears. The prince seems to be wooing for himself, as he is holding the hand of Hero. A man is seen climbing up to what looks to be Hero at her bedchamber, so she must have been soiled by touch. To reveal the truth, a ritual has to be made with the ladies being masked this time, as the disguised Hero is physically joined to Claudio by the giving of hands (5.4.52–60).

Benedick and Beatrice will at first deny their own 'hands' when their love letters are discovered until Benedick agrees to marry Beatrice, and calls for a dance 'ere they are married' (5.4.117). Leonato wishes to wait until after the wedding for another dance, when couples would have officially been joined, and there would be less risk in changing partners. However, Benedick at this point is determined to 'lighten our own hearts and our wives' heels' (ll. 117–18). Touching his partner in dance can ascertain whether his choice is 'shapely'.[39] Maybe this is the way Benedick can check that 'all the graces' can be found in Beatrice as the one woman he will actually wed (2.3.28). Even the capture of Don John cannot stop Benedick's desire for immediate dancing and he commands, 'Strike up, pipers' (5.4.127). A dance to lighten the heels of the ladies would include jumping, lifting and embracing. The ladies had made a sexual reference to these dance types earlier in the play (3.4). 'Light 'a Love' is a favourite dance of the serving maid Margaret, to which Beatrice adds further innuendo:

> Ye light 'a love with your heels! Then if your husband have stables enough, you'll see he shall lack no barns.(3.4.42–44)

In the final scene, dance remains part of the wooing process. The handhold of the partners during the dance would lead to kissing and embracing which would be seen by all those present, but the dance occasion would still allow private communication to occur between the individuals, before they have to make their public declarations at the wedding ceremony.

Fools in hand

So far, we have assumed that courtiers would know about the value of touching. The dance manuals offered instructions to explain which dances would allow touching and how social negotiation could occur with un-gloved hands, to enable courtly love to be achieved through physical contact with their special lady, or indeed with the ruling monarch. These gestures were, to the eyes of the puritan moralists, immoral moments as glaring as hell and brimstone. It is possible, however, to learn these dances and not realize the value of touch. There is none better than Shakespeare's Sir Andrew Aguecheek to demonstrate this ignorance. Although his legs were supposedly 'formed under the star of a galliard' (1.3.127–28), Sir Andrew represents the courtier who has received the requisite training but lacks the skill or intuition to understand the value of touching in early modern England.

In the first act of Shakespeare's *Twelfth Night*, Sir Toby invites his friend Sir Andrew to 'accost' his niece's chambermaid, Maria. Sir Andrew misunderstands the instruction. Maria displays her wit on wordplay based on the idea of touching:

> *Sir Andrew*: Fair lady, do you think you have fools in hand?
> *Maria*: Sir, I have not you by th' hand.
> *Sir Andrew*: Marry, but you shall have, and here's my hand.
> (1.3.61–65).

What follows is a sequence of jests with Maria keeping the upper hand in every way, as Andrew seems oblivious to the sexual innuendo that Maria is making. Even though they are holding hands, this particular male courtier is failing to communicate to his lady with the sense of touch. When she removes her hand and leaves, the dialogue with Sir Toby continues to expose Sir Andrew's lack of understanding of how these physical skills could be of value to a courtier. Sir Andrew may have learnt the 'kickshawses' (l. 111), which he assumes are specific dance steps, yet his scant knowledge of languages means he is unable to make the link with the French phrase 'quelque choses'. Physical skills such as dancing were included in a Renaissance education to demonstrate control of the body: 'Courtly dancing, like civility, instructed the ambitious if unrefined courtier to prepare and present his credentials by means of an "outward bodily propriety".'[40] However, such training may not have been fully understood nor achieved in practice by all. Even our poet of the dance, Sir John Davies, is mocked for his own bad dancing skills in practice.[41]

Sir Andrew has arrived in Illyria to woo the Lady Olivia. He may have learnt the appropriate courtly dances, but he is not aware about how to use dance in the art of wooing. He thinks he has the technique but he certainly doesn't know how to sense the 'fleshly motion' of the moves, nor understand how touch can communicate his desires. Not every courtier may have had the awareness of what this sense of touch could reveal, not being aware of the potential secret communication that could be made. In such a case this would be an example of 'hands against [their] hearts' (5.4.91–92), as Benedick feigns in *Much Ado* when he tries to deny writing his love letter to Beatrice. 'Hand against [...] hearts' is an ambiguous phrase, however: placing your hand *against* your own heart on your chest would also be the gesture for swearing the truth and expressing emotion. Touching hands can only communicate something with the appropriate physical sensation attached, and the touching moments allowed in social dance would need to be accompanied with shared aware-ness and mutual agreement if the activity of dancing was to initiate further social interaction between two physically joined human beings. In fact, when dancing courtly dances in practice, an opportunity to touch is such a special moment in the choreography that the parts of the dance where dancers are close but not able to touch can be more powerful, being sexually charged with the anticipation of physical contact when they will eventually 'embrace'. The dance manuals contradict those puritan writers who would have their readers believe that the dancing was saturated with overt sexual touching. Even the most lascivious *lavoltas* only allowed the man to touch the outside of the clothing, with the lady's body protected by layered skirts, corseted bodice and strengthened busk.

Touch was required to make a physical connection between dancing couples. To some, this may have signalled the moral danger of what could potentially follow such dancing activities. However, the dance itself may have frequently deceived the sense of sight of the onlookers. In actuality, the criticism of touching sensations in these 'dirty dances' may literally have been 'much ado about nothing'.

Notes

1 Constance Classen (ed.), *The Book of Touch*, Sensory Formations (Oxford: Berg, 2005), p. 1.
2 Philip Stubbes, *The anatomie of abuses* (1583), M8r–v. Further references are marked in the text.
3 John Northbrooke, *A treatise wherein Dicing, Dauncing, Vaine plaies [...] are reproved* (1579), fols. 66v–67r. Further references are marked in the text.
4 Christopher Fetherston, *A Dialogue against lewd and lascivious dancing wherein are refuted all those reason which the common people use to bring in defence thereof* (1582), D6r.

5　*A Treatise of daunses wherin it is shewed, that they are as it were accessories and depe[n] dants (or thinges annexed) to whoredome, where also by the way is touched and proued, that playes are ioyned and knit togeather in a rancke or rowe with them* (1581), A5r.

6　For examples of how dance was part of a humanist culture firmly established in the fifteenth century by dynastic marriages, see Jennifer Nevile, *The Eloquent Body: Dance and Humanist Culture in Fifteenth-century Italy* (Bloomington and Indianapolis: Indiana University Press, 2004), pp. 34–49, 52–57.

7　Sir Thomas Elyot, *The Book Named the Governor*, ed. by S.E. Lehmberg, Everyman's Library, 227 (London: Dent, 1962), p. 71. Further references are marked in the text.

8　D.R. Wilson, *The Basse Dance Handbook* (New York: Pendragon Press, 2012), pp. 143–48.

9　D.M. Loades (ed.), *Chronicles of the Tudor Kings* (Godalming: Bramley Books, 1996), pp. 145–46.

10　Wilson, p. 146.

11　Wilson discusses the vital skill needed to lead through the handhold, and even if he concludes that sometimes speech may be necessary, this would surely be a last resort. See *Basse Dance Handbook*, p. 280.

12　Thoinot (Jehan Tabourot) Arbeau, *Orchesographie* (Langres, 1589; 2nd edn 1596).

13　Thoinot Arbeau, *Orchesography*, trans. by Mary S. Evans, with introduction and notes by Julia Sutton and Laban notation by M. Becker and J. Sutton (New York: Dover Publications, 1967), p. 9. All further references are marked in the text.

14　Arbeau refers to Arena when discussing the reverence at the start of the dance: Arbeau, pp. 54–55.

15　There were nine editions of the Arena manual between 1529 and 1546, and a further eight in the 1570s. See Wilson, p. 149; Peggy Dixon, *Dances from the Courts of Europe*, 8 vols (London: Nonsuch, 1986–93), I, III, IV.

16　Wilson, p. 155.

17　Arbeau, p. 58.

18　Antonius Arena, 'Rules of Dancing', trans. by John Guthrie and Marino Zorzi, *Dance Research*, 4.2 (1986), 3–53 (p. 26).

19　Arbeau, p. 87.

20　Arbeau, pp. 119–21

21　Margaret M. McGowan, *Dance in the Renaissance* (New Haven, CT: Yale University Press, 2008), p. 100.

22　The exact translation of this technical term is debated: *Busq* translated as 'busk' or sometimes 'bust'.

23　Erroneously attributed to Stephen Gosson.

24　Ludovico Ariosto, *Orlando Furioso*, trans. by John Harington (1591), p. 116 (xv. 43).

25　See Nonsuch History and Dance's reconstruction film footage: www.nonsuchdance.co.uk (accessed 21 August 2013).

26　Penshurt Place painting of *lavolta*, reproduced in Nevile Williams, *The Life and Times of Elizabeth I* (London: Weidenfeld & Nicolson, 1992), p. 173.

27　McGowan, *Dance in the Renaissance*, Plate IV. Ball at the court of Henri III showing *la volta*. Anonymous sixteenth-century painting (Musee des Beaux Arts, Rennes).

28 McGowan, p. 8 n. 28.

29 McGowan, pp. 9, 15.

30 McGowan, p. 22 n. 87.

31 George Marson, 'The Nymphs and Shepherds Danced', in *The Triumph of Oriana*, compiled by Thomas Morley (1601), B4r-v.

32 John Ramsey's manuscript, 'Practise for Dauncinge', transcribed in D.R. Wilson, 'Dancing in the Inns of Court', *Historical Dance*, 2.5 (1986–87), 3–16 (p. 7).

33 Marcia Vale, *The Gentleman's Recreations* (Cambridge: Brewer, 1977), pp. 88–89.

34 John Davies, *Orchestra, or a Poeme of Dauncing Iudicially prouuing the true obseruation of time and measure, in the authenticall and laudable vse of dauncing* (1596).

35 Arbeau, p. 52.

36 Wilson, 'Dancing in the Inns of Court', pp. 3–16.

37 John M. Ward, 'Apropos "The Oulde Measures"', *Records of Early English Drama*, 18 (1993), 2–21.

38 Dixon, III–IV, 73–75.

39 Arbeau, p. 12.

40 Howard Skiles, *The Politics of Courtly Dancing in Early Modern England* (Amherst: University of Massachusetts Press, 1998), p. 31; quoting Norbert Elias, *The Civilizing Process: The History of Manners* (New York: Urizen Books, 1978), p. 201.

41 Hans S. Pawlisch, *Sir John Davies and the Conquest of Ireland* (Cambridge: Cambridge University Press, 1985), p. 18.

4

'Thou art like a punie–Barber (new come to the trade) thou pick'st our eares too deepe': barbery, earwax and snip–snaps

Eleanor Decamp

Why is there a barber in Ben Jonson's *The Epicoene*? Two comments about the play are my springboard to this chapter. William Kerwin explains that Cutbeard, the barber, 'is remarkable to the characters for his relation to sound [...] in a profession known for its garrulousness, he is able both to find a woman quiet enough [...] and to comport himself noiselessly enough'.[1] Writing on historical soundscapes, Emily Cockayne discusses the play's 'sonic theme' as a means to examine contemporary advice about seeking out 'aural ease'.[2] Kerwin highlights the barber's relationship to talkativeness, leaving unexplored 'sound' as a non-verbal concept; Cockayne focuses on the play's exploration of ambient city and domestic noise without reference to the barber.[3] But the barber is the linchpin in Jonson's satirical exploration of loquaciousness *and* sonority in the city, the impact of both verbal and non-verbal sound.

Jonson's choice of a barber character in *Epicoene* is a pertinent, dramaturgical one. In a play that satirizes aural experiences, the soundscapes of early modern London and those persons affected by noise, barbery and the barber are contextual and contextualizing constructs. Similarly, to underline the convention of gossip-mongering in *The Staple of News*, Jonson makes an ironic trailblazer out of Tom the Barber, who helps launch the news agency. Kerwin's dramaturgical point is that 'by making [Cutbeard] a barber, Jonson places him at the center of London's culture of appearances'.[4] But by making Cutbeard a barber, Jonson also places him at the centre of London's culture of sound where he functions as a sound control.

Morose asks Mute, 'And you have been with Cutbeard, the barber, to have him come to me? – Good. And, he will come presently?' (2.1.15–17). Morose is not waiting to have his beard trimmed. He is contemplating how to defend and distract himself from 'the labour of speech' (2.1.2), 'the discord of sounds' (l. 3) and 'noise' (l. 12). The irony of this 'Cutbeard' is that he is never connected to cutting beards; later he is a loquacious lawyer. Throats in *Epicoene* are not portrayed as places of hair-growth. When a horn is blown offstage Morose cries,

'What villain ... cut his throat, cut his throat!' (ll. 38–40), applying a murderous barbery threat which analogizes how to exterminate offensive sound. In the next scene, Morose complains of Truewit, 'Oh Cutbeard, Cutbeard, Cutbeard! Here has been a cutthroat with me' (2.2.147–48).

Cutbeard is associated with the misogynistic default that females talk too much, in particular supplied by Truewit: 'Why, you oppress me with wonder! A woman, and a barber, and love no noise!' (1.2.34–35). The barbery context can transpose the female voice into a musical instrument. Morose declares, 'I have married [the barber's] cittern, that's common to all men' (3.5.60): sound is prostituted in the shop.[5] When Epicoene begins to 'speak out', Morose calls, 'Oh immodesty! ... What, Cutbeard!' (3.4.39) blaming, 'That cursed barber!' (3.5.58). Referring to the racket he has endured at his antimasque-like wedding (as Truewit describes it, a cacophony of 'spitting', 'coughing', 'laugh[ing]', 'neezing', 'farting', and 'noise of the music' (4.1.7–8), as well as chatty, 'loud and commanding' (l. 9) females), Morose despairs, 'That I should be seduced by so foolish a devil as a barber will make!' (4.4.3–4).

This chapter examines the barber's shop as a sound-marked, cultural site of acoustic performance and practice and investigates how ears were treated, entertained and abused in barbery settings. Contemporary anthitheatrical-ists' condemnation of the theatre as a frivolous acoustic space corresponds to critiques of the barber's shop as an inevitably noisy environment, and I am interested in the connections between the site specificity and the 'earwitness' ('one who ... can testify to what he ... has heard') of the theatre and the shop.[6] My explorations are in dialogue with the growing body of criticism that investigates the ways in which sounds (noise, music and 'soundmarks')[7] can help us to think about identity, both individual and communal. Soundscape theorists such as R. Schafer and Barry Truax have provided a technical language for sonic studies, and have questioned how we view the relationship between humans and the sounds they encounter in their environment.[8] Bruce Smith, Cockayne, Wes Folkerth, David Garrioch and Bruce Johnson have drawn on these theorists and the language of acoustemology in their attempts to reconstruct the sound maps of the early modern past with reference to literary works: urban and rural acoustic landscapes, bell ringing, rough music, reverberating architectures, and the anatomy and experiential nature of the ear are the subject of some of their investigations.[9] I draw on the theory and historicity of these studies defining my own dramaturgical, and socially and medically situated acoustic field to uncover how barbery informed cultural conceptions of the early modern listening world.

The practitioners responsible for daily ear cleaning were the barbers: inventories and fictional sources reveal that the ear-pick[er] was one of the basic tools of the trade. In the museum at the Mary Rose Trust, one of the display items for the

Barber-Surgeon is of bone and ivory ear-scoops 'found behind the [medicine] chest' with barbery objects.[10] (The Trust's term 'ear-scoop' is modern.)[11] The 'Earepicker' is listed on the page devoted to an inventory of the 'Barbers Case' in John Woodall's _Surgions Mate_ and the 'Instruments of the Barber' in Randle Holme's _Armory_ include 'A _pair of Tweesers, or Twitchers:_ with an Ear pick at the other end of it' which 'cleanse[d] the eares from waxe, which often causeth a Deafness in the party'.[12] John Eliot deems '_An eare-picker, and a tooth-picker_' ('Une cure-dent & une cure-oreille') useful vocabulary for a barber's shop in his French handbook.[13] In John Lyly's _Midas_, the barber protests by his 'earpick' (5.2.178).[14] The order of faux-ritualized events in Phillip Stubbes's portrayal of the barber's shop, is telling: 'pleasant harmonie[s]' which 'tickle [ears with] vaine delight' are heard _after_ the client's ears have been picked.[15] In conceptual terms, therefore, the barber and his effective picking of ears is symbolic in enabling the _earwitness_. Cutbeard exposes Morose to unwelcome sounds by arranging his marriage: he has, figuratively speaking – although with a literal consequence – unblocked and therefore successfully picked Morose's ears.

While the early modern barber's responsibility with ears is not a controversial practice (and often takes comic paths), their association with them can be provocative because of the vulnerability and sensitivity of these organs. Over-exuberant digging in the ear with an inflexible instrument can puncture the delicate eardrum. Mrs Corlyon's household book (1606) describes several methods which tackle ear complaints, including a steam cure for the deaf made from Malmesye and cloves, and an extraction for earwigs from the ear using warm apples.[16] However, her book advises against common technique in ear treatment: 'lett those that will preserve theire hearing that speciall care that they picke not theire eares'.[17] In a metaphor in _Sir Thomas More_, 'Nor does the wanton tongue here screw itself | Into the ear, that like a vice drinks up | The iron instrument' (13.20–22), the instrument inserted into the ear, which conceptualizes the flatterer and his patron, easily takes on the qualities of a torture weapon. In barbery terms the ear-pick is a trivial version of the more intimidating razor: a barber – unskilled or malicious – might be a threat to customers' ears. Mocking the activities in a barber's shop, Stubbes writes, 'next the eares must be picked, and closed togither againe artificially forsooth', hinting at the potential perversions, or the perceived perversion, of barbery activities.[18] He suggests that barbers pick their customers' ears so vigorously that they actually pick them apart. Pick can mean 'to probe and penetrate ... to remove extraneous matter', but it can also mean 'To pierce, indent, or dig ... as to break up'.[19] Stubbes's reference to an artificial procedure suggests that the ear is not as it was before the barber sets to work upon it. The barber lingers in theatre's most renowned depiction of usurpation through the open-access ear: it was a barber-surgeon who admitted to the murder of the Duke of Urbino in 1538, which is widely believed to have inspired Old Hamlet's murder, by pouring poison into his ears.[20]

Responding to the scripted '*Lowde Musicke*' in the late Elizabethan play *Blurt Master-Constable*, the courtesan Imperia complains to the musicians, 'Oh, fie, fie, fie, forbeare, thou art like a punie-Barber (new come to the trade) thou pick'st our eares too deepe.'[21] The effects of some sounds, as Imperia suggests, are equivalent to bad ear-picking practice as well as bad playing. The courtesan objects to noise as an audience member and reminds us that audiences' ears should, like barbers' customers' ears, be handled with care. Her analogy has a reflexive effect: audiences might become more aware of what is demanded of their own ears in the theatre as the loud music for them too is intrusive. Hamlet knows that the groundlings' ears can be 'split' (3.2.10). Stephen Gosson's allusive reference that in the theatre there is 'Such masking in [the audience's] eares, I knowe not what', raises questions significant to my discussion.[22] Did, as the *OED* states, early modern people have a means to regulate, improve or deaden sounds in the theatre (or elsewhere) using materials or a substance?

Moreover, the probing action during ear-picking unsurprisingly relates to the sexually charged climate of barbers' shops. The barber's chair was sometimes synonymous with the prostitute, as the furniture that, according to one of Shakespeare's clowns, 'fits all buttocks' (*All's Well*, 2.2.16), and hair-plucking and trimming could encode acts of rape.[23] Imperia's objection to the uncomfortable picking-effect of sound occurs during some heavy petting. Tryphon the barber – a pathetic figure in Gervase Markham and William Sampson's *Herod and Antipater* – apostrophizes his ear-pick when fantasizing about Salumith:

> TRYPHON: Tooth-pick, deare Tooth-pick; Eare-pick, both of you
> Have beene her sweet Companions; with the one
> I've seene her picke her white Teeth; with the other
> Wriggle so finely worme-like in her Eare;
> That I have wisht, with envy (pardon me)
> I had beene made of your condition.[24]

In this play, the ear-pick is likely to be a stage property. If sound can be conceptualized as a sexual encounter with the ear, a physical equivalent exists in representations of the barber's ear-picking. If we regard Epicoene as Cutbeard's figurative ear-pick, we find that the play's gender politics are further interlaced: sodomitic notions of Epicoene as a penetrative object handled by a barber are suggestive before Epicoene is revealed to be male.

Morose's extreme hatred of noise, and his general gloom, is characterized as a humoral imbalance that needs treatment. Michael Flachmann discusses Morose's 'humourous ailment', although without specific reference to his ears. Taking his cue from Robert Burton's *Anatomy of Melancholy* (1621), he diagnoses Morose with melancholy verging on madness which 'can force a person into silence and seclusion'.[25] But Morose is not silent and he continues to seek out company (so long as it is mute), making Flachmann's melancholia reading questionable. Hudson Hallahan suggests that it is difficult for an audience to be particularly sympathetic to Morose because of his hypocrisy in speaking.[26] But his hypocrisy also lies in the fact that he does not seem to hear himself speak. The Boy suggests that if Morose's ears were not exercised properly, 'He would grow resty ... in his ease' (1.1.165–66). Holdsworth glosses 'resty' with 'sluggish', but given the next sentence's reference to 'rust' and Jonson's appetite for gritty depictions of urban and human filth, 'resty' in this context also refers to rancidity.[27] The Boy is commenting on Morose's physical complexion as well as his demeanour. The adjective is especially linked to grease and oil. Morose's ear canal is the subject of the Boy's attention, which is particularly foregrounded by the phonic similarity between 'ease' (in the text) and 'ears' (implied in the context). The homophone for the phrase is 'greasy in his ears'. In George Peele's *Old Wives' Tale*, Huanebango is, according to stage directions, '*deafe and cannot heare*'.[28] Zantippa cannot get his attention other than by breaking a pitcher over his head and exclaims, 'Foe, what greasie groome have wee here?' (E1ʳ). Additionally in *Epicoene*, the Boy's description of the 'street ... so narrow' (1.1.161) in which Morose lives, corresponds architecturally to the anatomy of intricate aural passages. Cutbeard is employed as picker and emulsifier of the excessive lipid-like substances in Morose's festering ears. To appease Morose, who does not appreciate the exposure, Truewit hopes that the barber will have to 'Eat ear-wax' (3.5.87) in order to stay alive after calamity has – in Truewit's imagination – struck the barber shop: Cutbeard's punishment should fit his crime.

Early modern writers often characterize the excrement of the ear by its bitter taste and generally explain earwax in terms of it being waste matter; its beneficial properties, which I discuss in the next paragraph, are usually portrayed by writers as secondary to the wax's execratory quality.[29] A French historiographer, Scipion Dupleix, questions the cause of wax's bitterness, concluding, 'It comes from a putrified and corrupt humour, which gathered together, thickens and heats there within, and being such, can bee no other then bitter; as are all things overcocted and rotten.'[30] Similar descriptions explain hair growth in the period, confirming the barber's trade as one that deals in bodily excrements.[31] Beard growth was even likened to the production of seminal excrement, associated, too, with heat.[32] One of Thersites's typically corporeal insults in *Troilus and Cressida* is that Agamemnon has 'not so much brain as ear-wax' (5.1.51–52): he applies the 'brains between legs' catchphrase, substituting one discharge for another.

Moderated removal of wax is usually deemed a necessary procedure. Filthy ears, states Pierre de La Primaudaye, 'must be oftentimes looked unto and cleansed'.[33] But writers do not always portray wax-free ears as a healthy condition. Variously spelled – with obvious innuendo – Cockadillio/Cockadilio/Cockadillia (and 'Cock' in speech prefixes) is the barber courtier in *Noble*

Soldier and a typical lackey.[34] In the following extract, the noble soldier, Baltazar, quickly detects corruption in court which threatens the monarch's bodily and political health.

BALTAZAR	Signeor is the King at leisure?
COCKADILLIO	To doe what?
BALTAZAR	To heare a Souldier speake.
COCKADILLIO	I am no ear-picker
	To sound his hearing that way.
BALTAZAR	Are you of Court, Sir?
COCKADILLIO	Yes, the Kings Barber
BALTAZAR	That's his eare-picker: your name, I pray.
COCKADILLIO	Don *Cockadilio*:
	If, Souldier, thou hast suits to begge at Court,
	shall descend so low as to betray
	Thy paper to the hand Royall.
BALTAZAR	[...]
	These excrements of Silke-wormes! oh that such flyes
	Doe buzze about the beames of Majesty!
	Like earwigs, tickling a Kings yeelding eare
	With that Court-Organ (Flattery)

(C2ʳ)

Baltazar characterizes Cockadillio as 'all ear-picker': 'To sound' means to probe and pierce. If the king is exposed to constant picking, no wax is left to protect his ears from, in physical terms, flies, and, in conceptual terms, flattery. Suggestively, Baltazar's outburst associates the barber with one colour in particular: a 'yellow hammer', a gold digger (as in Middleton's *A Chaste Maid in Cheapside*) but also a wax-tipped tool.

Of the flatterer (or 'willing slave[s] to another mans eare') Grey Chandos explains, 'his art is nothing but delightfull cosenage [...] In short he is the mouth of liberall mens coates, the earewig of the mightie.'[35] In a sermon on slander and flattery, Jeremy Taylor preaches that dangerous and smooth tongues, whisperers, tale-bearers and sycophants are 'like the earwig creeps in at the ear, and makes a diseased noyse, and scandalous murmur'.[36] Troublesome voices are characterized as non-verbal disturbances in the ear. Writers concede, therefore, that wax – like hair – is not without benefit to the body. Pierre de La Primaudaye explains that the 'yellow humour purged by the eares ... defendeth them against fleas, little flies and other small wormes and beastes, that might otherwise enter within them'.[37] Scipion Dupleix clarifies that:

> [earwax] is not unprofitable within the eares, but being thickened, fleas, and other little flyes which many insinuate within the eares, may trouble us, are there taken by this conglutinate humour.[38]

Baltazar suggests that the king's ears have been picked so much that the royal ear now harbours 'wormes', 'flyes' and 'earwigs'. In Richard Brome's *Love-Sick Court*, Tersules, once a tailor and – like the play's barber, Varillus – embracing the role of courtier, accuses Varillus: 'Your instruments are sharp as mine [...] you can pick more out of your Lords ears | Then I take from his Garments with my sheers.'[39] Careless, overly probing barbery activities leave the king's ear in *Noble Soldier* defenceless and vulnerable to infection. Royal ears are in danger of being open only to gratification (Baltazar recognizes the sodomitic undertones); ultimately this king faces civil war, the penalty for not keeping attentive to his subjects' grievances.

Morose tries to protect his ears in *Epicoene*. Truewit says that he has 'a huge turban of nightcaps on his head' (1.1.139–40). But total interference with ears' openness is contrary practice to that circulated by Protestant sermons which prioritized auricular concentration over ritualized practice. If 'faith cometh by hearing', God wanted discerning hearers.[40] The image of the blocked ear in early modernity is a troubled one because truth is also barred from it. Bloom highlights that the presiding lesson for women as well as good Christians was to be wary of the blurry line between 'constructive defense' and 'destructive deafness'.[41] Thomas Adams, a clergyman, despairs 'that the eare which should be open to complaint, is ... stopped up with the eare-waxe of partiality. Alas poore truth, that shee must now bee put to the charges of a golden eare-picke, or shee cannot be heard.'[42] Good barbery, ultimately, is good religious practice. The barber's need to strike a balance in ear-picking was the physical realization of the ideological balance that the listener was expected to achieve.

The early modern pulpit and the stage, as Bryan Crockett asserts, are comparable theatrical performing spaces which encourage aural alertness and instil the period's 'cult of the ear'.[43] Of church-going, Robert Wilkinson observes, 'Some come not to have their lives reformed, but to have their eares tickled even as at a play.'[44] Smith describes the South Bank theatres as 'instruments for producing, shaping, and propagating sound'.[45] The barber's shop is a similar nodal image of a sound-making site. In a Roman barber's shop a magpie hones its polyphonic skills: she would 'prate, and chatte [...] counting the speech of men [...], the voice of beasts, and sound of musicall instruments', and 'in deepe studie and through meditation [she] retired within herselfe, whiles her minde was busie and did prepare her voice like an instrument of musicke, for imitation'.[46] A shop, of course, is architecturally enclosed and, to some degree, separated from the polyphony of street cries and urban noises that intermingle outdoors: for Plutarch's magpie, the barber's shop is a place to filter, interiorize, rehearse and interpret sounds.[47]

The barber's shop not only contains sound but reverberates with it. When Rafe enters Barbaroso's lair in *Knight of the Burning Pestle* a particular acoustic delineates the scene: 'Knock, squire, upon this basin till it break | With the shrill strokes, or till the giant speak. [Tim *knocks*]' (3.320–21).[48] Earlier in the scene, the Host describes how 'Without [Barbaroso's] door [...] hang[s] | A copper basin [...] | At which no sooner gentle knights can knock | But the shrill sound fierce Barbaroso hears' (ll. 238–41). Celebrating the play's 'happy reconcilements' (5.2.386), the barber declares in Thomas Middleton's *Anything for a Quiet Life*, 'My basins shall all ring for joy' (ll. 383), indicating also theatrical finality.[49] The basin is both doorbell and church bell announcing the subject of barbery both inwards and outwards. Unlike a soundmark that refers simply to a 'community sound', these threshold sounds are, in Schafer's term, 'sound signals', 'sounds to which the attention is particularly directed' and which 'constitute acoustic warning devices'.[50] Indeed, the chiming barber's basin was acoustically tagged to denote something other than barbery practice: it was code for prostitution, the acoustic equivalent of a red light. In *Epicoene* Morose says, 'Let there be no bawd carted that year to employ a basin of [Cutbeard's]' (3.5.83–84). When Rafe knocks on Barbaroso's basins, he signals to the audience the subject of sexual indiscretion but he does not understand the social meaning of the sound he creates and misreads his purpose in the barber's lair.

Music-making is also a nodal image of activity in the barber's shop for which instruments – citterns, gitterns, lutes, virginals – were part of the furniture.[51] Characters perform songs in barbery settings in *1 Promos and Cassandra*, *Damon and Pithias* and *Midas*.[52] According to *The Trimming of Thomas Nashe* (a pamphlet produced in the wake of the Nashe–Harvey disputes), barbers have a 'great facilitie attaine to happiness': 'if idle, they pass that time in life-delighting musique'.[53] Intending 'to tickle with …vaine delight', as Stubbes makes clear, barbers claim an audience.[54] But, as with many well-established traditions, music in the barber's shop is subject to mockery. The competition between Pan and Apollo staged in John Lyly's *Midas* provides us with a blueprint: medicine's harmonic notes (represented by Apollo) supposedly produce one acoustic effect which is pleasing and associated with the God of healing; 'barbarous noise' (4.1.178) from the 'barbarous mouth of Pan!' (l. 20) produces another and is set against the play's barbery subplot in which the first song of the play is performed. A Latin song, translated by Henry Bold, envisages that barbers will form a musical society, beginning, 'In former time 't hath been upbrayded thus, | That Barbers Musick was most Barbarous', and playing on the nexus of etymological associations between 'barber' and 'barbarous', explored by Patricia Parker.[55] Stubbes's reference to 'pleasant harmonie[s]' is ironic: in his satire, these are 'barbarous notes'.

In *Midas*, music associated with barbery rarely seems to be convention-ally musical and this contributes to the perception that the barber's shop is somewhere where ears are under attack. One of the main lessons of *Midas* might be 'listen carefully' (to advice as well as to playing), but its subplot tests and ridicules this maxim: centred on the barber, it concentrates on sounds which, in non-theatrical settings, we might wish to filter out. Cries of pain, rattling, knacking, out of tune instruments, verbosities, slander and protests make a noisy soundscape. The given 'tune of "My Teeth Do Ache!"' (3.2.148, in the quarto as well as the 1632 edition) for the barber's song plays into the scene's parody of dentistry but it also ridicules the nature of the barber's shop music: the tune is not tuneful.

Smith reflects:

> The soundscape of early modern London was made up of a number of overlapping, shifting acoustic communities, centered on different soundmarks: parish bells, the speech of different nationalities, the sounds of trades, open-air markets, the noises of public gathering places. Moving among these soundmarks – indeed, *making* these soundmarks in the process – Londoners in their daily lives followed their own discursive logic.[56]

But if trades are 'soundmarked', and thereby have specificity in this acoustic form of representation, how do these identification tags function autonomously? In one seventeenth-century ballad barbery is characterized by sound alone: 'The Barber goes snip snap.'[57] This soundmark is not the creative device of a single balladeer. In the period, this barbery soundmark echoes across different literary media in a range of contexts, making it culturally stable. 'Snip snap', 'snap', 'snip', 'snipsnap', 'snip-snap', 'snipping' and 'snapping' as well as associative 'knacking' sounds are commonplace. 'Snip-snap' and 'knack' hover between various acoustic contexts and their flexibility as soundmarks corresponds to the linguistic slipperiness of the language generally attributed to barbers.

Barbery instruments (mainly scissors and razors) inherently produce sounds: the trade cannot be silent. In the catalogue of barbers' equipment recovered from the wreck of the *Mary Rose*, archaeologists list the variety of razors found: 'it is possible that any razor without [provision of arms] was opened simply by shaking the blade free'.[58] Although this implied action would not specifically constitute a 'snip snap', it suggests the noise made by metal scraping against metal. In his examination of ancient barbery tools, George Boon cites Plutarch, who comments on the barber's need frequently to 'strop the razor' and a customer's desire to have something to 'soften [his] stubble', writing, in addition, on Juvenal who 'recalls a young man's stiff growth "sounding" under the blade'.[59] In Charles Hoole's Latin dictionary a section on barbery defines the practitioner as 'one that snaps with the scissers'.[60] Drawing on Truax's description of soundscapes, Smith explains, 'the impinging of non-human sounds, all contribute to a given community's sense of self-identity'.[61]

For the most part writers do not suggest that these are solely incidental sounds from barbery work, but make clear that they are the result of barbers' affectations and rehearsed mannerisms. In *A Quip for an Upstart Courtier*, Greene implies that verbal communication can be matched with non-verbal sounds in the barber's shop, and that scissor sounds endorse faux penal gestures and rhetoric. He describes a barber lavishly waiting on Velvet Breeches: 'begins he to take his sissars in his hand and his combe, and so to snap with them as if he meant to give a warning to all the lice in his nittie lockes' (more infestations).[62] Excessive sound (even if these are not loud notes) associated with the practice of barbery appears frivolous and performance-driven. Motto reminds Dello in *Midas*, 'Thou knowest I have taught thee the knacking of the hands, the tickling on a man's hair, like the tuning of a cittern' (3.2.36–38). Often when sounds trouble us we characterize them as wholly unnecessary. In recent studies on early modern soundscapes, critics focus on the loud, iconoclastic sounds that characterize and organize the 'noisy' city, its bells and its street cries, for example. But intrusive sounds are not only the loud ones: the nature and the context of the sound affects people's reaction to it. Cockayne notes that 'the honourable Roger North explained that some sounds, such as the "clapping of a door", annoyed the hearer because, in contrast to musical sounds that have "equal time pulses", they have "unequal movements" and "uncertain periods"'.[63] If barbery sounds are like the 'tuning of a cittern' then they are not the predictable notes of a tune.

We seem particularly sensitive when body parts are responsible for the sound. In one production of *Titus Andronicus* (RSC, 1955) Peter Brook unlocked a greater potential to unnerve the audience. 'During the run, the *Express* reported: "Extra St John Ambulance volunteers have been called in. At least three people pass out nightly. Twenty fainted at one performance." A spokesman for the theatre pinpointed the "nice scrunch of bone off-stage when Titus cuts off his hand" as the crucial moment.'[64] Barbers' knacking fingers, rather like cracking knuckles, get too near the bone. Morose's satisfaction that his barber 'has not the knack with his shears or his fingers' (1.2.36–37) is not as peculiar as it initially sounds. Jonson's irascible protagonist might be associated with fanaticism, but he also parodies common human intolerances.

Sounds can also function beyond their immediate sonic impact; nails on a chalkboard, for example, codify unpleasant sound but also, more generally, a sensation of fleeting discomfort. A sound's effect can inform rhetorical and stylistic device, punitive gestures and onomastic choices. Barbery sounds are hardly deafening. However, if not the volume, then the nature of the sound, its sonic consistency, nettles the nerves. Moreover, objections to the noise are often explained by the proximity of its source to the ears of the client, as Bacon explains, and so the murmuring earwig is irritating. Of the giant barber in *Burning Pestle*, the Host proclaims: 'with his fingers and an instrument | With which he snaps his hair off, he doth fill | The wretch's ears with a most hideous noise' (3.249–51). This 'hideous noise' could be an allusion to the persistent chattiness of barbers, but given the references to 'fingers', 'instruments' and 'snaps', it is most likely to be a disturbance caused by non-verbal sounds. The sound produced by the barber is his vulgar, laboured proof that he is at work. Stubbes criticizes elaborate show in a barber's shop, emphasizing, 'what snipping & snapping of the sycers is there', which, in part, justifies the barber's extortions.[65]

Barbers' hands are a source of acoustic – as well as gesticular – performance. When Nashe refers to the *'knacke* of [the barber's] occupation' in *Have With You to Saffron-Walden*, he includes an addendum in the margin: *'Barbers knacking their fingers'.*[66] 'Knack' the skill is undermined by 'knack' the irritating noise, and the 'sounds' play off each other on the page. The literal mirroring of sounds in the barber's shop between instruments and fingers corresponds to the linguistic mirroring (puns and homophones) in the word. Today we would call 'knacking' 'clicking the fingers', the action which John Bulwer describes: 'knacking', is 'to compresse the middle-finger with the thumb by their complosion producing a sound so casting out our hand'. Bulwer later makes 'knacking' analogous with 'percussion'.[67]

In his entry on 'knacking' which constitutes a 'Contemno Gestus', Bulwer also refers to dancing in a 'Barbarian fashion' which he identifies as 'knacking … with … fingers' performed over the dancer's head.[68] Although Bulwer never specifically mentions barbers in *Chirologia*, the homophone in 'Barbarian' in this sentence is suggestive, reminding us of 'barbarous' Pan. Bulwer concludes that knacking 'expresse[s] the vanitie of things'.[69] Attending to the vanity of customers by fixing their complexions is part of the barber's professional activity, and so the trade's soundmark sonically encapsulates this pursuit. This doubling-up is suggested in the tailor's comparison between garments and ears in *Love-Sick Court* and the 'vaine delight' that music carries, according to Stubbes, in the barber's shop, both discussed earlier. In *Taming of the Shrew*, Petruchio says of the sleeve the tailor has made for Katherine, 'Heers snip, and nip, and cut, and slish and slash, | Like to a Censor in a barbers shoppe' (TLN 2075–76; 4.3.90–91).[70] Laurie Maguire has demonstrated that the original reading of 'Censor' (changed by many editors to 'censer' and by editors of *Complete Works* to 'scissor') was *'cittern* (or a variant spelling of that noun)'.[71] The itinerant sounds of barbery (which double-up with some soundmarks of the tailor, who also wields scissors), the implied musical instrument and the context of Petruchio's dissatisfaction at the fussiness of the garment, which is like an over-elaborate cittern-neck's engraving, here conflate. Although the context is sartorial, Petruchio's criticism plays out across onomatopoeias – barbery soundmarks (in that the tailor's scissor action is defined in terms of another context) – which provide an acoustic effect of excess. The point of the scene is that excess does not lie with the item (the sleeve) but with Petruchio's reaction to it: his argument based on acoustics supplants one based on vision. I began this chapter by separating the concepts of the culture of appearance and the culture of sound in *Epicoene*, but they are related.

In some references, the barber's finger movements signal the conclusion of the trimming process which constitutes a separate acoustic sign-posting: barbery is bounded by – as well as articulated through – soundmarks, which are structural. In *Damon and Pithias*, Snap is the porter at whose gates Wyll and Jacke 'be come … trimme Barbers'.[72] Snap's two entries around this scene encapsulate the trimming process (F1^r, G1^v). Finales are not described as a knacking-noise but as a single snap, an acoustic anti-climax after clanging basins herald a client's entrance. In 'New Trimming', the rhymer refers to 'the snap of [the barber's] Finger [that] then followes after' (stanza 6, line 4) the trimming routine as a rather pathetic flourish. Similarly, Stubbes describes how a barber concludes his services: 'Then snap go the fingers, ful bravely god wot. Thus this tragedy ended.'[73] Given the mundane subject, Stubbes's criticism of the excessive performances in barbers' shops easily emerges through his portrayal of an overly emphasized and trifling gesture as something heroic ('bravely') and within a grandiose context (a 'tragedy'). Both knacking and snapping are irritating and intrusive but, most significantly, they are not robust sounds: in their very nature they are incongruent with sounds we associate with grand matters (in performance contexts), such as alarums, thunder, drums, trumpets and bell chiming. Through the barber, therefore, we have a parody of sound, also exemplified earlier in this chapter by the effect of chiming basins. Stubbes and others construct this parody by playing with notions of volume, scale, context and the instrument which make a sound seem ridiculous; in the example of the ringing basin, parody is a matter of re-contextualization.

More generally, the noises associated with barbers are associated with coarse forms of expression. In Bulwer's *Chirologia*, 'certain Prevarications against the Rule of Rhetoricall Decorum' state that 'To use any Grammaticall gestures of compact, or any snapping of the *Fingers* … is very unsuitable to the gravity of an Oratour.' Elsewhere, *Cautio XXVIII* instructs, 'Avoyd knackings, and superflitious flextures of the *Fingers*, which the Ancients have not given in precept.'[74] The sound by which barbers are characterized informs the regular joke that barbers are terrific gossipmongers, but not necessarily great orators. Coarse, non-verbal sounds epitomize rough rhetoric (captured by Greene's description of a barber who 'at every word a [made a] snap with … [his] sissors'), and so this soundmark critiques oral expression.[75] Having noted that ex-barber Crispino is not thought to have many manners, Volterre declares that Crispino's 'fingers speake his profession' in James Shirley's *Humorous Courtier*.[76] Earlier I quoted from Smith on the soundmarks of trades who produce a discursive logic in a cityscape. More specifically, barbery's soundmark has a discursive logic in that it corresponds to barbers' oral habits and characterizes utterance.

At the end of *Trimming of Thomas Nashe* the author instructs, 'if heere I have been too prodigall in *snip snaps*, tell me of it, limit me with a Falt, and in short time you shall see me reformed'.[77] Lichfield suggests that his own writing might have snip snapped immoderately in chopping back Nashe's discourse wherein reproving '*snip snaps*' replace rhetorical attacks.[78] But the italics also highlight its intertextuality and parodic function: Lichfield adopts his reference to performing 'snip snaps' from the pamphlet to which he is responding. In his mock dedication to Lichfield, Nashe suggests that Lichfield should 'deal ... *Snip Snap* snappishly' with the Proctor of Saffron-Walden, indicating that if barbery and therefore barbers are characterized in terms of rhetorical prowess, the result is a rather feeble clicking of scissors and fingers which lacks efficacy.[79] '*Snip Snap* snappishly' is childish and over-alliterated.

Finally, the soundmark ('snip snap') is also supplied for onomastic purposes in literature. Disguised Young Franklin speaks in French, in his ludicrously poor disguise, and refers to Sweetball as '*ce poulain* Snip-snap' ('this young colt, Snip-snap'), replacing the barber's official name with an epithetical sound bite; the 'Snip-snap' is comic and does not need translation.[80] In *The Fancies Chaste and Noble*, Spadone refers to the barber as 'a snipper-snapper', transforming Secco into a minimizing onomatopoeia.[81] An epithetical use of 'snip' is also applied by the balladeer of 'The Northern Ladd'. The song tells of a female who is wooed by a number of different tradesmen, all of whom she refuses in favour of a ploughman. One of the maid's suitors is a mischievous barber:

> But I repell'd his rude address,
> and told him 'twas my greatest-cares,
> If wa'd a lowsie A-Snip, alas,
> when he's incens'd should keep my ears.[82]

As it did in *Quiet Life*, so 'Snip' ('A-Snip') in this quatrain can function as an antonomasia for the barber (i.e. 'if he were only a lousy barber').[83] However, it can also be an epithet for 'rude address', whereby the 'Snip' is a cutting or exposing remark (i.e. 'if his address was a rotten insult or intrusion').[84] In both senses the soundmark 'snip' is derogatory. The final line of the stanza suggests that the female's ears are under threat from the barber: 'should keep my ears' means 'should cover my ears'. The line means that when the barber becomes vulgar, or – to use Nashe and Lichfield's phrase – too 'prodigal in snip-snaps', the maid must plug her ears. Once again, the ears, figured here through the fraught status of the female ear which Bloom explores, are considered a vulnerable organ in the presence of the barber – moreover, a 'lowsie', lice-ridden, barber who by over-picking leaves the ear open to an unwelcome infestation. The performing 'Snip' in line three and reference to ears in line four of the stanza makes the connection in the ballad between barbery, sound-making and offence to the ear.

The barber and his trade supplied early modern culture with a particular acoustic currency and aural tropes which were absorbed into and shaped contemporary idiom and metaphor through a series of culturally stable signifiers: the tangibility of the ear-pick and the barber as the 'ear-picker', earwax as excrement, recurrent soundmarks, noisy instruments, practitioners' affectations, and the acoustically defined spatiality of the barber's shop. Sounds in early modernity had, as Smith argues, exceptional social meaning, and the figure of the barber – as a surrogate sound control and a parody of the courtier, preacher, musician and rhetorician – could help to characterize what it might mean to regulate or disturb aural experience. The barbers' ear-picking practices informed the whole concept of what it meant for something – material or otherwise – to enter the ear.[85]

Notes

1 William Kerwin, *Beyond the Body* (Amherst and Boston: University of Massachusetts Press, 2005), pp. 126–27.

2 Emily Cockayne, *Hubbub* (New Haven, CT: Yale University Press, 2007), pp. 106–30 (pp. 109–10).

3 Sounds other than the human voice offend Morose, including bearward's dogs, a fencer's drum, bells, snoring and creaking shoes. Some tradesmen ('chimney-sweepers', 'broom-men', 'any hammerman', 'brazier[s]', and 'pewterer[s]'s prentice[s]' (1.1.146–153)) are particularly irksome to him because of the tools or street cries they employ. (Quotations are taken from Ben Jonson, *Epicoene*, ed. by Roger Holdsworth, New Mermaids (London: A & C Black, 2005).)

4 Kerwin, p. 126. Cf. Farah Karim-Cooper, *Cosmetics in Shakespearean and Renaissance Drama* (Edinburgh: Edinburgh University Press, 2006), pp. 111–26.

5 See Laurie Maguire, 'Cultural Control in *The Taming of the Shrew*', *Renaissance Drama*, 26 (1995), 83–104 (pp. 92–93).

6 R. Murray Schafer, *The Soundscape* (Rochester, VT: Destiny Books, 1994), p. 272.

7 The term soundmark is 'derived from *landmark* to refer to a community sound which is unique or possesses qualities which make it specially regarded' (see Schafer, pp. 271–75).

8 See Barry Truax, *Acoustic Communication* (Santa Barbara, CA: Greenwood, 2001) and the Special Issue of Landscape Ecology: Soundscape Ecology (11/2011).

9 Bruce Smith, *The Acoustic World of Early Modern England* (Chicago: University of Chicago Press, 1999); Emily Cockayne, 'Cacophony, or Vile Scrapers on Vile Instruments', *Urban History*, 29 (2002), 35–47; Wes Folkerth, *The Sound of Shakespeare* (London: Routledge, 2002); David Garrioch, 'Sounds of the City', *Urban History*, 30 (2003), 5–25; Bruce Johnson, '*Hamlet*: Voice, Music, Sound', *Popular Music*, 24 (2005), 257–67; Allison K. Deutermann, '"Caviare to the general": Taste, Hearing, and Genre in *Hamlet*', *Shakespeare Quarterly*, 62 (2011), 230–55. Cf. Matthew Steggle, 'Notes Towards an Analysis of Early Modern Applause', in *Shakespearean Sensations*, ed. by Katharine A. Craik and Tanya Pollard (Cambridge: Cambridge University Press, 2013), pp. 118–37.

10 Three 'ear-scoops' numbered 80 A 1577, 81 A 1276, and 80 A 1524 at the Mary
    Rose Trust.

11 The *OED*'s first reference to 'Ear Scoop' is from 1895 (*ear*, n.1, III.16). See entries
    for 'Ear[e][-]pick[e]' in dictionaries by Richard Huloet (1572), sig. P1v, and Charles
    Hoole, *An Easie Entrance to the Latine Tongue* (1649), p. 244.

12 John Woodall, *The Surgions Mate* (1617), A4r; Randle Holme, *Academy of Armory*
    (Chester: [1688]), pp. 127, 427.

13 John Eliot, *Ortho-epia Gallica* (1593), I1r.

14 John Lyly, *Midas* in *Galatea/Midas*, ed. by George K. Hunter and David M.
    Bevington, The Revels Plays (Manchester: Manchester University Press, 2000).

15 Phillip Stubbes, *The Second Part of the Anatomie of Abuses Conteining the Display of
    Corruptions* (1583), H1r.

16 London, Wellcome MS 213, fo. 33–35. Cf. Cockayne, 'Experiences of the Deaf in
    Early Modern England', *The Historical Journal*, 46 (2003), 493–510 (esp. p. 498).

17 Wellcome, MS 213, fo. 33–34.

18 Stubbes, H1r.

19 *OED*, 'pick, v.1', I.2.a, I.1.c.

20 See Jennifer Rae McDermott, '"The Melodie of Heaven": Sermonizing the Open
    Ear in Early Modern England', *Religion and the Senses in Early Modern Europe*, ed.
    by Wietse de Boer and Christine Göttler (Leiden: Brill, 2013), p. 181.

21 Thomas Dekker, *Blurt Master-Constable* (1602), G3r.

22 Stephen Gosson, *The Schoole of Abuse* (1579), C1v. See *OED*, 'masking, n.2, †1'.

23 My thesis, 'Performing Barbers, Surgeons and Barber-Surgeons' (unpublished
    doctoral thesis, University of Oxford, 2012), explores Shakespeare's use of barbery
    metaphor for Lavinia's rape in *Titus Andronicus* (pp. 191–215).

24 Gervase Markham and William Sampson, *Herod and Antipater* (1622), G2r.

25 Michael Flachmann, '*Epicoene*: A Comic Hell for a Comic Sinner', *MaRDiE*, 1
    (1984), 131–42, see pp. 132–34 (esp. p. 132).

26 Hudson D. Hallahan, 'Silence, Eloquence, and Chatter in Jonson's *Epicoene*',
    Huntington Library Quarterly, 40 (1977), 117–27 (pp. 120–21).

27 Richard Dutton makes the same comment in his earlier edition for The Revels Plays
    (Manchester: Manchester University Press, 2003), 1.1.170-171n. See *OED*, † resty,
    adj.1. A variant of 'resty' is 'reasty', which also is etymologically linked to 'reasy'
    and 'rusty'.

28 George Peele, *The Old Wives Tale* (1595), s.d. E1r.

29 See Helkiah Crooke, *Mikrokosmographia* (1615), p. 576; Walter Charleton, *Natural
    History of Nutrition, Life, and Voluntary Motion* (1659), p. 97.

30 Scipion Dupleix, *The Resolver* (1635), P2v. Cf. Pierre de La Primaudaye, *The
    French Academie* (1618) p. 127.

31 See Crooke, pp. 66–70.

32 Will Fisher, 'Staging the Beard', in *Staged Properties in Early Modern English Drama*,
    ed. Jonathan Gil Harris and Natasha Korda (Cambridge: Cambridge University
    Press, 2002), pp. 230–57 (p. 234).

33 Pierre Primaudaye, *The Second Part of the French Acadamie* (1594), p. 127.

34 *The Noble Souldier* was authored, according to the Stationers Register by Thomas
    Dekker, but with the initials S. R. [Samuel Rowley] on the title page of the quarto,

1634.

35 Grey Brydges Chandos, *A Discourse Against Flatterie* (1611), C2r–v.

36 Jeremy Taylor, *XXV Sermons Preached at Golden-Grover* (1653), p. 312 (Sermon XXIV, Part III).

37 Primaudaye (1618), p. 399.

38 Dupleix, p. 316. Cf. Ambroise Paré, *The Workes*, trans. Th[omas] Johnson (1634), p. 190.

39 Richard Brome, *The Love-Sick Court* in *Five New Playes* (1659), sig. I6r.

40 Cockayne, 'Experiences of the Deaf', pp. 495–97; Folkerth, *Sound of Shakespeare*, pp. 44–51.

41 Gina Bloom, *Voice in Motion* (Philadelphia: University of Pennsylvania Press, 2007), pp. 111–59. Cf. Keith M. Botelho, *Renaissance Earwitnesses* (New York: Palgrave Macmillan, 2009); McDermott, pp. 177–97.

42 Thomas Adams, *The Happiness of the Church* (1619), p. 266. Cf. Thomas Taylor, *Peter his Repentance Shewing* (1653), I2r; Robert Wilkinson, *A Jewell for the Eare* (1610); William Harrison, *The Difference of Hearers* (1614); Stephen Egerton, *The Boring of the Eare* (1623).

43 See Bryan Crockett, *The Play of Paradox* (Philadelphia: University of Pennsylvania Press, 1995); Crockett, '"Holy Cozenage" and the Renaissance Cult of the Ear', *The Sixteenth Century Journal*, 24 (1993), 47–65.

44 Wilkinson, p. 34.

45 Smith, p. 206.

46 Plutarch, *The Philosophie*, trans. by Philemon Holland (1603), see pp. 966–67.

47 See Smith, pp. 63–70. Cf. Francis Bacon, *Sylva Sylvarum* (1627), G2r (138).

48 Francis Beaumont, *The Knight of the Burning Pestle*, ed. by Michael Hattaway, 2nd edn, New Mermaids (London: A & C Black, 2002).

49 Thomas Middleton, *Anything for a Quiet Life*, ed. by Leslie Thomson in *The Collected Works*, general editors Gary Taylor and John Lavagnino (Oxford: Clarendon Press, 2007).

50 Schafer, pp. 10, 275.

51 See Maguire, pp. 88–93.

52 Music in Lyly's plays has been the subject of debate since the early twentieth century. The quartos of his dramatic works include stage directions for singing, but song lyrics are absent. These were not published until Edward Blount's edition of Lyly's plays, *Sixe Court Comedies* (1632). Cf. Anon, 'The Rimers New Trimming' (c. 1614), a ballad.

53 Richard Lichfield[?], *Trimming of Thomas Nashe* (1597), B4v. On authorship, see Benjamin Griffin, 'Nashe's Dedicatees', *Notes and Queries*, 44 (1997), 47–49; Charles Nicholl, *A Cup Of News* (London: Routledge and Kegan Paul, 1984), pp. 233–36.

54 Stubbes, H1r.

55 Henry Bold, *Latine Songs With their English* (1685), sig. M4v–N1r; Patricia Parker, 'Barbers and Barbary', *Renaissance Drama*, 33 (2005), 201–44.

56 Smith, p. 56.

57 Anon., 'A Merry New Catch of All Trades' (c. 1620), stanza 5, line 2.

58 Gardiner, Julie, Michael J. Allen and Mary Anne Alburger (eds), *Before the Mast: Life and Death Aboard the Mary Rose* (Portsmouth: Mary Rose Trust, 2005), p. 217.

59 George C. Boon, '*Tonsor Humanus*', *Britannia*, 22 (1991), 21–32 (p. 27). *OED*, 'strop, *v*.1: To sharpen or smooth the edge of (a razor) with a strop. Also *transf.* and *fig.*'

60 Hoole, p. 299.

61 Smith, p. 47.

62 Robert Greene, *A Quip for an Upstart Courtier* (1592), C3v. Cf. Sweetball's exclamation in *Quiet Life*: incensed by Franklin's pranks, the barber declares, 'To him boldly; I will spend all the scissors in my shop, but I'll have him snapped' (3.2.15–16).

63 Cockayne, *Hubbub*, p. 36.

64 Quotations are from Samantha Ellis writing for *The Guardian*, 25 June 2003, on the production of *Titus Andronicus*, dir. Peter Brook for the RSC (Shakespeare Memorial Theatre: 1955).

65 Stubbes, G8v.

66 Thomas Nashe, *Have With You to Saffron-Walden* (1596), A3v; Lichfield[?] quotes directly from Nashe ('I espied *barbers knacking of their fingers*' (B3v)).

67 John Bulwer, *Chirologia* (1644), M8v, H3r (also N1r).

68 Bulwer, N1r.

69 Bulwer, part two, G1r.

70 Through Line Numbers follow the Norton facsimile of the 1623 text *The First Folio of Shakespeare*, ed. by Charlton Hinman and Peter Blayney, 2nd edn (London: Norton, 1996).

71 Maguire, 'Petruccio and the Barber's Shop', *Studies in Bibliography*, 51 (1998), 117–26 (esp. pp. 117–18). Editor Barbara Hodgdon, for The Arden Shakespeare Third Series (London: A & C Black, 2010), adopts Maguire's emendation.

72 Richard Edwards, *Damon and Pithias* (1571), F3v.

73 Stubbes, G8v.

74 Bulwer, part two, H1r, K8r.

75 *Upstart Courtier*, C4r.

76 James Shirley, *The Humorous Courtier* (1640), I3r.

77 Lichfield[?], G4v.

78 Italicization of '*snip snaps*' in the printed text highlights its performative role.

79 Nashe, *Saffron-Walden*, B2r.

80 *Quiet Life*, 3.2.136–37.

81 John Ford, *The Fancies, Chast and Noble* (1638), B1r.

82 Anon, 'The Northern Ladd' (1670–96), stanza 10.

83 Perhaps the capitalization of the 'A' suggests the proper noun.

84 In this instance that remark is bawdy with its innuendo, 'he would prick my master-Vein' (stanza 8, line 4).

85 This chapter emerges from my studies on barber-surgeons as a doctoral student at the University of Oxford. I am particularly grateful to Professor Laurie Maguire for her inspired supervision, to the Schools Competition Act Trust who funded my research, and to Pembroke College for a generous scholarship. With particular thanks also to Joy Thomas at Barbers' Hall and Simon Ware at the Mary Rose Trust.

5

Seeing smell

Holly Dugan

In January 2013, the Institute for Art and Olfaction commissioned graphic artist Micah Hahn and his design studio AutumnSeventy to create a series of prints on perfumery to commemorate its opening in Los Angeles.[1] The result was *Molecules, Series 1*, which depicts three of the most influential molecules that defined twentieth-century perfumery – aldehyde C12, Iso E Super®, and Galaxolide.[2] Gilded and embossed, the prints emphasize the chemical structure of these molecules, even as it renders them as fine art. That the prints are also lightly scented with each aromachemical depicted on it emphasizes the broader, and one might say synaesthetic, take on the mission of the institute: to connect fine art with olfaction. Although it is a visual representation of molecules that define modern perfumery, *Molecules, Series 1* thus joins a long art historical tradition of cross-modal representations of sensation, particularly smell.

Can a molecule be considered fine art? And, if so, which representation of that molecule best captures its olfactory beauty and renders it 'visible'? Consider, for example, Hahn's *Galaxolide* (Figure 3). It playfully invokes a wide variety of sensory modes to capture the aesthetic of Galaxolide. The print highlights both its chemical formula – $C_{18}H_{26}O$ – and its structural formula. Both are linked to its cultural associations with perfumery and public health. Galaxolide is a second-generation polycyclic synthetic musk, discovered in the 1960s, meant to synthesize the natural scent of deer musk. Translated into the language of public health, it is a hydrophobic but lipophilic 'toxin': it won't wash off in water and is easily stored in human fat.[3] Rendered into the language of commercial perfumery, however, it smells 'clean', a 'musky, flowery, woody odor' with a 'sweet, powdery nuance'.[4] Both its scent and its structure made it ideal for use in laundry detergents and soaps. And that association enables it to be a powerful 'note' in modern perfumes. What was known as the scent of *Comfort* brand laundry detergent became a key part of Estée Lauder's *White Linen,* Caron's *Parfum Sacre* and *Ralph* by Ralph Lauren.[5]

None of that history is easily visualized through either the molecular or chemical formula. But the print is also subtly scented with Galaxolide, connecting these visual representations with its olfactory counterpart and its many cultural

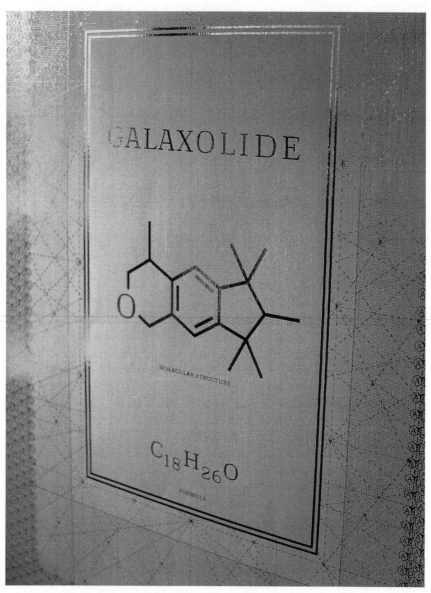

3 Micah Hahn, for the Institute for Art and Olfaction, 'Galaxolide',
in *Molecules Series 1*

associations. In doing so, the print playfully challenges its 'viewers' to consider whether or not perfume can be thought of as fine art by connecting olfaction with art historical traditions where vision is crucial. Staring at the embossed, shimmering representation of Galaxolide's structural bonds, breathing its scent of powdery, synthetic musk, one cannot help but wonder whether the union of art and olfaction necessarily demands a deeper interrogation of both categories and of the power of a *syn*aesthetic approach to fine art. Scent emerges as a postmodern riff on what Benjamin famously defined as the 'aura' of certain objects, the 'semblance of distance' between object and viewer (regardless of their spatial proximity) and a form of perception that endows the object with an ability to 'look back at us,' as we 'breathe' in its wake.[6] Modernity, especially its technologies of reproduction using film and video, shifted multisensorial, atmospheric, and *syn*aesthetic modes of perception towards two-dimensional visual fields, seemingly sacrificing olfaction in the process.[7] Exhibits that stage olfaction as part of the aesthetic experience redirect this more traditional 'view' of art appreciation towards a different aesthetic approach to design and materiality.[8] The aura of *Molecules, Series 1* may very well be the effervescent scent that wafts from the print. But it is also its resonance with other cultural codes, codes that demonstrate the unspoken and powerful ways in which olfaction defines our interaction with the social worlds we inhabit.

The Institute for Art and Olfaction is not alone in making the claim that a molecule might indeed be fine art. In an attempt to emphasize the design of iconic perfumes like *Chanel No. 5*, *Jicky*, and *Drakkar Noir* (rather than the design of their containers), the Museum of Arts and Design in its *The Art of Scent, 1889–2012* exhibition went to great lengths (and expense) to exhibit perfume as itself an art object, one that corresponds with other aesthetic movements. It may seem odd to classify Olivier Cresp's fragrance *Light Blue* (2001) as a still life, yet the exhibition did, asking visitors to perform a kind of olfactory ekphrasis – to think through the category of one medium (painting) to address another (perfume). In doing so, the object in question – and perhaps also the space of the museum itself – emerged anew, or at least that was the hope. Explaining that the problem of perfume's lack of aesthetic lustre connects to its status as a commodity, Chandler Burr, the exhibit's curator, emphasized that one kind of cross-sensory mode has stood in the way of others: the relationship between language and olfaction.[9] Seeking to change the terms one uses to describe modern perfume, Burr's exhibition elevated scent through its association with the traditions of visual art.

Such an approach suggests the complex biological and cultural 'loops' through which we process sensation; some of these include aesthetic form while others engage more directly with lived experiences.[10] To 'see' smell is thus to engage with a synaesthetic mode of art appreciation that probes the limits of both biological and cultural definitions of sensation. Though such an approach may seem impossible, synaesthesia – as both an embodied condition and an aesthetic trope – offers a useful reminder that sensation is always a cultural interface between the body and the world at large; it reminds us of the varied, multisensorial ways in which we have, and we might, perceive the world without insisting on ahistorical, trans-historical, or universally able-bodied experiences of embodiment. To 'see' smell in this way is to engage with both multisensorial meanings of art and olfaction in the present and a synaesthetic approach to their meanings in the past. As both Hahn's *Galaxolide* as well as *The Art of Scent* exhibition suggest, the art of olfaction and the olfactory components of art are not necessarily the same thing, which becomes immediately clear when one switches from modern or postmodern art objects to early modern examples.

Postmodern art like Hahn's *Galaxolide* is not the first to ask its audience to 'breathe' in its splendour or the scent of musk: many pre-modern objects were valued in Renaissance culture precisely for their redolent qualities.[11] Of the wide variety of ingredients used to do this, musk was one of the most highly prized (and most expensive) scent-ingredient. Valued for its strength and its ability to be diffused, musk has been used to scent a wide variety of objects since late antiquity, though its value as a renaissance perfume ingredient derives more from its associations with the East than with the classical past. As early as the ninth century, Persia imported musk from the Tonkin region of Tibet and China through dedicated 'musk routes', routes similar to those of the Silk routes but connecting central and east Asia with the medieval Islamic world.[12] From the Arabic *misk*, Persian *mushk*, and probably from the Sanskrit *mushká* for 'scrotum', musk was harvested from adult male deer, one of several species of *Moschus*, which produced musk in a vesicle near its genitals. Inside the vesicle, the animal's glandular secretions formed irregular 'grains' of musk.[13] Once the deer was killed and the vesicle removed, these grains were dried preferably in their pod, developing a rich and distinctive scent. Used for thousands of years in Buddhist, Hindu, Jewish and Islamic rituals as both a perfume and a medicinal cure, musk was rediscovered by Europeans (along with other aromatic ingredients) through travel and trade associated with the crusades in the medieval period.

Though it is possible to remove musk without killing the deer, this was rarely done; musk deer were hunted to the point of endangerment. By the early nineteenth century, musk was in short supply and still in high demand, which led to experiments in domestication in the mid-nineteenth century. But the domesticated deer produced fewer musk grains and those had poor aromatic quality, which in turn fuelled its synthesizing after Albert Baur, a German chemist, seeking to develop a more effective version of trinitrotoluene (TNT), discovered one of his synthetic compounds smelled similar to musk. These early 'nitro' musks – musk ketone, musk acetate and musk xylene – were key components of major perfumes of the early twentieth century, including

Chanel No. 5.[14] Though their smell lacked the faecal quality of animal musk, their unique scent was highly valued in commercial perfumery. Nitro-musks, however, are highly unstable and potentially neurotoxic, which led to second-generation polycyclic musk synthetics like Galaxolide.

Hahn's *Molecules 1* explicitly names Galaxolide, yet, for most of us, we see and smell musk. In this way, it offers a useful reminder of the wide variety of art objects that worked similarly in the past, resonating across cultural, chemical and art histories to create an aesthetic effect. Vision and olfaction have been linked in the past and remain linked in the present, a point brought home when one adds to this discussion the numerous pre-modern art objects associated with the history of perfume, many of which are on 'display' in museums because of their ornate materiality. Objects like gold censers, elaborately embroidered leather gloves, ceramic potpourri vases, ivory snuff boxes, silver vinaigrettes and the more familiar crystal and glass perfumer bottles are valued mostly for that visual materiality. That they were once defined by the long-since-faded scents they dispensed seems hard to reconcile within current cultures of display. Exhibited in ways that render them meaningful within modern and postmodern sensory hierarchies and emphasize their visual materiality, these objects' olfactory qualities are rendered obsolete.

Emphasizing visual strategies of display makes a certain amount of sense, given the educational goals and aesthetic objectives of most museums in Europe and North America.[15] Objects must be exhibited in ways that render them meaningful to contemporary audiences. Although some museums are staging multisensorial exhibitions, including those that involve haptic and olfactory encounters, vision is still the dominant mode through which aesthetic beauty or cultural value is defined.[16] The power to touch or smell an object is now associated with intimacy we associate with possession, because too many hands could potentially destroy that which makes it valuable. The object is preserved for the future by limiting access: sight, rather than touch or smell or taste, defines its display.

This was not always the case: both private and public collections often emphasized other sensory modes of display, fostering different kinds of understanding of an object's materiality. Many medieval and renaissance copies of the Holy Sepulchre, including the Jerusalem Chapel in Bruges and the *Sacro Monte* in Varallo, deliberately eschewed visual accuracy in favour of haptic, olfactory and gustatory sensory verisimilitude: this dampening of vision sought to mimic the sensory experience recorded by most Christian pilgrims to the Holy Sepulchre in Jerusalem, which could only be visited at night.[17] Some renaissance art theorists believed that the aesthetic value of sculpture was best understood through touch: in fact Lorenzo Ghiberti in his fifteenth-century treatise on tactility in Italian sculpture argued that there were elements of sculpture only discernible through touch.[18] Likewise, seventeenth-century collections designed to invoke curiosity about nature emphasized that all aspects of perception were needed to evaluate materiality. Edward Leigh, for instance, decried that fact that some numismatists evaluated a coin's worth by 'the base handling and smelling' better than 'others not altogether strangers to them could by sight'.[19] Although Ken Arnold, historian and head of Public Programmes at the Wellcome Trust, emphasizes that this approach was not the norm, it was equally rare to find experts who did not rely on a multisensorial approach to materiality. Sensory perception was part of an emerging scientific method: Robert Hooke advised that the best way to examine an object studied was to evaluate its 'sonorousness or dullness, smell or taste'.[20] And Renaissance collectors often encouraged visitors to take a sensuous approach to certain objects: early modern English diarist John Evelyn records his visit to the collection of Signor Septalla, when he smelled Indian wood 'that has the perfect scent of civet'.[21] Robert Plot, naturalist, chemist and first keeper of the Ashmolean Museum, evaluated objects for the collection based on taste and smell, declaring one specimen worthy after ascertaining it was 'tart enough' and another after it had yielded 'a strong ungrateful smell'.[22]

Such an approach is counterintuitive to most contemporary cultures of display, which, of course, reflect modern ocular-centrism but also strategies for preservation: creating distance between objects and visitors helped to preserve many objects from the intense wear and tear that resulted from such handling – it is hard to imagine allowing all visitors the opportunity to sniff the *Mona Lisa*. Though digital imaging and cataloguing has enabled museums to offer new modes of interaction, including digital reproductions that record the sound, feel and even smell of an object, it raises questions about the intrinsic value of the object's materiality. As Ken Arnold queries: 'If all the remote attributes of an object can be recorded and mastered elsewhere and all the direct ones matched and even surpassed through simulacra, why bother with the real thing at all?' Arnold and others emphasize that digital techniques are most effective when combined with experiences *in situ,* allowing museums to provoke wonder in much the same way as pre-modern cultures of display.[23]

Smell, as a mode of appreciating art and cultural objects, is generally associated more with an irreducible 'aura' of authenticity than with technologies of reproduction, seeming to offer a visceral truth about an encounter with art that seems more 'real' than others, especially those involving synthetic, technological or digital reproductions. But to take seriously the ways in which olfaction has participated in the history of art requires a more nuanced understanding of this visceral effect, particularly the ways in which it too has been culturally and historically constructed. Galaxolide, for instance, does not smell exactly like natural musk; it lacks a faecal quality. Yet this might be lost on most people who have not smelled it in its natural form. Modern perfume also involves a very different twist of space and time than what Benjamin evokes in his definition of aura. It is designed to fade, and thus might be better likened to more ephemeral media such as performance art (as author Alyssa Harad has argued), or opera (as perfumer Christophe Laudimiel has explored in his 'scent opera'), or theatre (as the famous 'smell-o-vision' experiments of the 1960s argued, as did John Water's 'odorama' sniff cards that accompanied *Polyester*).[24] Finally, we 'breathe' in much more than just the aura of art in the space of the museum, as experimental exhibits such as Laib's wax rooms or Martynka Wawrzyniak's 'Smell Me' olfactory self-portrait show. In this way, the ephemerality of scent connects to other kinds of contemporary art that challenge an aesthetic of permanence.[25]

Staged in this way, perfume and its history connect these recent artistic movements to a longer, sensuous history of collection and display. As the perfume exhibit at the Museum of Arts and Design highlighted, it might itself be the 'object' on display, requiring a radical reconfiguration of the space of the museum and reminding visitors that aesthetic effects unfold in distinct time and space. Because scent is ephemeral, it also implicitly thwarts curatorial modes designed to emphasize preservation. Like other objects whose value may reside in the allure of use, especially those whose use we may no longer fully understand, the aesthetic of perfume is one that requires a different mode of appreciation. It reminds us that there is a 'beauty in letting go' of preservation, as archaeologist Sven Ouzman has argued, allowing new questions and relationships to form so that people may 'marvel at objects' but 'in ways that make the apprehender aware of the object's place in a continuum of humanistic and material practice' and of how their own perception of it is implicated in those histories.[26]

Early modern perfume had its own complex relationship to materiality; neither visible nor permanent, early modern perfume thwarts modern definitions of perceptible objects. Edmund Husserl, for instance, in his landmark study of phenomenology, argued that objects are things that can be handled, displayed and most importantly seen.[27] Yet sensation as a historical phenomenon included a more complex approach to materiality than Husserl allows. For example, a fifteenth-century English censer highlighted in the Victoria and Albert Museum's 'Making Sense of an Object' series is, literally, defined by its olfactory use.[28] Though it is implied by its name, its scent, frankincense, rarely accompanies its display; even if it did, modern frankincense stems from a different species of plant than either ancient or medieval frankincense.[29] Its scent is closer to ancient rather than medieval incense. Likewise, our cultural associations with its smell may or may not be linked to Catholic liturgy; incense is a common note in modern perfumes, for example.

Yet to discount olfaction entirely is to misunderstand a large component of the object's history. English censers are almost always staged behind glass: objects like this one are incredibly rare, since most were destroyed in the many religious reforms of the sixteenth century. This particular example was found hidden in the walls of a house, where it was undoubtedly placed to protect it from such reform. In order to make sense of the object, the museum focuses on explaining its use through the conservation work involved in repairing its chains. The chains are key to understanding its complex cultural history: they facilitated its swinging, which was integral to its liturgical use. Frankincense and other resins were poured over hot coals placed inside the metal chamber, producing a sweetly scented smoke that emerged from the holes at its top; the smell marked the divine transformation of transubstantiation, signalling the presence of the divine.

Though small, it was a powerful dispenser, capable of filling even a cathedral with its scent. Although this one has little decorative detail, most medieval censers were shaped in the architectural form of the church, connecting their use with that space.[30] Yet this object's scent history remains elliptical, reduced to its broken chains. The length of those chains, for instance, reveal if it was designed to hang or swing; by the late Middle Ages, censers had become larger, with four chains and an internal chamber to stabilize hot coals to better facilitate swinging. These advances all directly relate to more elaborate uses of liturgical incense, yet this particular object's worth is more readily measured through its visual materiality, a point that resonates in the tantalizing snippet of its history in the sixteenth century. How did it remain hidden in the walls of the house for so long, escaping detection when so many other censers did not? Its striking, historical narrative is left unanswered. It is easy to presume that, given its size, it was not easy to spot. Such a conclusion, however, fails to interpret the censer within other sensory registers: it left a rather large olfactory footprint. To make 'sense' of this object, one needs to grapple simultaneously with its tangible, visual and ephemeral materiality. Otherwise, our historical assumptions about the boundaries between visible and invisible matter obscures its material history: we value that which we can see (its metalwork, inscriptions, even donation history) rather than its aspects most familiar to late medieval men and women – its smoky, scented exhalations. How we define the materiality of our evidence matters, especially in attempts to collect, display or historicize material objects associated with the history of the senses. Put another way, one might ask: what does it mean to 'see' smell in the past after its materiality has long since faded?

Such a question is integral to understanding the history of early modern pomanders. Indeed, it is hard to argue that art and olfaction are not linked when considering the cultural history of early modern pomanders, yet it is equally difficult to say precisely how they connect to one another. Both were key to the power of pomanders within renaissance culture: part jewellery, talisman and medicinal cure, pomanders and the scents that defined them were integral to protecting those who wore them. Yet the relationship between the two –

between a pomander's ornate exterior and the aromatics it contained – remains underexplored, particularly as an aesthetic one. Part of this has to do with the conventions of early modern art. As François Quiviger has argued, the relationship between these two sensory modes in Italian renaissance art is complex: flowers, for instance, are common allegories of both visual and olfactory beauty. Likewise, the sensory horrors of plague, particularly the stench associated with death, are rarely depicted visually, and are usually signified by a single figure, holding his nose.[31] Beyond signifying a good or bad scent, what do visual clues signify? When olfaction is depicted extensively, it is often in foul detail.[32]

Elevated to allegorical abstraction or reduced to obscene fart jokes, olfaction remains an enigma within the aesthetics of early modern art. Pomanders, as decorative and scent objects, may provide some insight. Like censers, pomanders are literally defined by their olfactory use. From the French *pomme d'ambre*, or apple of amber, a pomander was a ball of aromatic paste, usually ambergris, musk or civet, mixed with other aromatics (floral petals, spices or animal secretions). Unlike most European renaissance censers, however, which were

4 Pomander in the shape of a ship, the Walters Art Museum, Baltimore 44.464

5 Silver pomander in the form of a book, Science Museum A641827

6 Pendant perfume-ball, British Museum AF.2863

7 Pomander case, British Museum 1854,0124.1

primarily used by Catholic priests to dispense incense, renaissance pomanders varied greatly in both their scents and their uses. The term described a particular scent, but it became a complex signifier of perfume more generally along with the technology used to dispense it – by the fourteenth century the name also described the elaborate metal casings that contained them (and now define their storage and display).

These small, yet often ornate, objects exist in a wide range of forms; some hint at complex allegorical associations – such as the enamel seventeenth-century pomander in the shape of a ship (Figure 4), or the seventeenth-century silver pomander in the shape of a book with a rat engraved on its cover (Figure 5) – while others are comprised solely of aromatics, such as the ball of benzoin studded with emeralds (Figure 6), or designed to protect and dispense a similar mass of aromatics (Figure 7). Pomanders like these last two examples were made up of a simple and often costly mass of aromatic paste made from ambergris, benzoin, civet, musk, or some amalgamation of these ingredients; others most likely housed a more affordable paste made from floral petals and fixatives.

Even the most simple of pomanders in terms of design, however, may provide some insight into both its scents and their cultural uses. Those affixed with gemstones may have served as aromatic jewellery, hanging from belts or necks and perfuming the wearer and his or her clothes; its elevated ornamentation emphasizes the costliness of the aromatics most likely contained within it. The more elaborate the container, one presumes, the more expensive its ingredient (with musk generally the costliest of aromatic ingredients). Some, carved out of wood with simple cutouts as design elements, were most likely used in prayer, hanging from rosary beads made from a similar paste as that inside – ground rose petals mixed with aromatic fixatives. These rose-scented pomanders and beads fostered multisensorial (haptic and olfactory) meditation on the Virgin Mary, whose purity was allegorically linked to the rose. To 'see' this particular smell in renaissance art requires we look for it using synaesthetic clues to its material history rather than its allegorical signification. Bartholomäus Braun's *Portrait of a Woman* (1547), for example, depicts its subject in prayer, holding just such a pomander and rosary beads, its scent seemingly signalled by a floral attribute placed nearby. Yet the flower is a pink carnation, not a rose; its presence works in visual, rather than olfactory ways, suggesting both the young woman's faith and, most likely, her recent betrothal.[33] The scent of the rose resonates through the colour of the red rosary beads that are entwined through her fingers, a pinky extended towards the pomander.

That extension may be figurative, but such a gesture also subtly connotes how these objects were used. A pomander needed to be opened or set in motion to release its scent. Worn close at hand, hung from chains around the neck and waist, pomanders were thus both decorative and utilitarian. This unique combination of visual form and olfactory function created intimate, aesthetic effects, linking a pomander's visual and olfactory qualities through an intimate, and haptic, engagement with both. Only part of its cultural value emerges through static display. Pomanders that work as *memento mori*, for instance, engage directly with anamorphic perspective; the handling required to achieve the desired visual effect undoubtedly released fragrance, raising questions about how that scent connected to the aesthetic representation unfolding for the viewer. The Danish pomander (circa 1600) that later belonged to Queen Sophie Amalie of Denmark, for instance, visually mimics the bright red colour of rosary beads, but its six 'beads' are made instead from red coral, four of which are carved into the shape of skulls – something its owner would have known intimately by touch. The remaining two beads explicitly connect beauty with death, with one side carved with an image of a crowned woman and the other a crowned skull. These beads are strung on a chain with an enamel pomander of double their size shaped as a skull, crowned with rubies. Inside it are six compartments, engraved with scent ingredients – 'schlag', 'canel', 'citron', 'malorca', 'rosen' and 'negelen' [musk, cinnamon, lemon, orange, rose and clove] – as well as a sponge for a vinaigrette.[34] The vinaigrette released its scent with every twist and turn of the chain; the internal compartments contained specimens useful to have at hand should disease and death manifest itself in something other than allegorical form.

The Danish queen's 'death's head pomander/vinaigrette' performs a visual and olfactory twist on pomanders of prayer even as it worked as medicinal protection from foul airs.[35] Pomanders were often shaped as *memento mori*, adding additional olfactory meanings to their visual signification. One sixteenth-century example demonstrates how this worked: on one side is engraved the face of a woman, on the other, a skull. It warns those who read its engraving '*sum fui*'. Yet the perfume it contained also complicates this temporal narrative, infusing it with an even more sinister meaning: in this instance, the scent of the pomander works as an olfactory reminder of the visual lesson – beauty not only fades but is perhaps already dead, since the fragrance emerges only from dead or dried botanical and animal matter. The anamorphic perspective required to 'read' the *memento mori*'s warning engages the pomander's scent: one heeds the warning only after breathing in the pomander's scent. '*Sum*' is engraved on the woman's throat; '*fui*' on the top of the skull. This oddly asymmetrical placement of text requires that one turn and flip the pomander in order to read the message, which might be explained by the fact that the empty eye sockets of the skull open to the inside, allowing scent to escape from them during this action. [36]

That a sweet smell could signal the presence of disease and death was a paradox all too real for most early modern men and women; plague prevention required extensive use of aromatics to protect the body's vulnerable orifices from contagion. Pomanders worked especially well when patterns of contagion were erratic, as they often were in England; although some geographic areas were linked with higher threats of contagion, and some plague outbreaks were more uniform than others, for the most part dangerous air could be anywhere, requiring one have perfumed protection close at hand.[37] Strong scents worked as a shield, blocking more dangerous, contaminated air from entering the body. Yet this practice ironically worked to connect perfume with the presence of plague, linking the fragrant with the foul in complex and nuanced ways. Pomanders, as *memento mori*, enact this paradox in highly ornate ways. Shaped into coffins and skulls, these pomanders connected the technology of perfume with the latent risk in smelling. The olfactory paradox of smell – that death might smell sweet – is revealed through its visual form. Other images emphasize the paradox of its size in relationship to its cultural necessity. Pomanders were often shaped as snails, which seems abstract until one considers the animal's ability to withdraw into itself for self-protection. Snails were thus a symbol of the pomander's power: though one could not retreat from the disease, one could retreat into one's own air.[38] Its perfumes were thus an extension of the self, rather than a mode of self-presentation for others. Such a conclusion helps

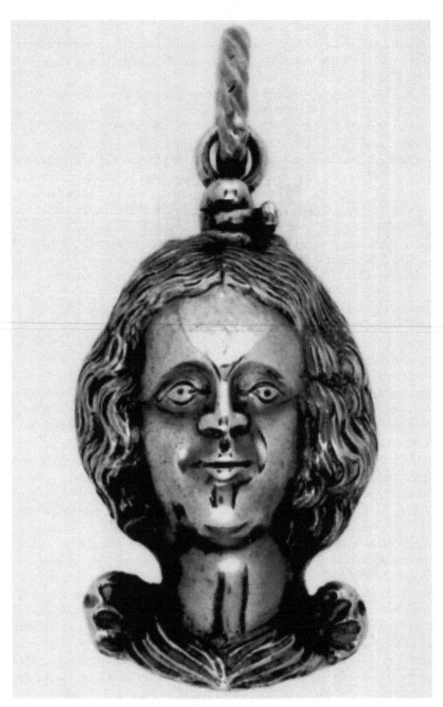

8 Silver pomander in the form of a female head, British Museum 1978,1002.220

explain a seventeenth-century English pomander in the shape of a woman's head (Figure 8): it may have served as a self-portrait, connecting the pomander's scents with those that protected its young wearer from harm.

Given their use, some pomanders were affixed with written amulets: one Birgittine nun sent gifts of musk-scented pomanders to her friend and her children to defend them from the bad vapours associated with the plague. Noting their small size – she calls them *bisamäpfelien* or 'little musk apples' – the nun also notes that each was affixed with a feather that contained a scroll of paper with the Greek letter *tau* written on it. As art historians Corine Schlief and Volker Schier argue, a letter that accompanied this gift suggests the expansiveness of 'sensory and cognitive experiences' that comprised the 'spiritual and material life' that comprised the everyday life of the faithful.[39] In it, the nun explains how the gift was intended to engage all of the senses of its wearer: the feather reminds the wearer of its hidden, written scroll (inscribed with its symbol of the cross), a symbol of everlasting life in the presence of death just as the sweet scent of musk promised to defend against any 'bad vapours'. Its small size perhaps suggests its intimacy; it may reflect a private, but powerful bond between women. Such epistolary evidence documents that seeing, smelling and feeling the pomander rendered it meaningful as a gift.

Some pomanders have internal compartments that are engraved with the names for various spices and aromatics. This sixteenth-century example (Figure 9), for instance, includes engraved compartments for 'moscat', 'rosen' and 'rosemarin' (nutmeg, rose and rosemary), with images of foliage on its internal

9 Gilt pomander, Science Museum A629413

sides. Outside it is also decorated with images of fruit and foliage. The emphasis on spices – rather than more costly aromatics such as civet, musk or storax – suggests that this object was valued less for its scent ingredients and more for its cultural use, though such a conclusion limits the design of the object to our ability to 'read' its olfactory materiality through the engraved names alone. Could its more abstract qualities suggest something else? The emphasis on fruit and foliage suggests a correspondence with the botanical scents and spices contained within it. Might the pomander's scents be meant to work together in a cohesive way? Some have argued that the complexity of this design suggests that they were not; separate chambers require more time to open the pomander and then select an internal chamber to open and inhale.[40] This seems to be a very different action than merely sniffing an open-work pomander that protects an aromatic ball of paste. But what one loses in immediacy, one gains in specificity, raising questions about the cultural significance of specific scents. For this style of pomander, the named scent of rose or musk may signal a complexity of signification akin to those of Galaxolide discussed above.

And what of pomanders that use engravings to differentiate between compartments? One, for instance, has four compartments, each side engraved with an images of a saint – Dorothy, John, Barbara, Andrew, Mary Magdalene, Paul, Catherine and Peter.[41] When closed it forms an image of a sky, with a sun and clouds. As one cataloguer notes, it resembles a prayer nut when closed, an object that drew upon medicinal traditions based on morphology as well as sensuous prayer rituals.[42] Do these visual clues work in cross-modal ways as well – do they 'signify' scents? Did St Catherine of Alexandria – often invoked in early modern Catholic art as a protector of virginity – connect with nutmeg, cloves and balsam, scents associated with the Virgin?[43] Though it is not depicted on the pomander, St Dorothy's attribute of apples and roses may have been signalled through the presence of scent.

In this chapter, I have surveyed only a few of the many early modern pomanders housed in private and public collections. Though they vary greatly – in design, ornamentation and provenance – most share one thing: they are now empty. To understand the cultural signification of early modern pomanders thus requires a synaesthetic approach: we must train ourselves to 'see' smell in the past. Pomanders, like most objects in museums, are catalogued, displayed and organized to make meaning within our sensory world. We define them primarily by their visual components; as a result they join a variety of other objects stacked in drawers and displayed behind glass whose meanings remain occluded; to understand their meaning in the past is to engage with a multisensorial approach to history. In this way, pomanders remind us of the complex ways in which olfaction challenges traditional approaches to materiality and representation. To see smell in the twentieth and twenty-first centuries involves fine arts and photography, the chemicals that we recognize as perfume transcribed into abstraction, either through elevating their chemical bonds into gilded prints or capturing their reaction through photography. The synaes- thetic loop is visual; early modern pomanders may have worked in a similar way but they also engaged haptic and perhaps even gustatory meanings as well as sensory modes vastly different from our own. We may not be able to access those meanings, but to view, hear, touch, taste or smell an object is to wonder about those sensorial meanings as they unfolded in strikingly different times and places. I can attest that it is a very different experience to hold and sniff an early modern pomander, given its historical association with plague, than to view it. Even the absence of scent reminds us of its once potent power; the act of sniffing is itself a potentially fraught, yet unavoidable action. As such, pomanders remind us not only of the strong links between art and olfaction in our own cultural moment, but also of their connection in the past. They challenge us to engage in a *syn*aesthetic approach to materiality so that we might begin to approach a multisensorial understanding of history.

Notes

1 For more, see the institute's website http://artandolfaction.com/special-projects/ molecule-prints/ [accessed 18 June 2013].

2 Aldehyde C12 is best associated with the fizzy, sparkly scent of *Chanel No.5*; Iso E Super is the trademarked name of 7-acetyl, 1,2,3,4,5,6,7,8-octahydro-1,1,6,7-tetra- methyl naphthalene, a woody-amber scent (when combined with other molecules) and a clean scent (on its own) that is used in so many modern perfumes that it is hard to label one as representative; Galaxolide is a synthetic musk used in perfumes like *Tresor* and *White Linen*.

3 For the extent to which it has been found in humans, see the Environmental Working Group's Human Toxome Project www.ewg.org/sites/humantoxome/ [accessed 13 June 2013].

4 See perfume blogger Elena Vosnaki's essay on musk http://perfumeshrine.blogs- pot.com/2009/12/musk-series-2-natural-and-everything.html [accessed 13 June 2013].

5 Vosnaki, http://perfumeshrine.blogspot.com/2009/12/musk-series-2-natural- and-everything.html [accessed 13 June 2013].

6 Walter Benjamin, 'Little History of Photography', trans. by Jephcott and Kingsley Shorter, *SW*, 3:104, cited in Miriam Hansen's 'Benjamin's Aura', *Critical Inquiry*, 34 (2008): 336–76 (p. 340).

7 For more on synaesthisa and modernist art, see Caro Verbeek's research: www. caroverbeek.nl.

8 For more on directed viewing, especially of the productive arts, see Caren Yglesias, 'Seeing Air', *Visuality/Materiality: Images, Objects, and Practices* (Farnham: Ashgate, 2012), pp. 85–108 (p. 87).

9 "'To a degree it's a problem of language", Mr Burr said. "We have not had anything other than a marketing language applied to these works."' Quoted in Carol Kino, 'Fragrances as Art, Displayed Squirt by Squirt', *New York Times*, 15 Nov. 2012

www.nytimes.com/2012/11/16/arts/design/the-art-of-scent-at-the-museum-of-arts-and-design.html?pagewanted=all [accessed 19 June 2013].

10　David Howes, 'Introduction', in *Empires of the Senses: The Sensual Culture Reader*, ed. by David Howes (Oxford: Berg, 2005), p. 5; see also his essay, 'Hearing Scents, Tasting Sights: Toward a Cross-Cultural Multi-Modal Theory of Aesthetics', in *Art and the Senses*, ed. by Francesca Bacci and David Melcher (Oxford: Oxford University Press, 2011), pp. 161–81.

11　Holly Dugan, *Ephemeral History of Perfume: Scent and Sense in Early Modern England* (Baltimore, MD: Johns Hopkins University Press, 2011), pp. 6–7.

12　Ronit Yoeli-Tlalim, 'Islam and Tibet: Cultural Interactions – An Introduction', in *Islam and Tibet: Cultural Interactions Along the Musk Route*, ed. by Anna Akasoy, Charles S. Burnett and Ronit Yoeli-Tlalim (Aldershot: Ashgate, 2011), pp. 1–16 (p. 8).

13　R.A. Donkin, *Dragon's Brain Perfume: An Historical Geography of Camphor* (Leiden: Brill, 1999), p. 2; Anya King, 'Tibetan Musk and Medieval Arab Perfumery', in Akasoy, Burnett and Yoeli-Tlalim (eds), pp. 145–62 (p. 147).

14　Tilar Mazzeo, *The Secret of Chanel No. 5: The Intimate History of the World's Most Famous Fragrance* (New York: Harper Collins, 2010), p. 208.

15　See Constance Classen and David Howes, 'The Museum as Sensescape: Western Sensibilities and Indigenous Artifacts', in *Sensible Objects: Colonialism, Museums, and Material Culture*, ed. by Elizabeth Edwards, Chris Gosden and Ruth Phillips (Oxford: Berg, 2002), pp. 199–222 (p. 200).

16　Other exhibits have worked from the opposite premise – that scent can expand our experience of visual art. Tate Britain's *Pre-Raphaelites: Victorian Avant-Garde* exhibit, for example, included an ambulatory 'scent' tour, led by art historian Christina Bradstreet and olfactory event planner Odette Toillete, whose goal was 'to explore the historical associations of scent and its influence upon the interpretation of the paintings'. See 'Scented Visions: A Multisensory Tour of the Pre-Raphaelites Exhibition and Private View', www.tate.org.uk/whats-on/tate-britain/private-view-special-event/scented-visions-multisensory-tour-pre-raphaelites [accessed 13 June 2013].

17　Laura Gelfand, 'Sense and Simulacra: Manipulation of the Senses in Medieval Copies of Jerusalem', *Postmedieval*, 3 (2012), 407–22.

18　'I have seen by diffused light … a statue of an Hermaphrodite … which had been made with admirable skil … In this [statue] there was the greatest refinement, which the eye would not have discovered had not the hand sought it out', Lorenzo Ghiberti, *I Commentari*, ed. by O. Morisani (Naples: Riccardo Ricciardi, 1947), pp. 54–55, quoted in Geraldine A. Johnson, 'Touch, Tactility, and the Reception of Sculpture in Early Modern Italy', in *A Companion to Art Theory*, ed. by Paul Smith and Carolyn Wilde (Oxford: Blackwell, 2002), pp. 61–75 (p. 64).

19　Edward Leigh, *Three Diatribes* (1671), p. 42, cited in Ken Arnold, *Cabinets for the Curious: Looking Back at Early English Museums* (Aldershot: Ashgate, 2006), p. 76.

20　Robert Hooke, *Posthumous Works of Robert Hooke*, ed. by Richard Westfall (New York: Johnson Reprint Corp., 1969), p. 36.

21　John Evelyn, *Diary of John Evelyn, Esq.*, ed. by William Bray (London: Bickers, 1906), p. 275.

22 Arnold, p. 56.

23 Arnold, p. 256.

24 Alyssa Harad, 'Perfume is Not an Object: A Few Thoughts', www.alyssaharad.com/scent/perfume-is-not-an-object-a-few-thoughts-about-perfume-and-art [accessed 1 May 2013]; Christophe Laudamiel, Nico Muhly and Valgeir Sigurdsson, 'Green Aria Scent Opera'; for more on smell-o-vision and *Polyester*, see Rachel Herz, *Scent of Desire: Discovering our Enigmatic Sense of Smell* (New York: Harper Perennial, 2007), p. 230.

25 See Helen Pheby, 'Contemporary Art', in *Museum Materialities: Objects, Engagements, Interpretations* (New York: Routledge, 2010), pp. 71–88 (p. 81).

26 Sven Ouzman, 'Beauty of Letting Go: Fragmentary Museums and Archaeologies of Archives', in *Sensible Objects: Colonialism, Museums, and Material Culture*, ed. by Elizabeth Edwards, Chris Gosden and Ruth B. Phillips (Oxford: Berg, 2006), pp. 269–301 (p. 293).

27 Edmund Husserl, 'A Phenomenology of Reason', in *General Introduction to a Pure Phenomenology* (The Hague: Nijhof, 1982), p. 31.

28 See 'Censer: Making Sense of an Object', in *Conservation Journal*, 39 (2001), www.vam.ac.uk/content/journals/conservation-journal/issue-39/censer_making_sense_of_an_object/hduga [accessed 24 June 2013].

29 Dugan, p. 31.

30 Fifteenth-century Florentine censer, Victoria and Albert Museum, no. 549-1889.

31 François Quiviger, *The Sensory World of Italian Renaissance Art* (London: Reaktion, 2010), pp. 126, 134.

32 Alice Sanger and Siv Tove Kulbrandstad Walker, 'Introduction: Making Sense of the Senses', in *Sense and the Senses in Early Modern Art and Cultural Practice*, ed. by Alice Sanger and Siv Tove Kulbrandstad Walker (Farnham: Ashgate, 2012), pp. 1–16 (p. 14 n. 4).

33 See Maryan Ainsworth and Joshua Vaterman, *German Paintings in the Metropolitan Museum of Art, 1350–1600* (New York: Metropolitan Museum of Art, 2013), p. 283 n. 10.

34 Danish Royal Collection, Rosenborg Palace, Copenhagen, http://dkks.dk/Pomander-2 [accessed 2 July 2013].

35 The titles of both Richard Whitford's *Pomander of Prayer* (1531) as well as Thomas Becon's *Pomander of Prayer* (1563) suggest that the term also accrued literary and metaphorical meanings in the sixteenth century.

36 Edmund Launert, *Perfume and Pomanders: Scent and Scent Bottles* (Munich: Potterton, 1987), p. 110.

37 Dugan, pp. 110–11.

38 Launert, p. 22.

39 Corine Schlief and Volker Schier, *Katarina's Windows: Donation and Devotion, Art and Music, as Heard and Seen in the Writings of a Birgittine Nun* (State College, PA: Penn State University Press, 2009), p. 241.

40 Luisa Coscarelli, 'Do I Smell? The Pomander and its Materiality', *Unmaking Things: 2012–2013*, Royal College of Art and Victoria and Albert Museum http://unmakingthings.rca.ac.uk/2013/do-i-smell-the-pomander-and-its-materiality/ [accessed 21 June 2013].

41　Launert, p. 106.

42　Launert, pp. 20, 106.

43　C.M. Woolgar, *The Senses in Late Medieval England* (New Haven, CT: Yale University Press, 2006), p. 243.

Part II

The senses in context

6

Robert Herrick and the five (or six) senses

Natalie K. Eschenbaum

When you descend to the lower level of the Art Museum of New South Wales, you are greeted with an intense, pungent, but welcoming aroma. Cinnamon, cardamom and cloves – the same spices that lured English Renaissance traders to India – draw you into a room that houses Ernesto Neto's installation, *Just Like Drops in Time, Nothing*.[1] Dozens of massive semi-transparent tubes of stocking-like fabric hang from the ceiling, weighted down by hundreds of pounds of ground spices. As Neto's title prompts, the spices look and act 'like drops' of liquid; their access to the sense of smell is as important as their material nature. The museum's Director Curatorial, Anthony Bond, explains how the body and its senses are central to Neto's work: '[The] spice[s] swell the fabric in voluptuous almost bodily forms that fill the gallery space and our olfactory organs with [their] aromatic intensity.' To engage with this art is to become part of it, because your 'body ingests the work and is simultaneously ingested by it'. Neto uses the sense of smell to question the boundaries between people and things: 'Scent entails the physical invasion of the body by its particles unlike vision that always exists as a translation conveyed to the eye by light from a distance.'[2] He forces viewers to smell his art, inviting the possibility that sensation is always invasive.

Although Neto's installation, as well as Bond's description of it, stem from a modern understanding (or imagining) of sensation, Robert Herrick's early modern English verse similarly explores the surfaces of bodies, their sensing orifices and the liquefying experiences of sensation. Herrick, however, does imagine all five senses to enable 'physical invasion of the body'. In 'The Argument of his Book', he provides a partial table of contents for *Hesperides* (1648), his collection of over 1400 poems. The things emphasized at the midpoint of the verse catalogue are liquids and sensual objects: 'I sing of *Dewes*, of *Raines*, and piece by piece | Of *Balme*, of *Oyle*, of *Spice*, and *Amber-Greece*' (ll. 7–8).[3] Throughout *Hesperides*, Herrick sings of things that enliven the senses, and he describes sensation as a process of absorption or consumption. For instance, like Neto's spices, the body absorbs the ambergris-based perfume through the sense of smell. In this chapter, I argue that Herrick's poetics reveal that all objects act like fluids when they are seen, tasted, touched, heard or smelled – or, rather, when they are textualized or poeticized as sensible things.

Critical interest in the senses in early modern literature has increased steadily in recent years, as evidenced by this collection. Sense experiences are historically specific, and, Susan Stewart explains, the 'forms of their articulation and expression in works of art give us an historical account of how such experiences [...] are transformed'.[4] In early modern England, most writers agreed with Aristotle's general assertion that knowledge happens via the senses: 'if one perceived nothing one would learn nothing'.[5] Sensation allowed early moderns to, quite literally, make sense of their realities.

By the time Herrick published *Hesperides* there was a long tradition of poetic sensoria, or verses specifically devoted to the five senses. Examples include Richard de Fournival's *Bestiare d'amour* (*c*. 1240), Edmund Spenser's *The Faerie Queen* 2.11 (1590), George Chapman's *Ovid's Banquet of Sence* (1595), Thomas Tomkis's play *Lingua* (1607) and Michael Drayton's *Idea XXIX*, 'To the Senses' (1616). The narrator of Drayton's sonnet, for example, calls upon each sense in his attempt to thwart Love's attack on his heart:

> But he with beauty first corrupted sight,
> My hearing bribed with her tongue's harmony,
> My taste by her sweet lips drawn with delight,
> My smelling won with her breath's spicery,
>   But when my touching came to play his part
> The king of senses, greater than the rest,
> He yields Love up the keys unto my heart[.][6]

In *The Five Senses: Studies in a Literary Tradition*, Louise Vinge offers an impressive survey of these sensual verse catalogues. She mentions Cowley's 'The Soul' (1647) and Cleveland's 'To the State of Love, Or, the Senses' Festival' (1651) to demonstrate how the five senses *topos* persisted in mid-seventeenth-century love poetry.[7] Herrick, publishing at this time, would have been aware of the tradition. But *Hesperides* is not part of Vinge's survey because Herrick does not have a single poem, or a defined series of poems, that catalogues all five senses. 'Of Love. A Sonet' is the closest he comes to this tradition:

> How Love came in, I do not know,
> Whether by th'eye, or eare, or no:
> Or whether with the soule it came
> (At first) infused with the same:
> Whether in part 'tis here or there,
> Or, like the soule, whole every where:
> This troubles me: but I as well
> As any other, this can tell;
> That when from hence she does depart,
> The out-let then is from the heart.

Herrick nods to the sensorium tradition, but does something different here. His narrator admits that the science of sensation, as it relates to love, confuses him. He knows he is in love because his heart aches when his beloved departs. When in love, the usual ways in which we gain knowledge and confirm reality – our bodily senses – are not helpful. When in love, our bodies are infused with the feeling and, perhaps, with the soul of our beloved.

Herrick's choice of the word *infuse* (from the Latin, *infundĕre*, meaning 'to pour in') predicts the way in which he describes the liquefying function of the five senses throughout *Hesperides*.[8] Even though his collection does not include a traditional poetic sensorium, and even though 'Of Love. A Sonet' seems to dismiss the senses, Herrick writes dozens of poems about seeing, hearing, smelling, tasting and touching things and people. In *Hesperides*, to sensually engage with things or people is usually to infuse with them, to melt into them, to liquefy.

Herrick's poems about seeing his beloved Julia are probably the best examples of the effects of intrusive, liquid sensation. Take, for instance, the oft-anthologized 'Upon Julia's Clothes':

> When as in silks my *Julia* goes,
> Then, then (me thinks) how sweetly flowes
> That liquefaction of her clothes
>
> Next, when I cast mine eyes and see
> That brave Vibration each way free;
> O how that glittering taketh me!

The description of Julia's clothing reflects the experience of visual sensation. The effect of the vision mirrors the vision itself. In the first stanza, the narrator describes Julia's silk clothing flowing like a river. The parenthetical 'me thinks' implies that he does not yet see the clothing, but is simply imagining the undulating liquid cloth. The second stanza then opens with him seeing the clothes by 'cast[ing]' his eyes, like a fisherman throwing his line into a river. The narrator does not just see the silken river, but he throws his eyeballs into it. He then realizes that he is at the wrong end of the fishing pole (as is often the case in these sorts of fishing allusions). He cannot capture the glittering, liquid clothing, but rather is taken, or captured, by it. The experience of seeing the river is the experience of becoming a river. To see is to liquefy and to become one with that which you see. Seeing is infusion.

Herrick describes a similar experience of visual sensation in 'Julia's Petticoat'. Here, the narrator 'behold[s]' an 'Azure Robe' (l. 1). The wonderfully tactile verb, 'behold', suggests a physical joining of the seer with the thing seen. The petticoat comes to life in the narrator's vision of it; it goes 'wandring' and ''two'd pant, and sigh, and heave' (ll. 3, 5). But seeing the petticoat's animated movements causes the narrator to liquefy again:

Sometimes away 'two'd wildly fling;
Then to thy thighs so closely cling,
That some conceit did melt me downe,
As Lovers fall into a swoone:
And all confus'd, I there did lie
Drown'd in Delights; but co'd not die.
That Leading Cloud, I follow'd still,
Hoping t'ave seene of it my fill;
But ah! I co'd not: sho'd it move
To Life Eternal, I co'd love.
(ll. 13–22)

The blue petticoat flows when Julia moves, periodically 'cling[ing]' to her thighs and revealing her body's outline. This visual image conjures in the narrator's mind a 'conceit', or a 'fanciful notion', that makes him melt and then drown.[9] One can only guess what sort of 'fanciful notion' he conjures, but the poem cares less about what is imagined than it does about the physical effects of seeing. He is not content simply to lie 'Drown'd in [the] Delights' of what he has imagined, but he needs to keep drinking in the vision of the petticoat. He keeps following that 'Cloud' – a billowing, moving body of liquid – and says he hopes 't'ave seene of it my fill'. To see is to ingest, as you would drink or food. Sight is sustenance, even if it, like love, is insatiable.

In these poems about Julia's clothing, seeing is a liquid process that conjoins the viewer with that which is seen. Herrick's poems about hearing similarly melt together the listener with that which is heard. In another Julia poem, 'Upon Julia's Voice', the narrator describes her singing:

So smooth, so sweet, so silv'ry is thy voice,
As, could they hear, the Damn'd would make no noise,
But listen to thee, (walking in thy chamber)
Melting melodious words, to Lutes of Amber.

Julia's voice, accompanied by lutes, is so beautiful that even those suffering in Hell would be silenced if they could hear her. They would simply stand, mesmerized, and drink in the sound of her voice (like the narrator who is sustained by drinking in the vision of her moving petticoat). Herrick's own language depicts the beauty of Julia's singing through alliterative onomatopoeia. The first and fourth lines melt their own 'melodious words'; like her voice, his poetry is '[s]o smooth, so sweet, so silv'ry'. Herrick's poetic voice mirrors, or melts into, Julia's. Her voice is his poetry, and his poetry is her voice.

In 'Againe', the poem immediately following 'Upon Julia's Voice', the narrator hears her voice and claims to lose his own:

When I thy singing next shall heare,
Ile wish I might turne all to eare,

To drink in Notes, and Numbers; such
As blessed soules cann't heare too much:
Then melted down, there let me lye
Entranc'd, and lost confusedly:
And by thy Musique strucken mute,
Die, and be turn'd into a Lute.

Here, the ear is given the mouth-like ability to drink in liquid music. Herrick's narrator asks to 'turne all to eare', so that his entire being can consume (and be consumed by) Julia's voice. He asks to be like 'blessed soules' who are not limited by physical bodies and their senses. Souls, as we saw in 'Of Love. A Sonet', are like liquids that can be poured into and out of bodies. The narrator wants to immerse himself in listening so completely that he loses himself and becomes the sound that entrances him. Indeed, he refers to himself as 'I' – a subject – three times in the first two lines. As soon as he wishes to be turned into an ear – an object – the first person subject disappears. The listener (or, rather, the 'ear') melts down with complete consumption of the liquid music, where he (or, rather, it) asks passively to be 'let' to 'lye'. As a melted, entranced, confused object (confused, because he is no longer an 'I'), the listener relinquishes all control to the music.

In both of these poems, sounds have metamorphic power. They can change solids to liquids and people to things. Herrick gives scents this same power. As Neto demonstrates with his spiced art installation, smelling is a more intrusive sense. We can smell from afar, but scents (like tastes, but less voluntary) are drawn into the body. Perhaps predictably, *Hesperides* also includes a poem about smelling Julia. In 'Upon Julia's sweat' Herrick's narrator asks if we would like 'oyle of Blossomes', or a floral perfume, and informs us that we can 'Take it from my *Julia's* sweat' (ll. 1–2). Her sweat, he says, smells like lilies and lavender and should be bottled. Similarly, when she breathes we can capture 'rich spices' that 'flow' from her mouth (l. 6). Like visions and sounds, scents act like liquids when they 'flow' from a person's body. 'To Dewes. A Song' also describes scents, but this time to capture the feeling of being in love. It begins with the narrator asking liquid dew to 'consume' the fire of Love that burns within him, '[a]lthough the Pile be all perfume' (ll. 3–4). The funeral pile might smell sweet, like Julia's breath, but it is incinerating him nonetheless. He continues:

Alas! the heat and death's the same;
Whether by choice, or common flame:
To be in Oyle of *Roses* drown'd,
Or water; where's the comfort found?
Both bring one death; and I die here [...]
(ll. 5–9)

To drown is to die, whether the vehicle is plain water or scented rose oil. What this means, though, is that being in love feels like burning in spice or drowning in floral perfume. Being in love feels like being overwhelmed by, and losing yourself in, your beloved's scents. Smelling, like seeing and hearing, is a liquid process that directly affects the sensor.

In *Hesperides*, scents change things as well as people. One of Herrick's epigrams, 'The Custard', describes a piping hot dessert that is delivered to a dinner table. A man named Furze, 'three or foure times with his cheeks did blow | Upon the Custard, and thus cooled so' (ll. 3–4). Furze cools the custard, but the narrator informs us that now 'none co'd eate it, 'cause it stunk so much' (l. 6). Unlike Julia, who would have spiced the custard with her scented breath, Furze's disgusting breath taints the custard, making it inedible. Lungs, another foul-breathed individual, does not even need to blow on food to corrupt it; he just sits at the table and 'his breath do's Fly-blow all the meate' ('Upon Lungs. Epigram', l. 2). Lungs's breath is so foul that meat begins to decompose, to crawl with maggots, simply when he is in its presence. Scents are powerful. Whether you are custard, meat or a person, smells get under your skin and change your composition, for better or for worse.

The epigrams about tainted foodstuffs are as much about the sense of taste as they are about smell. The noxious smells emanating from the custard and meat are warnings that the food should not be tasted. Because of its connection with eating and drinking, taste is the sense that most obviously draws substances into, and changes, the body. In 'Upon Jack and Jill' Herrick describes the physical effects of taste while playfully poking fun at his own art:

> When *Jill* complaines to *Jack* for want of meate;
> *Jack* kisses *Jill*, and bids her freely eate:
> *Jill* sayes, of what? sayes *Jack*, on that sweet kisse,
> Which full of Nectar and Ambrosia is,
> The food of Poets; so I thought sayes *Jill*,
> That makes them looke so lanke, so Ghost-like still.
> Let Poets feed on aire, or what they will;
> Let me feed full, till that I fart, sayes *Jill*.

Jill dismisses the substitution of tasty kisses for solid food because, she says, sweet tastes are not enough. She wants to be full enough to fart, which will only happen if she consumes substantial food or drink. But even though the poem dismisses figurative language (kisses taste like nectar and ambrosia), much like that which we have seen Herrick himself use (sweat smells like perfume), Jill reveals how it still has tangible effects. When poets feed on metaphors, or nothing, or air, their bodies become 'lanke, so Ghost-like'. The effects of *not* eating solid food, of solely tasting ambrosial kisses, are equally real and substantially change the composition of bodies. Also, Jill responds to Jack's sweet metaphor by creating her own figurative image (poets feed on air). Poetry begets more poetry.

'Upon Loach' provides a very different kind of 'sweet' taste:

Seeal'd up with Night-gum, *Loach* each morning lyes,
Till his Wife licking, so unglews his eyes.
No question then, but such a lick is sweet,
When a warm tongue do's with such Ambers meet.

Taste is another fluid sense. It is connected to liquid saliva, which can taste like nectar (Jack's kisses) or dissolve eye-gum (Mrs Loach's licks). But 'Upon Loach' reveals that taste is fluid in another manner; tastes change based on who does the tasting. I might find Loach's coagulated eye drainage to be salty and disgusting, but his wife makes the action and taste 'sweet' because she loves him. As William Miller explains, rules of disgust 'mark the boundaries of self; the relaxing of them marks privilege, intimacy, duty, [...] caring'.[10] Herrick confirms the fluid nature of taste in 'Upon Teares': 'Teares, though th'are here below the sinners brine, | Above they are the Angels spiced wine'. Depending on who does the tasting, brine can be wine, and wine can be brine. We saw that smells change the composition of people and things; tastes work in similar, fluid ways, and reveal that experiences of sensation differ from person to person.

To taste is also to touch, but, outside of tasting, this fifth bodily sense is the least explored in *Hesperides*. Indeed, Herrick frequently has been charged with fetishism because his narrator desires from a distance. Lillian Schanfield demonstrates this critical tendency in '"Tickled with Desire": A View of Eroticism in Herrick's Poetry' when she says Herrick is a 'silent, prowling visitor from that all-too-Freudian world of repressed fantasies and sublimated sexual energies'.[11] According to Schanfield, Herrick 'mentally disrobes', 'praises' and 'sniffs' his mistresses, but undressing, kissing or otherwise touching them exists only in the space of fantasy.[12] *Hesperides* certainly includes a number of poems about imagined contact with women (an illustrative example is 'The Vine', where the narrator dreams his vine-like penis is exploring his mistress's body), but Herrick's narrator does reach out from time to time. For instance, in 'Upon Julia's Breasts', he asks Julia to display her breasts, so that he can first 'Behold' them (l. 2), and then touch (and taste) them: 'Betweene whose glories, there my lips Ile lay, | Ravisht, in that faire *Via Lactea*' (ll. 3–4). He compares her breasts to the Milky Way, probably to describe both their pale colour and their physical function. By laying his lips on her breasts, he could simply be nuzzling them, but he also could be kissing and perhaps even suckling from them. Considering he places his lips 'betweene' her breasts, this final reading is unlikely. But even if the poem is not a description of lactophilia, Herrick describes touch as another fluid sense. Touching Julia's breasts is like drinking them in, and this sensation ravishes the narrator in the same way that the vision of her silken skirts and the sound of her singing did.

Another poem about Julia confirms this fluid reading of touch. 'Upon Julia's

Washing Her Self in the River' begins with vision and ends (perhaps?) with touch:

> How fierce was I, when I did see
> My *Julia* wash her self in thee!
> So *Lillies* thorough Christall look:
> So purest pebbles in the brooke:
> As in the River *Julia* did,
> Halfe with a Lawne of water hid,
> Into thy streames my self I threw,
> And strugling there, I kist thee too;
> And more had done (it is confest)
> Had not thy waves forbad the rest.

When Herrick's narrator gazes at Julia's naked body he grows jealous of the river that caresses and partially conceals her. Instead of trying to touch her, he throws himself into the river. As he thrashes around, he finds himself kissing the river and admitting that 'more had done' if the water had been calmer. He attempts to make love to the river, because touching the river *is* touching Julia. The river has absorbed her being; by touching the river, he can touch her.[13]

This tour through Herrick's sensorium complicates our understanding of early modern sensation. First, in Herrick's imagination, sensation is a liquid process that infuses the sensor with what, or who, is sensed. When we sense, we do not simply drink the world in through five portals; rather, to sense is to melt, to conjoin with what is sensed, and to change the composition of our selves as well as the things and people we encounter. Second, sensation is frequently, and perhaps always, related to love or lust. The poems that describe one or more of the senses do so because they also describe desire. And, third, Herrick suggests that poetry itself functions like the people and things that are sensed. This is, in part, because poetry is music and has the same liquid and transformative powers as anything else that is sensed. When seen or heard, poems get under our skin. Those that focus on the five senses may even have the power to change how we understand and experience sensation at large.

To begin to make sense of Herrick's sensorium of liquids, lusts and lyrics, we must turn to the philosophical and medical texts that defined sensation for him and his contemporaries. Louise Vinge explains:

> what was said in literary works about the sense-organs and their functions depended on natural science and anatomy. Several ideas and images originally came from treatises by philosophers – Aristotle of course being the most influential – and physicians, and by repeating their phrases in compilations, medieval scholars handed them on.[14]

By the seventeenth century, most descriptions of the five senses acknowledge, if they do not parrot, Aristotle's philosophy from *De Anima* (*On the Soul*). Aristotle is frequently credited with categorizing and defining the senses as five, although Vinge reminds us that the 'division [...] had been accepted long before and was even subjected to criticism. But naturally it later gained a position that was almost unshakable simply because it was authorized by Aristotle.'[15] Even the order in which most writers describe the senses, from high to low (sight, hearing, smell, taste, touch), is the one Aristotle provides in his seminal text (II.6–11; pp. 172–87).

At least two of Aristotle's observations are worth considering alongside Herrick's verse. In *De Anima*, Aristotle asserts that sense perception is the faculty of receiving the forms of objects independently of the matter of which they are composed. He draws an analogy to explain how the 'sense is the recipient of the perceived forms without their matter, as the wax takes the sign from the ring without the iron and gold – it takes, that is, the gold or bronze sign, but not *as* gold or bronze' (II.12; p. 187). Our senses are like soft wax, he says, and when we come into contact with something, the sensed object will only leave a matter-less imprint on the sense. If it is a gold ring we see, for instance, only an image of that ring will impress itself on to our sight; no gold will actually travel into our eyeballs. So far, it seems Herrick might disagree. When his characters sense, their bodies are physically affected, and people have the ability to infuse with that which they sense. Later on, however, Aristotle qualifies his statement by limiting it to the three highest senses: 'Neither light nor darkness nor sound nor smell has any effect on bodies. [...] But the tangible objects and the flavours do affect them directly' (II.12; p. 188). According to Aristotle, when we taste or touch things their matter does have a direct effect on our bodies. Herrick imagines all five senses to function like taste and touch, the senses that have the ability to draw matter into the body.

Although Aristotle says sight, hearing and smell do not transfer matter, he does tell us that all bodily senses require a medium for perception to occur. The sense organs never act directly. For instance, in the case of sight: 'If someone puts what has colour on the sight-organ itself, he will not see it. In fact, colour moves the transparent, the air, say, and by this if continuous the sense-organ is moved' (II.7; p. 175). He continues:

> the same account can be given in the case of sound and smell. For none of them produces the sensation by touching the sense-organ, rather it is the medium that is moved by smell and sound and each of the sense-organs by this. And when anyone puts the sound or smell source on the organ itself, this produces no sensation. It is the same situation, only not apparently so, with touch and taste. (II.7; p. 175)

Aristotle argues that for sensation to occur there needs to be distance between the sense organ and what is sensed. This distance is not empty space, but it is filled with a substance (air, water, spit) that carries the sensual impression. So, even if *matter* is not transferred via the medium, the medium itself has to touch the origin and the destination. You could argue, then, that the medium conjoins the sensor with what is sensed. This is what Herrick might be exploring in a poem like 'Upon Julia's Washing Her Self in the River', where the narrator literally embraces the medium (water) that physically separates him from his beloved.

Aristotle's philosophy probably influenced Herrick, but the depictions of sensation in *Hesperides* align more intriguingly with the Epicurean ideas of Lucretius in *De rerum natura* (*On the Nature of the Universe*). In *Sensible Flesh*, Elizabeth Harvey describes Lucretius as an early 'materialist' who believed 'touch forms the basis for the other four senses'.[16] Lucretius claims there is a material connection between people and that which they sense. Sights, sounds, smells, tastes and textures do not just travel through media; small particles actually break off what is sensed and travel into the person who senses. All sensed objects touch the body of the sensor. Misty Anderson articulates this philosophy well: 'Sensory perceptions that "penetrate" the body though [*sic*] touch are Lucretius's paradigm for sensation and hence knowledge.'[17] For example, Lucretius describes how theatre awnings physically touch people and things with their colour particles. The awnings '[spray] particles from their surfaces this way and that', and these particles instantaneously settle on the actors and their props.[18] The people and things 'are made to glow and flow with the colours of the canopy' that flaps above them (IV.78–79; p. 97). In another example, when stars twinkle above a calm lake, 'immediately the sparkling constellations of the firmament in all their unclouded splendour twinkle back reproduced in the water' (IV.212–14; p. 100). The stars in the water are made up of 'flimsy tissues' that are thrown off from the actual stars (IV.158; p. 99). If Herrick's narrator were to dive into this water, he would conjoin with actual star particles. Perhaps Julia's reflection in the river is not just a reflection; it is a tissue made up of pieces of her. When he dives into the reflective water, the narrator actually conjoins with these pieces and so with her.

Everything in the world is matter, according to Epicurean philosophy (and unlike Aristotelian philosophy), and sensation only happens when bodies collide with other bodies, no matter the sense. As Lucretius notes, hearing works like seeing:

> all forms of *sound and vocal utterance* become audible when they have slipped into the ear and provoked sensation by the impact of their own bodies. The fact that voices and other sounds can impinge on the senses is itself a proof of their corporeal nature. (IV.525–29; p. 108)

This material understanding of sensation demonstrates why, when it comes to taste, some corporeal collisions are pleasant, while others are unpleasant: 'When something sweet to one is bitter to another, it must be because its smoothest particles caressingly penetrate the palate of the former, whereas the latter's gullet is evidently invaded by particles that are rough and jagged' (IV.658–61; p. 112). This philosophy helps to explain, for instance, why Lungs's stinky breath spoils meat. Diseased, smelly particles throw themselves out of Lungs's mouth and infuse themselves with the meat.

It is tempting to argue that Herrick read Lucretius and these philosophies made their way into *Hesperides*. Here is what we do know: *De rerum natura* was rediscovered and published in Italy in the early 1500s;[19] it was probably translated into English by the memoirist Lucy Hutchinson in the 1640s or 1650s;[20] it gained popularity in the late seventeenth century and a handful of editions were published in both Latin and English (most notably, John Evelyn and John Dryden translated excerpts);[21] and biographies often describe Herrick as an Epicurean.[22] It is possible that Herrick was ahead of his time, and that he embraced this philosophy before his compeers. But it is equally possible that Herrick was influenced by other theories of sensation that saw the process as physical and intrusive. In *The Key of Green*, Bruce Smith explains how the seventeenth century experienced a dramatic 'shift in thought about thought'. Smith describes a pre-Cartesian understanding of sensation:

> According to the model of the mind [...] inherited from Aristotle, Galen, Avicenna, Averroës, St. Augustine, and Aristotle's scholastic disciples, all knowledge begins with sense experience. [...] The route from the senses to the intellect was not, however, the direct electrical connection between sense organs and brain mapped by modern physiology. [...] Rather, a circuit through the heart via the vaporous fluid *spiritus* was imagined to act as the body's internal communication system. As a result, sensation was a whole-body experience.

To sense something was to invite the 'vaporous fluid *spiritus*' to course through, and to necessarily affect, your entire body. The effect would be felt with the 'excitation [...] of the body's four humors according to whether the heart dilated in desire or contracted in avoidance'. And then you would experience 'this rush of humors throughout the body as passion of one sort or another'.[23] In this way, seventeenth-century sensation is akin to liquefaction, as Herrick suggests in his verse.

Herrick may or may not have read Lucretius, but he certainly was aware of Galenic theories of the bodily humours and the resulting passions. Numerous poems in *Hesperides* mention the humours, and Smith notes that 'more than thirty books with "passions" in the title were published in England' in the mid-seventeenth century.[24] In *Bodies and Selves in Early Modern England*, Michael Schoenfeldt explains, 'Galenic medicine provided [...] writers with a rich and malleable discourse able to articulate and explain the vagaries of human emotion in corporeal terms.' In a way, Galenic humours and passions made *all* sensation fluid as well as physical. Schoenfeldt reminds us that our post-Cartesian perspective makes it difficult to comprehend a time when selves were not separate from bodies. In seventeenth-century England, 'embodiments of emotion [are] not [...] enactments of dead metaphors but rather explorations of the corporeal nature of self'.[25] When Herrick's narrator says he drowns in the vision of Julia's petticoat, Herrick probably does not use 'drown' as a simile. When he sees her petticoat, he does not feel *like* he is drowning. He *is* drowning.

Schoenfeldt takes a compelling passage from Peter Brown's *The Body and Society* to illustrate just how embodied bodies were in the period:

> Here were little fiery universes, through whose heart, brain, and veins there pulsed the same heat and vital spirit as glowed in the stars. To make love was to bring one's blood to the boil, as the fiery vital spirit swept through the beings, turning the blood into the whitened foam of semen. It was a process in which the body as a whole – the brain cavity, the marrow of the backbone, the kidneys, and the lower bowel region – was brought into play, 'as in a mighty choir'. The genital regions were mere points of passage. They were the outlets of a human Espresso machine. It was the body as a whole, and not merely the genitals, that made orgasm possible.[26]

Brown uses orgasm as a vivid example of early modern, specifically Galenic, bodily experience, and reminds us that sex and sensation are intimately connected. Indeed, the fourth book of *De rerum natura* is entitled 'Sensation and Sex'. Lucretius confirms Brown's description, in part, when he explains how the 'seed [...] travels through every member of the body, concentrating in certain reservoirs in the loins, and promptly awakens the generative organs' (IV.1041–43; p. 122). These awoken genitals then seek out the source of desire ('whether [...] a lad with womanish limbs or a woman radiating love from her whole body') so that the lover can 'ejaculate the fluid drawn from out of his body into that body' (IV.1054–55, 1057; p. 122). But, Lucretius explains, when it comes to desire, ejaculation is just one liquefying part of a sensual whole body experience:

> Venus teases lovers with images. They cannot glut their eyes by gazing on the beloved form, however closely. Their hands can rub nothing from off those dainty limbs in their aimless roving over all the body. Then comes the moment when with limbs entwined they pluck the flower of youth. Their bodies thrill with the joy to come, and Venus is just about to sow the seed in the female fields. Body clings greedily to body; they mingle the saliva of their mouths and breathe hard down each other's mouths pressing them with their teeth. But all to no purpose. One can remove nothing from the other by rubbing, nor enter right in and be wholly absorbed, body in body; for sometimes it seems that that is what they are craving and striving to do, so hungrily do they cling together in Venus' fetters, while their limbs are unnerved and liquefied by the intensity of pleasure. At length, when the build-up of lust has burst out of their groin, there comes a slight intermission in the raging fever. But not for long. Soon the same frenzy returns. (IV.1100–17; pp. 123–24)

This intensely erotic description suggests a few things. First, sex is not solely genital. Intercourse is one step in a process that involves seeing, touching, tasting and, one imagines, smelling and hearing too. Second, the bodily senses fail when it comes to desire. Elsewhere in *De rerum natura* Lucretius insists on the material nature of sensation. If 'from every object flows a stream of matter' (IV.224–25; p. 110), then why can our hands 'rub nothing from off' our beloveds when we caress them (IV.1102–03; p. 123)? Lucretius either contradicts himself in his description of sex, or he suggests that, when it comes to love, the 'flimsy tissues and filmy shapes' that float off our beloveds simply are not enough (IV.158; p. 99). Like Herrick's narrator, we want to melt into one with our *Julias*, but we only are 'tease[d] [...] with images' that do not contain enough matter to satisfy. This leads to a third point, which has to do with insatiability. Even the genitals are essentially useless when it comes to the satisfaction of desire; intercourse and ejaculation may provide a 'slight intermission' from desire, but they have as little purpose as seeing, touching and tasting. Seeing Julia's undulating petticoat, hearing her melodious voice or smelling her perfumed breath are just as sexually satisfying as genital sex (that is, *not satisfying at all*).

Lucretius does imply that at least parts of our body liquefy when they are engaged in sexual intercourse. During sex, the 'limbs are unnerved and liquefied by the intensity of pleasure'. Here, the body's liquefaction is linked with its unnerving, which could mean the loss of sensation. But it could also mean that, during sex, the limbs are sensed so fully that their ability to sense is saturated. A handful of early modern writers argue that sexual desire does not just affect the abilities of the five senses; they say sexual desire *is* a sixth bodily sense, and because it holds power over the other senses it should be considered the true king of the senses. For instance, in *The Anatomy of Melancholy* (1621) Richard Burton mentions this sixth sense when he begins his discussion of the traditional five: 'Of *Touching, Hearing, Seeing, Smelling, Tasting*: to which you may adde *Scaligers* sixt sense of *Titillation*, if you please.'[27] Francis Bacon similarly cites Scaliger in *Sylua syluarum* (1627):

> The *Pleasure* in the *Act* of *Venus* is the greatest of the *Pleasures* of the *Senses*: [...] *Scaliger* doth well, to make the *Pleasure* of *Generation* a *Sixth Sense*; And if there were any other differing *Organs*, and Qualified *Perforations* for the spirits to passe; there would be more than the *Fiue Senses*.[28]

Bacon claims sexual titillation is a sense because, like the other five senses, it has an organ and a portal that allows fluid spirits to exit (and enter) the body. To classify venery as a sense is to link it with knowledge ('carnal knowledge' takes on a new meaning here), as well as with pleasure. Venery might stupefy the other senses, but it does this by intensifying their pleasures.

In *Exotericarvm Exercitationvm* (1557) Julius Caesar Scaliger originally suggested that titillation was a sixth sense for a different reason. Daniel Jaeckle explains, 'in a section on touch and taste, Scaliger argues that the desire to copulate depends on a sixth sense that somehow includes touch and sight and results in titillation'.[29] Scaliger says that this 'sextus quidam sensus, sicut & gustus: uterque non sine tactu: sed tamen aliud & ab illo & inter se'. The sixth sense is similar to taste and correlated with touch, yet it is different and something between these two senses. He continues, 'Gustus indiuiduo datus: alter ob speciem. Etenim si non allicerêntur illa voloptate: quotus quisque coire vellet?' Taste is granted for the individual, but the sixth sense is granted for the human species. The sixth sense is necessary, Scaliger argues, because if we were not satisfied with this 'illa uoloptate' (extreme pleasure) then we would rarely be willing to have sex.[30] The sixth sense is a generative sense that is purposefully pleasurable because it is absolutely essential for the perpetuation of the species.

Scaliger states that, with the sixth sense, pleasure is a means to an end. But Bacon implies that sexual pleasure *is* the sixth sense; he calls it the '*Pleasure* of *Generation*'.[31] We might say that sexual pleasure is to generation as taste is to sustenance. Taste helps us to discover foods and drinks that are necessary for survival, but, more often, we use the sense of taste for pleasure. The sixth sense works in the same way. Sex may be related to generation, but the sixth sense is focused on the pleasures (and pains) of sexual desire in general.

It is Bacon's sixth sense that finally helps to explain Herrick's liquefying depictions of the five traditional senses. In *Hesperides*, the desire for sexual pleasure defines the experience of sensation. Seeing, hearing, smelling, tasting and touching are all akin to sex. All are driven by the desire of individuals to (or not to) infuse with the people and objects they encounter. It is pleasurable to drink in a vision of Julia's undulating petticoat or to imagine inhaling her sweet scents. Even though Herrick's narrator cannot actually infuse with Julia (as Lucretius laments), poetic language can capture the truly desired terminus of love, which is the liquefaction and infusion of two sensual bodies.

Herrick's poetry is both about sensation and a demonstration of the experience of sensation, much like the spiced art installation that opened this chapter. The museum's curator suggests that we do not just view Neto's artwork, but we ingest it, are ingested by it, and become one with it.[32] The same happens when we hear Herrick's verse. 'The Night-piece, to Julia' exemplifies this in its aim to enchant both its subject, Julia, and us, its readers. The first three stanzas paint a beautiful picture of Julia, walking at night, led by faeries, elves and other spirits. At line 16, Herrick states a transitional 'Then':

> 4. Then *Julia* let me wooe thee,
> Thus, thus to come unto me:
> And when I shall meet
> Thy silv'ry feet,
> My soule Ile poure into thee.
> (ll. 16–20)

Once Julia has (and we have) been enchanted by poetry, *then* Herrick has access to woo her (and us). She (as we) will have been softened, or melted, by the lovely music that drew her to him. What the repeated 'Thus, thus' refers to is unclear; however, it could be read as a reference back to the first three lyric stanzas. He will woo her 'thus, thus', with poetry like that which we have just experienced. When Julia reaches Herrick in the fourth stanza, she becomes the poetry he writes; her 'silv'ry feet' are the poetic feet that comprise the lines of his verse. As a poem, or even simply as a woman wooed with poetry, Herrick can infuse his liquid soul with Julia, and with us, his readers.

Herrick's liquefying senses might make the most sense when we remember that the language of poetry is always the language of bodily sensation. In *Poetry and the Fate of the Senses*, Susan Stewart says the 'task of aesthetic production and reception in general is to make visible, tangible, and audible the figures of persons, whether such persons are expressing the particulars of sense impressions or the abstractions of reason'.[33] Poetry is an artistic expression of sensation that is '[e]rotic and rhetorical at once'.[34] Herrick reminds us that poetry physically touches us; we are supposed to *feel* something when we read it, hear it, touch it, *sense* it. And because his poems are themselves sensible objects, we might imagine that a little bit of Herrick infuses with us every time we open our senses to his verse.[35]

Notes

1 Ernesto Neto, *Just like Drops in Time, Nothing*. Textile and spices, 2002. Art Gallery of New South Wales (276.2002) www.artgallery.nsw.gov.au/collection/works/276.2002/ [accessed 6 June 2013].

2 Anthony Bond, 'Sensing Space and the Place of Body', curator's essay for Art Gallery of New South Wales (1997) www.anthonybond.com.au/exhibitions/ernesto-neto-agnsw-1997/ [accessed 6 June 2013] (para. 5 of 14).

3 All verse quotations are from *The Complete Poetry of Robert Herrick*, ed. by J. Max Patrick, rev. edn (New York: Norton, 1968); titles and line numbers are cited in the text.

4 Susan Stewart, 'Remembering the Senses', *in Empire of the Senses: The Sensual Culture Reader*, ed. by David Howes (Oxford: Berg, 2005), pp. 59–69 (p. 59).

5 Aristotle, *De Anima* (*On the Soul*), trans. by Hugh Lawson-Tancred (London: Penguin, 1986), III.8; p. 210. Hereafter cited in the text.

6 Michael Drayton, *Idea XXIX*, 'To the Senses', in *Elizabethan Sonnet-Cycles*, ed. by Martha Foote Crow (Chicago: McClurg, 1897), p. 38; ll. 5–11.

7 Louise Vinge, *The Five Senses: Studies in a Literary Tradition* (Lund: LiberLäromedel, 1975), p. 113.

8 Etymology of 'infuse, v.' from *OED*.

9 Definition of 'conceit, n.' from *OED*.

10 William Ian Miller, *The Anatomy of Disgust* (Cambridge, MA: Harvard University Press, 1997), p. xi.

11 Lillian Schanfield, '"Tickled with Desire": A View of Eroticism in Herrick's Poetry', *Literature & Psychology*, 39 (1993), 63–83 (p. 81).

12 Schanfield, p. 63.

13 Thanks to Anita Butler (King's College London) for connecting my analysis of this poem to Heraclitus, who said 'you can't step into the same river twice'. In his assertion that the river absorbs part of his mistress, Herrick seems to disagree with the Heraclitean idea of perpetual change.

14 Vinge, p. 12.

15 Vinge, p. 15.

16 Elizabeth Harvey, 'Introduction: The "Sense of All Senses"', in *Sensible Flesh: On Touch in Early Modern Culture*, ed. by Elizabeth Harvey (Philadelphia: Pennsylvania University Press, 2003), pp. 1–21 (p. 4).

17 Misty Anderson, 'Living in a Material World: Margaret Cavendish's *The Convent of Pleasure*', in *Sensible Flesh*, ed. by Harvey, pp. 187–204 (p. 189).

18 Lucretius, *On the Nature of the Universe*, trans. by R.E. Latham, rev. edn (London: Penguin, 1994), iv.86–87; p. 97. Hereafter cited in the text.

19 John Godwin, 'Introduction,' in Lucretius, *Nature of the Universe*, trans. by Latham, p. xxxv.

20 A.E. Stallings, 'A Note on the Text and Translation', in Lucretius, *The Nature of Things*, trans. by A.E. Stallings (London: Penguin, 2007), p. xxviii.

21 John Evelyn, *An essay on the first book of T. Lucretius Carus De rerum natura. Interpreted and made English verse by J. Evelyn Esq* (1656); John Dryden, *The Annual miscellany, for the year 1694 being the fourth part of Miscellany poems: containing great variety of new translations and original copies* (1694).

22 For instance, the Poetry Foundation says, 'Like the serious Epicurean, Herrick seeks to maximize pleasure and minimize pain'. 'Biography: Robert Herrick, 1591–1674', *Poetry Foundation* (2013) www.poetryfoundation.org/bio/robert-herrick [accessed 10 June 2013].

23 Bruce Smith, *The Key of Green: Passion and Perception in Renaissance Culture* (Chicago: University of Chicago Press, 2009), pp. 29–30.

24 Smith, p. 30.

25 Michael Schoenfeldt, *Bodies and Selves in Early Modern England* (Cambridge: Cambridge University Press, 1999), pp. 6, 11, 8.

26 Peter Brown, *The Body and Society: Men, Women, and Sexual Renunciation in Early Christianity* (New York: Columbia University Press, 1988), p. 17.

27 Richard Burton, *The Anatomy of Melancholy* (Oxford, 1621), C[1]r: Part 1, Section 1, Member 2, Subsection 6.

28 Francis Bacon, *Sylua Syluarum, or A Naturall Historie* (1627), p. 173.

29 Daniel Jaeckle, 'The Sixth Sense in Cleveland's "The Hecatomb to his Mistresse"', *Notes and Queries*, 54 (2007), 411–12 (p. 412).

30 Julius Caesar Scaliger, *Exotericarvm Exercitationvm* (Paris, 1557), Exercitatio cclxxxvi.3. Thanks to Eric Kraemer (University of Wisconsin, La Crosse) and Annie Wattez for their translation assistance.

31 Bacon, p. 173.

32 Bond, para. 5 of 14.

33 Susan Stewart, *Poetry and the Fate of the Senses* (Chicago: University of Chicago Press, 2002), p. 2.

34 Stewart, p. 26.

35 Thanks to Rick Rambuss (Brown University) for his mentorship when I began working on Herrick at Emory University. Thanks also to the University of Wisconsin, La Crosse, for grants that enabled me to conduct research at the Folger Shakespeare Library, to draft this essay, and to travel to the London Renaissance Seminar (Shakespeare's Globe and Birkbeck, University of London) where I met the kind people who believed it had a place in this collection.

7

'Did we lie downe, because 'twas night?': John Donne, George Chapman and the senses of night in the 1590s

Susan Wiseman

Above the now lost bough of the rood, in the highest panel of the Doom picture in St Peter's, Wenhaston, Christ judges the world, whose fate is spread below him. He is seated on a rainbow flanked by the sun to his right and the moon to his left.[1] In the early 1500s the story of light and dark expressed in the representation of sun, moon and rainbow above darkness held a clear but also complex and evocative message concerning God's power. The force of such precise and suggestive symbols was changed, not abolished, by subsequent events. If, in 1500, light and dark were at God's command in the heavens, so were they in 1668 when Milton's fallen angels wander amongst 'shades of death' in 'A Universe of death, which God by curse | Created evil' (*Paradise Lost*, II.622–23). Milton's darkness, like that of the Doom, holds an assumed relationship between sensory perception and cognition. Light and darkness are known within the symbolic lexicon which automatically sorts light with life and dark with deprivation, wickedness.[2] However, Milton's angels wander in a 'universe' – by the time Milton writes, the heavens themselves have changed. In assessing this world the senses were both a prime tool and an impediment, and were understood as such.

As we know, between the Doom and *Paradise Lost*, a subject's relationship with visuality was reshaped – in part by the Reformation; in part by the innovations and controversies over the moving universe. Within the narrower sphere of night and light, at the same time as we find conceptual shifts, Craig Koslofsky argues, the whole of Renaissance Europe saw a crucial shift in people's sensory and other relationships to time as improved illumination opened up precincts of the day hitherto less explored, and changed, patchily, the previous pattern of first and second sleep which had filled the lightless hours.[3] The sensory and material changing of the nocturnal environment and practices as the long darkness was gradually artificially illuminated, particularly when set alongside changes to the heavens and steadily louder ticking of clock time, invites further exploration in relation to literary texts. Night, light and shadow changed as ground for thought. Framed by the large question of whether changing perceptions and experiences of night constitute an epochal shift, this essay works on a small scale to investigate the place of the senses in understandings of light, dark and shadow in the post-Reformation period, using the evidence of the writings of two contrasting poets, John Donne and George Chapman. Both use night as a testing ground for ideas concerning sensory perception, but in what appear to be quite different ways. Their writings stage experiential scenes where we see situations that engage the main discourses on night, light and shadow – religious, philosophical and classical. This essay explores how they use night, light and shadow to engage the reader in debates about their world.

We can begin with Donne's will, where he disposes of his personal time keeping technology:

> And my will & desire is that my verie worthie frend and kind Brother in law *S'Thomas Grymes* [...] be Overseer of this my Will To whome I give hereby the Strykinge clocke wch ordinarilye I weare [...] Item my will is that the fower large pictures [...] shall remayne still in those places As also the Marble Table Sonne Dyall and Pictures wch I haue placed in the Garden[.][4]

The striking clock was the first bequest, and to a person of both emotional and practical importance. The sundial is counted among the things to be inventoried in order that it remain, with table and pictures, as part of an enduring philosophical environment inviting those who enter the garden to learn by looking.

Donne's attitude to time has been the subject of much critical enquiry but is almost always framed in terms of attitudes found in later devotional writing.[5] However, as we see, even at the very end of his life the sundial, with its sensory orientation in the apprehension of time, was at the centre of his thoughts. The dial, and particularly the sensory environment of light it uses, is very little investigated in relation to Donne's writing, notwithstanding that engagement with the senses and with night, light and shadow is sharp and analytical in Donne's 'Songs and Sonnets' (1635). Donne's creative destruction of earlier forms (the sonnet, the sequence) and addressees (the lover replaced in his poetry by apparently multiple lovers and addressees) involves the strategic but unforegrounded importance of the significatory power of the senses. If his poems re-examine contemporary forms then, this investigation suggests, they also take the night, light and particularly shadow as prompts to thought. As a treatise from the 1590s puts it, 'The Skeptick doth neither affirm nor deny any position'; Donne's use of night, light and especially shadow both elaborate and draw on their place as a ground of philosophical thought.[6]

An example of the key role of the senses in Donne's early poetry is the 'Lecture Upon the Shadow'. The poem is generally regarded as needing explication, and critics tend to explain the use of shadows shortening and lengthening in the poem as standing for the uncertainties that shade the lovers' frankness in the early, morning stages of love, disappearing at love's zenith only to be replaced by shadows facing the other way:[7]

Except our loves at this noone stay,
We shall new shadowes make the other way.
As the first were made to blinde
Others, these which come behinde
Will work upon our selves, and blind our eyes.
If our loves faint, and westwardly decline,
To me thou, falsely, thine,
And I to thee mine actions shall disguise.
(ll. 14–21)[8]

The possibility of continuing love is introduced almost parenthetically and semi-subjectively; 'Except' the love stays at frank, 'reduc'd', undisguised noon, there is no alternative but that love will decline and so be shadowed by disguise, feigned openness, lies. If 'morning shadowes wear away' these 'grow longer all the day'. The problem is gathered up in the final lines, into the problem of love, time and night:

But oh, love's day is short, if love decay.
Love is a growing, or full constant light,
And his first minute, after noone, is night.
(ll. 24–26)

It appears that, ultimately, the lecturer abandons the link between love and diurnal sequence because the time of love is more extreme, fast and absolute than the path of dawn to dusk and if not growing or noon, is nothing. In this reading, light and dark, noon and night, become failed metaphors, and so shadow's part in love is, in fact, minimal, implied only in its growing phase. In this, usual, understanding, the shadow becomes almost a ruse; a proposition finally abandoned as inappropriate. In this logic, love is ultimately severed from the metaphoric link with light and dark and one 'point' of the poem, therefore, is to lead us to see love and sensorily measured time as distinct. If we follow this understanding, then the poem works in something like the same way as 'The Computation', which sets up an elaborate sum translating 24 hours into 2400 years, only to end by brushing aside the metaphor with an expostulation – 'Can ghosts die?' (l. 10). To understand 'Lecture' in this way invites the question of why the poem goes to such lengths to build an image of human behaviour which insists on the very link that it apparently abolishes between a sensory apprehension of time (as daylight, shadow, night) and love. This is particularly significant, given the slightly tortuous ways it does so (hence the explication so often provided).

What happens if we give more weight to the strong focus on the shadow? The title might justify this, in that it is the poem's exploration of visual technologies of measurement that make it a philosophical 'lecture'. Moreover, the poem explores the relationship between love and time using the idea of a sundial and it is clear that in doing so the poem is also interested in the physical and sensory world. As Christopher Bardt writes, sundials 'are catchers, recording instruments, translators of light into time' and the poem both uses this translating quality of light to time and adds its own translation, back and forth between the lovers' shadows and the measurements of the sundial.[9] The poem explores the subjection of sensory experience to technology of thought and measurement. As Thomas Fale noted in 1593, once 'the reason and proportion of shadowes' had been discovered, dials could show time.[10] The poem prompts us to think in numbers, but also in terms of sight – declining, reclining, and in degrees with an implied zenith and nadir – as Fale describes.[11] Critics, however, tend not to consider the dial a driving vocabulary in the poem, perhaps because sundial time and the time of love are understood as split in the final lines. Love's decay is understood as different from sundial time because 'his first minute, after noon, is night' (l. 25). However, and as the comparison with 'The Computation' illuminates, in this poem the use of sense and technology are held together linguistically; even in the last line the poem goes on translating between time and light.

The continuity of the patterning of time, love and light to the end of the poem invites us to re-read it with attention to time and shadow. The final lines see the appearance of 'he', Cupid, who is not present when love is growing. If Cupid prompts us to think about Venus it might be a reminder of the poem's concentration on the physical, venereal love of 'tread', and we should also, perhaps, be reminded that Donne read, and wrote, riddles; the 'Songs and Sonnets' uses such structures.[12] In that spirit, we can recall that elsewhere Donne thought of Venus as a planet and so in the poem's last line, Cupid, as the son of Venus, and so coming after her. This can remind us to think in planetary hours.[13] The planetary hours of a day, while still being 12, measure not from midnight to midnight but from dawn to dusk (in day hours) and dusk to dawn (in night hours), and the further one is from the equinox the greater the difference between day and night hours.[14] As Fale puts it, we need to think of the movement to and from twelve as in 'unequall houres'.[15] In order to 'know the hower of the day when the Sun shineth', Fale directs his reader to 'seeke in some Calender in what Signe and degree the Sun is that day'.[16]

If the concept of the short planetary day is in play in the poem's final lines then, using a kind of time appropriately based in the senses because cued by light and dark, we are able to see that the poem really does go on translating between light-time and love, or desire and dark (or night-time), and the death of love or desire after consummation. The 'unequall', planetary hours were not so short that noon was, literally, followed by night but they were regularized in the sundial's use of the interior of a hemisphere; sundials not only translate light but also translate time, from the sensory and planetary time of dawn to dusk into the regular hours.[17] The dial technology, emphatically present throughout, seems in part to link the sensory light of day and night's 'unequall hours'. If the poem separates love and clock time, simultaneously it suggests that both love and time rely on the senses.

'Lecture' is not literally a riddle; its chains of association are looser and more allusive than riddles permit. However, it shares with riddles the making strange of human behaviour for, clearly, in deriving human qualities from the behaviour of shadows, the poem allows light, dark and shadow to drive the poem, making human love correspond to the translation of light into time. If the final lines seem to abandon, even reject, the lecture's premise of a relation between love and hours, they simultaneously maintain that link. The time of the sundial 'is' hours, but not as a clock; a sundial shows apparent time in a local context but, to stretch a point, the translation of unequal into equal hours is itself a kind of disguise. Time and love are both, we can speculate, undisguised – and maybe both are, therefore, disclosed as both sensory for time is light and shadow, love – desire? Whether or not this reading holds, it is clear that attending to the poem's meditation on light, dark and shadow and on its translation of light into time illuminates Donne's engagement with the technology of light-time as significant in his writing on time, eternal and human. Indeed, in the early modern environment time was marked most accurately by bells and light; in Henry VIII's tower at Nonsuch the clock sits between the sundial and the bell. It is not surprising that Donne uses the effects of light as a ground for argument.

'Lecture' is far from alone in Donne's earlier writing as an investigative use of the senses, more specifically light, dark and shadow. In 'A Nocturnall Upon St. Lucie's Day', the senses are interwoven with alchemical language and an elaboration, even multiplication, of the absence of light, the world of dark. The poem has been read as referring to the death of Anne More but also paired with the 'Lecture' as solstice and shortest day.[18] 'Nocturnall' uses the senses as a ground of thought, but where the 'Lecture' restricts the frames of reference to which they apply, 'Nocturnall' multiplies discourses within which the senses signify.[19] These vocabularies might be read as reinforcing the information derived from the senses but, equally, as contradicting it.

The Christian calendar marks St Lucy's Day as 13 December, remembering the meagre 'seaven houres' daylight of the 'yeares midnight' (ll. 1–2). St Lucy, straddling Catholic and Protestant traditions, is a sensory saint, in the best-known version of her story carrying her eyes before her on a plate (they have been torn out but God has healed her). Paradoxically and appropriately, St Lucy is patron saint of the blind and celebrated in a festival of light; the multiplying dark nothings, deaths and absences of the poem – 'the Sunne is spent', 'life is shrunke, | Dead and enterr'd' (ll. 6–7) – are framed by the day's festival reputation. The speaker, made by love's 'Alchimie', 'A quintessence even from nothingnesse' (ll. 13–15), in the aftermath of his lover's ambiguous 'death (which word wrongs her)' (l. 28) is 're-begot | Of absence, darknesse, death; things which are not' (ll. 17–18). Donne ties the vast, operatic excesses of amatory and sexual loss (whereby the world is drowned in the lovers' tears, they became 'Chaosses', their literal, sexual or spiritual 'absences' made them 'carcasses' (ll. 22–27)) to a precise distillation of nothing – 'the grave | Of all, that's nothing' (l. 21) and 'Of the first nothing, the Elixer' (l. 29). Working downwards through the vital Aristotelian hierarchy the poem demonstrates the speaker's absence:

> Were I a man, that I were one,
> I needs must knowe; I should preferre,
>   If I were any beast,
> Some ends, some means; Yea plants, yea stones detest,
> And love. All, all some properties invest;
> If I an ordinary nothing were,
> As a shadow, a light, and body must be here.
> (ll. 30–36)

'But', we are told, 'I am None'. Donne's speaker is precise in an enumeration of the absent qualities of nothing by an opposition of the vital souls of the world from human to stone, all of which, including stones as the vital matter of the world, had life and so, sense. This speaker is not human – 'Were I a man [...] I needs must knowe.' The final movement of the poem challenges the temporal schema of death and renewal at the level of its component parts. Sun, multiplied as a 'lesser Sunne', is sent on sexual errands to bring lower lovers more desire and the astrological implication of the 'limbecke' (l. 21) distillation is diverted into an astrological joke on the 'Goat' (l. 39). The poem's alchemy for the speaker and his lover is his lover's canonization and St Lucy's day's rededication as her 'Vigill, and her Eve' (l. 44). The three schemas of light and dark (the annual and Christian cycle, the alchemy of spring and of transformation through love), as well as the reverse alchemy of his epitaphic nothingness, have all been working together to celebrate the lover's 'long night's festivall' (l. 42). The sudden juxtaposition of the parts of the descriptive vocabulary turns the inward orientation of the nothing-speaker back towards the world and the present in a final (but not conclusive) alignment of his night, his lover's night and the festival of St Lucy.

The shadow, specifically, in the 'Lecture' and 'Nocturnall' is distinct from night and light in being strongly associated with the body it registers both in the metaphor of the lovers' shadows and in the 'ordinary nothing' of a shadow that implies 'a light, and body must be here' (l. 36). Thus, Donne's speculations on the shadow remind us that, while he uses gradations of light in distinct ways as poetic visualization, when he was writing, shadows were present in other cultural precincts; like the planets, the shadow was subject to enquiry. Used by Leonardo da Vinci in relation to perspective, it was also explored in two significant myths.

The shadow has a distinct life as a key component in the understanding of visual representation, through the story of the birth of painting told by Pliny, which 'all agree [...] began with tracing an outline around a man's shadow and consequently that pictures were originally done in this way'. Pliny told an additional story in which a girl loves a young man and 'drew in outline on the wall the shadow of his face thrown by the lamp' and her father later made a clay statue.[20] At the same time, the tracing of the shadow was the ground against which the development of painting as an art measured itself. As Quintilian put it: 'For what, I ask again, would have been the result if no one had done more than his predecessors? [...] the art of painting would be restricted to tracing a line around a shadow in the sunlight.'[21]

The story of the shadow outlined was at the origin of how painting thought about itself as a constantly improving art, though it seems also to have implications for the nature of desire and sensory fulfilment.[22] For the present argument, painting is significant not only because it attends to the shadow in theory and practice, but also because of the very specific role of the shadow in this story of the creation of art. The shadow, not the physical body, is what is outlined in the story; it is the shadow of the form, not the form, which sets going the competition in representation. The shadow has an ambiguous but crucial status. It is thrown by light, so it is natural, but in stimulating the leap to representation it comes to have a semi-representational status itself – readily used as such if framed or theatricalized as in the puppet theatre, the myth of real and illusory in Plato's cave, or the shadow almost lost and so painfully returned in *Peter Pan* (see for example visual meditations on the shadow by Tim Noble and Sue Webster).[23]

Plato's cave uses the shadow's interstitial properties to explore the relationship between experience (sense) and knowledge. The shadow's important presence in the scenes of knowledge described in Plato's cave is only the best known philosophical use, widely known in the Renaissance. Dwellers in Plato's cave have their reality mediated and manipulated. Here, the sensory apprehension of shadows both substitutes and unfits the humans for the experience of full, actual, light.

Obviously, like all other referents the shadow signifies according to representational context. Donne's poems do not develop philosophical arguments on the shadow; rather, they put to work a feature of sensory and cognitive experience that is strongly linked to both sense and questioning: light and dark, but particularly the shadow, were emerging in sixteenth-century England as a ground for thought. The mythic lineage of visuality in thought and art, in which the contrast of light and dark is the ground of thought of various kinds, is suggestive about the way in which Donne's poetry uses the sensory apprehension of light and dark and, specifically, the shadow. In the 'Lecture' the shadow operates as a ground on which the poem is built in a way reminiscent of the myth of painting as initiated by the prompt of the shadow. In the 'Nocturnall', light and dark are the starting place for the elaboration and overthrowing of the poem's metaphorical and analogous sequence. In each case, light and dark are the starting place of the poem in the dual sense of preceding the poem's ideas but also prompting them. The myths of light and art schematize and consider the obvious fact that apprehension of the effects of light and dark are bound up with cognition which, in turn, rests on assumptions about the world's organization – something which, as far as light was concerned, had changed cataclysmically in the period before Donne began writing and continued to do so. Donne was engaged with the transformation of the heavens.

Johann Kepler, in his Galilean 'optick' story of the moon, writes that 'I suspect that the author of that impudent satire, the *Conclave of Ignatius*, had got hold of a copy of this little work, for he pricks me by name at the very beginning. Further on, he brings poor Copernicus to the Judgement seat of Pluto.'[24] As Marjorie Hope-Nicolson explores, *Ignatius* discloses Donne's awareness of contemporary developments in the theory of the Earth's relationship to the universe. These are articulated where his speaker experiences an ecstatic voyage to another world, in this case Hell and the moon. While 'in an Extasie' his 'Soule':

> had liberty to wander through all places, and to suruey and reckon all the roomes, and all the volumes of the heavens, and to comprehend the situation, the dimensions, the nature of the people, and the policy, both of the swimming Islands, the *Planets*, and of those that are fixed in the firmament.[25]

The speaker should be silent on this topic, he says, since Galileo has 'of late summoned the other worlds, the Stars to come neerer to him, and giue an account of themselues', and since Kepler, following Tycho Brahe's death, 'hath receiued it into his care, that no new thing should be done in heauen without his knowledge'. This knowledge is so detailed that Hope-Nicolson considered it to be possible, even likely, that Donne had read Kepler's controversial *Somnium* in manuscript.[26] Whether or not this was the case, and Hope-Nicolson's account is convincing, there is no doubt that Donne brought the implications of the new world to his thinking on the senses and to the Christian, moralized thinking on light and night bound up with that. Overall, then, while in 'Songs and Sonnets' Donne's poetic focus on night, sight, light and shadow uses sensory data as a ground of knowledge which can be repeatedly undercut, when we add this active engagement with the changing movement of the heavens we can see that sensory data not only makes experience vivid but feeds into more systematic kinds of knowledge.

A year earlier than *Ignatius*, in 1610, Donne had written 'The First Anniversary', canvassing 'the Starres which boast that they do runne | In Circle still, none ends where he begunne' (ll. 275–76) because 'Man hath weav'd out a net, and this net throwne, | Upon the Heavens' (ll. 279–80), a capture undermined relentlessly by human time and darkness within which 'mankinde decayes so soone, | We're scarce our Father's shadows cast at noone' (ll. 143–44).[27] While all scholars accept that Donne was thinking about the changes in the heavens, what he thought, and the grounds for making such an assessment are debated. However, without asking, for example, whether different narrators are to be considered as disclosing his opinion, we can ask whether the sensory apprehension of light and dark, so closely aligned with time and death, mark for Donne the extraordinary new part the heavens were known to play in the diurnal cycle. In the 'Songs and Sonnets' we can see that the senses were repeatedly interrogated as indices of situations. If in 'Lecture' the senses are crucial but problematic in the apprehension of time and love, in the 'Nocturnall' the whole implication of day, night and light on the darkest day is rearticulated in the final stanza. As we see in these poems, perhaps most forcefully in 'Breake of Day', the sensory perception of night and light is consistently foregrounded as the ground of thought:

> 'Tis true, 'tis day, what though it be?
> O wilt thou therefore rise from me?
> Why, should we rise, because 'tis light?
> Did we lie downe, because 'twas night?
> (ll. 1–4)

'Love', which in 'spight of darkness' brought the lovers to their encounter should override 'light' (ll. 5–6) too but, in fact, is itself overridden by 'businesse' (l. 18). The senses are part of action but not the whole; humans can override night and light, yet the senses remain the ground of metaphor and thought. Donne's 'Songs and Sonnets' put the senses to work in researching the world.[28]

Charles Coffin has noted Donne as a non-pastoral poet.[29] However, even as Coffin seems to bypass Donne's engagement with the senses, he engages sharply with their key discursive location in Donne's systematic thinking – scepticism. Coffin has influentially framed Donne as caught between two ways of interpreting the world, one 'scholastic' and synthetic, the other Galilean as 'new facts made a cleavage between the realms of the physical and metaphysical'.[30] Coffin's tendency to see this as Donne's problem has been highly influential, with the result that the place of the senses and experience in the 'Songs and Sonnets' tends to be elided into the poet's later, theological, explorations of doubt. However, contemporaries saw it differently; in 1606 Sir Toby Matthew described Donne and associates as 'mere libertines'.[31] In 'Songs and Sonnets', certainly, doubt is the condition of the poems as events and distinct interpretative frameworks are synthesized and disassembled with a speed calculated to maintain uncertainty. What Coffin sees as Donne's ultimately resolved problem of doubt and faith, these poems present as an opportunity for troubling, but bravura, explorations of the world and knowledge.

Even if Donne's scepticism was later channelled to debate faith we can productively read early poems as exploring doubt and certainty – what Montaigne called 'experience'.[32] Within this, the senses, including the visual sense, play a key role in conveying an immediate set of implications that are ready to be challenged. The eye's evidence is crucial, but to take it at face value would be foolish. Whatever the right answer might be to 'Did we lie downe, because 'twas night?', it is not uncomplicatedly 'Yes' or 'No', though the sensory knowledge of night is helpful in working out the answer.

Although the sermons, offering explicit answers to doubt, tend to focus discussion of Donne's scepticism, we know that Donne read Michel de Montaigne and Agrippa, both of whom explored doubt.[33] The 'nothing' that speaks the 'Nocturnall' tells us that were he a man something would tell him that he was so. This sounds strikingly like the paradox enunciated by Francisco Sanchez: 'I do not even know this – that I know nothing.'[34] 'Lecture' and 'Nocturnall' take the senses as the primary location of the sceptical attempt to know the world, using sensory data and accepted cognitive nuggets to evoke a frontline scepticism – scepticism shaped as an encounter with experience. These poetic texts, unlike the sermons, don't provide assessments of scepticism itself or answer doubts. We know about this aspect of Donne's thinking from the sermons. If scepticism names the debate about how and what we know, though, the poems we have considered use the senses and particularly the examples of light and dark and of visual stimulus like shadow, used so often in classical and Renaissance scepticism as the location where problems are experienced. Victoria Kahn's comment on Montaigne's 'recognition of our inability to suspend the activity of judgement in a single and fatal dismantling of the architectonic self' is perhaps more helpful in thinking about Donne's attitude to both the senses and doubt than the pursuit of his theology and logical refutations of doubt in the sermons.[35] Donne, too, keeps in play the assertion of the self, and its dismantling – the nothing, 'I am none' of the 'Nocturnall', is an assertion of sense and desire in the world even in the mode of its abolition. There is, then, a connection between Donne's use of the senses in the 'Songs and Sonnets' and the anniversary poems and his later working through of 'doubt'. Yet the distinction between sensory scepticism in 'Lecture' and 'Nocturnall' and the sermons' arguments of doubt is crucial.

So, if we agree that Donne is using the sensory apprehension of night, light and shadow to establish a sceptical poetic practice in these early poems, we can set them against other contemporary writings. The specificity of Donne's use of light, dark and shadow can be seen more clearly in comparison with George Chapman's 'The Shadow of Night' (1594). Chapman's poem's dense obscurity put it at the heart of the 'School of Night' controversy, and has been critically explored in terms of melancholy, as contrasting active and contemplative life or as, simply, obscure.[36] The 'Hymnus in Noctem' explores night in terms of the senses, but also derives substantial sections from Natale Comes's allegorical fables.[37]

Chapman's showy introduction bids for notice, and the poem promises a trans-valuation of the schema that aligns day and divine power, night and sin, as a time which sends mortals 'bolde reliefe'.[38] In its first appearance, un-named except in the title 'Hymnus in Noctem', night brings emotional and sensory respite:

> now let humour giue
> Seas to mine eyes, that I may quicklie weepe
> The shipwracke of the world: or let me sleepe
> (Binding my sences) lose my working soule[.]
> (ll. 8–11)

Working with an Aristotelian frame of sense, Chapman imagines sleep as an alternative to the problematic daylight world when:

> forth their sundrie roofes of rest,
> All sorts of men, to sorted taskes addrest.
> Spreade this inferior element: and yield
> Labour his due: the souldier to the field,
> States-men to counsel, Iudges to their pleas,
> Merchants to commerce, mariners to seas:
> All beasts, and birds, the groue and forests range,
> To fill all corners of this round Exchange,
> Till thou (deare Night, o goddesse of most worth),
> Letst thy sweet seas of golden humour forth
> And eagle like dost with thy starrie wings,
> Beate in the foules, and beasts To Somnus lodgings,
> And haughtie Day to the infernall deepe,
> Proclaiming scilence studie, ease, and sleepe.
> (ll. 205–18)

The day initiates work, characterized as drudgery and presses 'taskes' on all men; the very animals must 'groue and forests range' for food. Busy and burdened creatures are saved by the 'starrie wings' of night, sweeping 'haughtie Day' to 'the infernall deepe'. Day is 'driuen' from 'heauen' – 'In hell then let her sit'. In replacing involuntary labour with 'scilence studie, ease, and sleepe', night returns animals and humans to a state presented as both more congenial and truer than the daylight cacophony.

Chapman engages night very differently from Donne in exploring it as a freestanding topic. Initially night is a time which sends mortals 'bolde reliefe', emotional and sensory respite. However, peace ends when 'the gloomy shadow of the night [...] | [...] dims the welkin with her pitchy breath' (Christopher Marlowe, *Doctor Faustus*, 1.3.1–4), and, like Faustus, the poem's speaking voice begins his incantations:[39]

Now make him leaue the world to Night and dreames.
Neuer were vertues labours so enuy'd
As in this light: shoote, shoote, and stoope his pride:
Suffer no more his lustfull rayes to get
The Earth with issue: let him still be set
In Somnus thickets: bound about the browes,
VVith pitchie vapours, and with Ebone bowes.
Rich-tapird sanctuarie of the blest,
Pallace of Ruth, made all of teares, and rest,
To thy blacke shades and desolation,
I consecrate my life; and liuing mone,
Where furies shall for euer fighting be,
And adders hisse the world for hating me,
Foxes shall barke, and Night-rauens belch in grones,
And owles shall hollow my confusions:
There will I furnish vp my funerall bed,
Strewd with the bones and relickes of the dead.
(ll. 261–77)

Invoking the complete defeat of day, whose 'lustfull rayes', impregnating the whole world, are to be imprisoned in 'Somnus thickets', the speaker consecrates his life to a world of night whose palace, 'sanctuarie of the blest', is now figured as a grotesque charnel house where adders 'hisse the world'. The earlier nirvana-like calm of night gives way to a subjective evocation of a flight to night's 'sanctuarie' motivated by worldly rejection. The vocabulary of the invocation is multisensory, brash and works not by a comprehensive shift of values but by inversion of values from the Doom's moral schema.

If the senses are explicitly allocated to the day under the sign of excess, then the evocation of night as free from the senses is compromised by the poem's rich imagining of a sensorily saturated grotesque cell of night, where the subject resides amongst animal 'barkes', haunted by 'ghosts' unquietly seeking revenge. Apparently invited to join the speaker in the hymn's act of occult worship, in unpoliced shifts between description of repose and fervid advocacy, the reader is invited to 'Come to this house of mourning, serve the night', and when the goddess appears she is busily 'Circkled with charmes' (l. 396) and 'with meteors, comets, lightenings' (l. 400). Thus, once the incantation starts the absence of activity gives way to a forcefully sensory world of night.

In re-evaluating night and darkness Chapman produces a poem that is both intensely visual in its very focus on darkness and inevitably foregrounds the dominance of other sensations at night. The poem is alive with sounds and particularly those of animals inhabiting a world in which their senses are much more sharply attuned than those of humans. In electing to live by night Chapman's speaker is compromised because, as Laurie Shannon puts it, the night belongs to others; to animals, for example, whose senses operate better without light and whose sounds dominate the world of the night devotee.[40] Chapman's poem seeks a re-evaluation of night cast in visual terms, but night does not belong to the sight but to the senses that work better at that time – primarily sound and touch. Moreover, for all his attempts to make a new set of values for night, the sensory emphasis of the poem seems to tug the reader towards old associations of the senses – described in medieval times by animals and by visual representations of the human body as a giantly overgrown sense organ (ear, mouth, eye).[41] As night approaches it is visual, but once present the human is partly overwhelmed, as perhaps is Chapman's poem, by a sensory world that operates a different hierarchy.

The night, in Chapman's poem, is visually re-imagined using classical iconography. However, as the incantation starts we see the poem using the sensory and moral schema of day and night and, as the night world invades the poem, we see clearly the ways in which the senses are automatically allocated familiar morality. The icons and sounds of the incantation are imbricated in the value system of the Doom which renders the night torrid rather than a nirvana. Night is the subject's last retreat, but it is now a charnel house:

> There will I furnish vp my funerall bed,
> Strewd with the bones and relickes of the dead.
> Atlas shall let th'Olimpick burthen fall,
> To couer my vntombed face withall.
> (ll. 276–79)

We can imagine a specificity to this scene of charnel 'sanctuarie' as a retreat from the world partly conceptualized as a retreat from sense in the only recently redundant chambers and annexes to the pre-Reformation church in which anchorites voluntarily withdrew themselves from the realm of the senses. The anchorite's literal entombment was emphasized by the initiation ceremony's use of light and the administration of extreme unction in which the subject's sense organs were anointed as a token of a reparation and forgiveness before death.[42] The ceremony explains that, "'These things being done, let the grave be opened'" and the recluse entered singing, "'This shall be my rest for ever'", before dust was scattered and the house of enclosure built up.[43] The anchorite symbolically relinquished sense. This was a way of life within living memory; in just 1548 we hear of Katherine Man, a former recluse of the Blackfriars, giving up her right to the house in exchange for a pension.[44]

Yet if Chapman's transvaluation of night's associations seems ultimately to be embroiled in the past, and in the very moralized schemes of sense, night and light that it seeks to overthrow, it is also addressing preoccupations of its contemporary world in looking again at sense and sight in its questioning of sight. In registering the value of optics, thinking about sight and sense led to questions of illusion. As Jonathan Hudston discusses, Chapman used the optical tricks associated with perspective and more specifically the viewer's perspective.[45] In *Ovid's Banquet of Sense* (1591) the fountain described at the start is:

> So cunningly to optic reason wrought
> That farre of, it showed a woman's face,
> Heavie and weeping but more neerely viewed,
> Not weeping, heavy, nor a woman shewed[.]
> (III. 24–27) [46]

One way to think about 'Hymnus in Noctem' is as developing such a comparative game into a prolonged exploration of the senses at night and rule at night. In a different mode, 'Hymnus in Noctem' also presents the world as a question of 'optic reason' or perspective and set alongside these other versions of changed visuality, or perspective, showing a 'truer' situation.

In 'Hymnus in Noctem' night is not simply a perspectival puzzle in which knowledge is disrupted through visual effects, but is drawn out from the point of view of a devotee of the night. If the speaker recalls the anchorite, the poem also recalls the world of optic unreliability. Given that 'day, or light' does 'but serve the eye' which 'enflames the heart, and learnes the soule abuse' (ll. 362–65), the visual sense itself must be reformed if the night is to be seen in its true form. As Jacqueline Watson reminds us in this volume, sight was in theory the highest of the senses but was also very likely to lead a viewer astray. 'The Shadow of Night' addresses this situation on terrain that is in some ways surprisingly close to Donne's. Where it seems, then, that Donne is exploring night philosophically whereas Chapman is, perhaps quixotically, attempting to investigate night itself from the point of view of a passionate bid for re-evaluation, a more complex situation is suggested by this comparison of the two poems. If Donne explored light, night and shadow as a ground of thought, Chapman follows through a re-evaluation of night and explores the sensory stumbling blocks to full human possession of that world. In doing so, his work, too, leads us back to the grounds of knowledge from the distinct vantage point of faith as it encounters the unreliability of sensory apprehension. As *The Skeptick*, a version of Sextus Empiricus's *Outlines of Pyrrhonism* tells us, paintings can appear to sight in one way, 'but to the touch they seem not to be so' – the very senses cannot agree on how we know the world, and Chapman's poem recognizes faith's struggle with this.[47]

Finally, how can we set Donne and Chapman's worlds of night, light and shadow in relation to the large questions with which we opened – of Reformation, knowledge, and, potentially, sensory change? If we return, for a moment, to the world of the Doom, here is a medieval summary of the senses at work:

> Kepe well x and flee from VII
> Rule well V and come to Heaven.[48]

It is clear that this is not describing Donne and Chapman's sensory world, but it allows us to see the problem of how to investigate the sensory aspects of a changing world. As Alain Corbin suggests, the 'sensory environment' has changed massively, but finding methods to track that change is complex. Corbin argues that at moments of conflict, 'abrupt confrontations of systems of perception' illuminate sensory change.[49] For sight, then, key moments might be street-lights, the growth of cities, legislation for brick buildings, changes in labour, and Koslofsky writes a part of that as an epochal story. However, approaching Corbin's problem of a paucity of textual records, it is also possible to put together different kinds of evidence. Thus, that *The Skeptick* was circulating in the 1590s is an indication of vernacular debate on the role of the senses, and sensory experience, in producing knowledge. The writing is much more exemplary than a modern philosophical text and even, to a limited extent, shares with poetry the quality of an 'essay' testing elaborations on evidence. At the same time, in the poems analysed, both Donne and Chapman seem to investigate and use the implications of the 'old', Catholic world of night. With the Reformation, of course, the mapping of time on to the life of Christ, the hours, was superseded.

We can, then, see a link between Reformation and a potential change in the 'sensory environment'. The dark and light of the hours was reshaped by morning and evening prayer, with evening prayer linking God and light with the 'peace' of evening. The emergence of a labouring day and religious change are, it seems, marked together in the very texts of the church as the *Book of Common Prayer* formalizes 'Morning' and 'Evening' prayer. The day marked by morning and evening prayer represents a dedication of temporal and sensory being clearly as forceful as Corbin's points of conflict, and every bit as complex in terms of the questions its suggests about change driven 'top down' or 'bottom up'. These markers of time and light bring with them questions of sleep and labour, the potential reinvention of a role for the senses in 'evening', a time to become so important in eighteenth-century writing on the self. What the distinct orientations towards sensory knowledge found in the poetry of Donne and Chapman may suggest is that when thinking again about the sensory environment, texts from a range of different precincts of culture, not only those telling directly of sense experience, allow us to track hints of sensory worlds at particular moments, not only in epochal sweeps. And, above all, conceptual and sensory change are bound together, albeit in enigmatic ways.

Notes

1 For images of the Doom see www.wenhaston.net/doom/ [accessed 1 July 2013].

2 John Milton, *Paradise Lost* www.dartmouth.edu/~milton/reading_room/pl/ book_2/ [accessed 23 July 2014]; *Paradise Lost*, ed. by Alastair Fowler (London: Longman, 1968), p. 118.

3 Craig Koslofsky, *Evening's Empire: A History of the Night in Early Modern Europe* (Cambridge: Cambridge University Press, 2011), pp. 1–2; on 'segmented' sleep, see p. 6.

4 R.C. Bald, 'Donne's Will', in *John Donne: A Life* (Oxford: Clarendon Press, 1970), pp. 563–67 (pp. 563–64).

5 G.F. Waller, 'John Donne's Changing Attitudes to Time', *Studies in English Literature, 1500–1900*, 14.1 (1974), 79–89; Theresa M. DiPasquale, 'From Here to Aeviternity: Donne's Atemporal Clocks', *Modern Philology*, 110.2 (2012), 226–52.

6 William M. Hamlin, 'A Lost Translation Found? An Edition of *The Skeptick* (*c.* 1590) Based on Extant Manuscripts', *English Literary Renaissance*, 31.1 (2001), 34–51 (p. 42).

7 The earliest may be Edward Dowden, 'The Poetry of John Donne', in *New Studies in Literature* (London: Kegan Paul, 1895), pp. 90–120 (pp. 105–6). See John T. Shawcross (ed.), *The Complete Poetry of John Donne* (New York: Anchor, 1967) p. 410n; see also the discussion of explication of the shadows in Roger Cognard, 'The Solstice Metaphor in Donne's "Lecture Upon the Shadow"', *Essays in Literature*, 7.1 (1980), 11–20 (pp. 12–13).

8 John Donne, 'Lecture Upon the Shadow', in *The Complete Poetry of John Donne*, ed. by Shawcross, pp. 86–87. All references to Donne's poems follow Shawcross, with line numbers hereafter cited in the text.

9 Christopher Bardt, 'Constructing Light', *Journal of Architectural Education*, 58.2 (2004), 14–18 (p. 14).

10 Thomas Fale, *Horologiographia* (1652), A2r.

11 See also DiPasquale, p. 431.

12 See Alison R. Reike, 'Donne's Riddles', *Journal of English and German Philology*, 83.1 (1984), 1–20.

13 In 'Problem X', Donne explores Venus and shadow using a strikingly similar vocabulary of Venus (John Donne, *Problems and Paradoxes*, ed. by Helen Peters (Oxford: Clarendon Press, 1980) pp. 33–35.

14 'The system of planetary hours divided daylight hours into 12 equal parts and the night also into 12 equal parts. Thus the length of the hours varied through the seasons as the days grew longer or shorter, and daylight hours were only the same length as night hours at the two equinoxes.' Hester Higton, *Sundials at Greenwich* (Oxford: Oxford University Press and National Maritime Museum, 2002), p. 448.

15 Fale, L4v; 'the placing of the houres unequall', N3v.

16 Fale, O4r.

17 See Michael R. Matthews, *Time For Science Education* (New York: Plenum, 2000), pp. 49–50.

18 See Cognard.

19 Shawcross (ed.), p. 402n.

20 The material on the shadow in painting works follows the discussion of Victor I. Stoichita in *A Short History of the Shadow* (London: Reaktion, 1997), pp. 42–67. Pliny, *Natural History* (London: Loeb, 1952), p. 43 (xxxv.15), quoted in Stoichita, p. 11.

21 Quoted in Stoichita, p. 42.

22 See Stoichita, pp. 42–43.

23 See Bartolomé Esteban Murillo, *The Origin of Painting* (1660–65). Tim Noble and Sue Webster's work, see www.timnobleandsuewebster.com/artwerks.html [accessed 6 September 2013]; www.timnobleandsuewebster.com/metal_fucking_rats_2006.html [accessed 6 September 2013]; and, Youngman www.timnobleandsuewebster.com/youngman_2012.html [accessed 6 September 2013].

24 See Marjorie Hope-Nicolson, 'Kepler, The *Somnium*, and John Donne', *Journal of the History of Ideas*, 1.3 (1940), 259–80 (p. 268).

25 John Donne, *Ignatius his Conclave* (1611; repr. Amsterdam and Norwood, NJ: Walter Johnson, 1977), p. 2; Marjorie Hope-Nicolson, *passim*.

26 Hope-Nicolson, pp. 268–71.

27 Shawcross, pp. 276–86.

28 Shawcross, p. 106; see DiPasquale, *passim*.

29 Charles Coffin, *John Donne and the New Philosophy* (New York: Columbia University Press, 1937), p. 283.

30 Coffin, *John* Donne, p. 284. See e.g. Kenneth Gross, 'John Donne's Lyric Skepticism: In Strange Way', *Modern Philology*, 101.3 (2004), 371–99: 'even if the poems compel and indulge […] suspicion they are wise enough to let us know that we cannot stop there. Love is at the limit, and a continual promise' (p. 399).

31 Sir Toby Matthew, *A True Historical Relation of the Conversion of Sir Tobie Matthew*, ed. by A.H. Matthew (1904), pp. 90–91; quoted in Bald, pp. 188–89.

32 Michel de Montaigne, 'Of Experience', in *Essays*, trans. by John Florio, 3 vols (London: Dent, 1921; repr. 1938), iii, 322–86.

33 Don Cameron Allen, *Doubt's Boundless Sea* (New York: Arno, 1979), pp. 115–19; Bald, p. 2.

34 See Allen, pp. 77–78.

35 Victoria Kahn, *Rhetoric, Prudence and Skepticism* (Ithaca, NY: Cornell University Press, 1985), p. 151.

36 Frances Yates, *Occult Philosophy in the Elizabethan Age* (London: Routledge, 1979; repr 2001), pp. 171–75.

37 *Natale Conti's Mythologiae*, trans. and annotated by John Mulryan and Steven Brown, 2 vols, Medieval and Renaissance Texts and Studies, 316 (Tempe, AZ: Arizona Center for Medieval and Renaissance Studies, 2006).

38 All references and line numbering for 'Hymnus in Noctem' are to George Chapman, *Plays and Poems*, ed. by Jonathan Hudston (London: Penguin, 1998), pp. 223–37. The text is from *The Shaddow of night containing two poeticall hymnes* (1594), STC 190:16.

39 Christopher Marlowe, *Doctor Faustus* ed. by J.B. Steane (Harmondsworth: Penguin, 1969).

40 Laurie Shannon, *The Accommodated Animal: Cosmopolity in Shakespearean Locales* (Chicago and London: University of Chicago Press, 2013), p. 174.

41 See Carl Nordenfalk, 'The Five Senses in Late Medieval and Renaissance Art', *Journal of the Warburg and Courtauld Institutes*, 48 (1985), 1–22.

42 Nordenfalk, p. 3.

43 Rotha Mary Clay, *The Hermits and Anchorites of England* (London: Methuen, 1914), pp. 76, 94–98.

44 Francesca M. Steele, *Anchoresses of the West* (Derby, Darley Dale: no pub., 1903), p. 100.

45 See Hudston (ed.), p. xvii; see also discussion pp. xxxii–xxxiii, n. 6. See *Hero and Leander*, iii, 125–26, quoted in Hudston (ed.), p. xxii.

46 Quoted in Jonathan Hudston, 'Introduction', in Chapman, *Plays and Poems*, see also discussion pp. xxxii–xxxiii, n. 6. See *Hero and Leander*, iii, 125–26, quoted in Hudston, 'Introduction', p. xxii.

47 Hamlin, p. 50.

48 *Secular Lyrics of the XIVth and XVth Centuries*, ed. by Rossell Hope Robbins (Oxford: Clarendon Press, 1955), p. 80; quoted in Nordenfalk, p. 4.

49 Alain Corbin, 'A History and Anthropology of the Senses', in *Time, Desire and Horror: Towards a History of the Senses*, trans. by Jean Birrell (Cambridge: Polity Press, 1995), pp. 181–95 (p. 183).

8

Love melancholy and the senses in Mary Wroth's works

Aurélie Griffin

In his *Anatomy of Melancholy* (1621), Robert Burton defines the effects of love on humankind:

> How it tickles the hearts of mortall men,
>   *Horresco referens*, —
> I am almost afraid to relate, amazed, and ashamed, it hath wrought such stupend and prodigious effects, such foule offences. Love indeed (I may not deny) first united Provinces, built citties, and by a perpetuall generation, makes and preserves mankind, propagates the Church; but if it is rage it is no more Love, but burning lust, a disease, Phrensie, Madnesse, Hell. *Est orcus ille, vis est immedicabilis, est rabies insana*; 'tis no vertuous habit this, but a vehement perturbation of the minde, a monster of nature, witte and art.[1]

In Burton's account, love is characterized by its excessive, often violent nature, which has devastating consequences over the world as well as over people's minds. As it turns out, love was rarely a happy feeling in the Renaissance, and was repeatedly associated with melancholy. Love melancholy, to which the third (and longest) part of Burton's *Anatomy* was entirely devoted, was considered at the time one of the three main species of melancholy, together with scholarly melancholy and religious melancholy.[2]

Burton sets himself the considerable task of defining both melancholy and love, finding intimate connections between the two.[3] While all melancholy is not love, love must be understood as a form of melancholy, which Burton, quoting various authorities on the matter, indifferently calls 'a disease', 'a species of madnesse' and 'a melancholy passion', concluding that:

> most Physitians make it [love] a species, or kinde of melancholy (as it will appeare by the Symptomes) and treat of it apart: whom I meane to imitate, and to discusse it in all his kindes, to examine his severall causes, to shew his symptomes, indications, prognosticks, effects, that so it may be with more facility cured.[4]

Burton indicates that love, just like melancholy, can be detected through a number of symptoms, which are similar to the symptoms of melancholy that are consistently identified in the medical literature of the period.[5] 'Symptoms of the body' include paleness, leanness, languor, sighs, tears and a tendency to stay close to the ground, since earth was the element associated with melancholy. 'Symptoms of the mind', on the other hand, entail fear without cause, doubt and a distinct taste for obscurity.[6] Another symptom, which concerns both the body and the mind, is the perturbation of the senses.

In this chapter, I will study the effects of love melancholy over the senses in the works of an early modern woman writer, Mary Wroth. Her romance *The Countess of Montgomery's Urania* (1621), her closet drama *Love's Victory* and her sonnet sequence, *Pamphilia to Amphilanthus*, all deal with love melancholy, and consistently evoke its effects over the characters in terms of an opposition between the 'external' and the 'internal senses'. This distinction was formulated by Thomas Aquinas in the Middle Ages and had an important influence on Renaissance medicine, as I will demonstrate. I will then examine several examples taken first from *Urania*, then from *Love's Victory*, and finally from *Pamphilia to Amphilanthus*, which best illustrate Wroth's understanding of love melancholy as a disruption of the division between the 'external' and the 'internal senses'.

In the early modern period, 'the senses' not only referred to the five senses we know today (sight, hearing, smell, taste and touch), or even to the sixth sense of 'titillation' evoked by Eschenbaum in her chapter. These were known as the 'external senses', but there were also three 'internal senses': the common sense, the imagination and the memory. Early modern medicine and philosophy often referred to this distinction, following the doctrine of Thomas Aquinas to which I turn presently.

Aquinas's definition of the senses is part of his attempt to define man; more specifically the nature of the soul and the relation between the soul and the body. This definition is rooted in his reading of Aristotle's *De Anima*.[7] According to Aquinas's *Summa Theologia*, the senses – both external and internal – are 'preliminary to the intellect'. The senses are counted among the 'powers of the soul', the soul itself being composed of three parts (although they cannot be separated): the vegetative soul, which is closest to the body in that it is linked to man's needs; the sensitive soul, which deals with the senses and the passions; and the rational soul, which is specific to humankind in so far as it is the seat of reason. The senses are thus part of the soul, but they operate through the body. Aquinas defines a hierarchy in which the external senses are inferior to the internal senses, sight being 'the most perfect, and the most spiritual' of the external senses.[8] The external senses only perceive sensations, while the internal senses are necessary to receive those sensations. The external senses enable one to establish contact with the world through sensations such as 'hot and cold, wet and dry', but the internal senses allow those sensations to reach the soul properly (in other words, to be internalized). The purpose of the internal senses is to allow the sensations received through the external senses to access the rational soul, 'which so far exceeds the corporeal nature that it is not even performed by any corporeal organ'.[9]

The three internal senses all have distinct roles, but they are all linked as well.[10] The common sense is used 'for the reception of sensible forms', which is the first step of the internalization of sensation. The imagination, 'which is as it were a storehouse of forms received through the senses', is devoted to 'the retention and preservation of those forms'. Finally, the 'estimative and memorative powers' (which Aquinas reduces to one, memory) take care of 'intentions which are not received through the senses'. To define those 'intentions', which actually go beyond the mere external senses, Aquinas takes an example from the animal world:

> the animal needs to seek or to avoid certain things not only because they are pleasing or otherwise to the senses, but also on account of other advantages and uses, or disadvantages; just as the sheep runs away when it sees an approaching wolf not on account of its colour or shape, but as a natural enemy; and again a bird gathers together straw, not because they are pleasant to the sense, but because they are useful for building its nest. Animals, therefore, need to perceive such intentions, which the exterior sense does not perceive.[11]

The ability to detect 'intentions' could also be defined as the power of anticipation, as in guessing one's enemy's reactions or imagining uses of objects beyond the mere perception of their physical qualities. Interestingly, the example of the sheep and the wolf was used in very similar terms – although without quoting its source – by French physician André du Laurens, which testifies to Aquinas's influence on Renaissance medicine.[12]

Aquinas actually had an important influence on Renaissance theories of the senses. In his classic study on melancholy entitled *The Elizabethan Malady*, Lawrence Babb explains that Aquinas's division of the senses was part and parcel of the early modern conception of man.[13] Indeed, many of the treatises dealing with the passions and melancholy are indebted to Aquinas, and several quote his doctrine extensively. Thomas Wright's *The Passions of the Mind in Generall* (1601), André du Laurens's *A Discourse of the Preservation of Sight* (1599) and Nicolas Coeffeteau's *A Table of Humane Passions* (1621), for instance, all begin with a presentation of the external senses and the internal senses.[14] Timothy Bright's *A Treatise of Melancholie* (1586) and Robert Burton's *Anatomy of Melancholy* (1621) also refer to the internal and the external senses respectively.[15]

Contemporary medical and philosophical treatises such as these repeatedly describe melancholy as an affection of the senses – but are they referring to the external senses, to the internal senses, or to both? For Nicolas Coeffeteau, love is 'a true alienation of the sences, which ariseth, from that the spirit and will of him that loveth, being wholly imployed in the contemplation and enjoying of the thing beloved'.[16] Coeffeteau's 'alienation of the sences' seems to embrace both the external and the internal senses, as the lover's senses are completely focused on the beloved and become, so to speak, severed from the lover's body and mind. Lovers thus prove unable to use their senses to grasp any other object than their beloved. Another French scholar, Jacques Ferrand, provides his reader with concrete, even grotesque examples of such an alienation:

> doe we not oftimes see young spruce Gallants enamoured with some old, crooked, deformed *Hecuba*, with a furrowed forehead, long hairy eyebrows[,] bleare eyes, long hanging ears, a sadd nose, thick blabber lips, black stinking teeth, with a long terrible chin hang[ing] downe to her girdle; which yet they w[ill] swear is a second *Helen* [...] If she have her neck all bedaubed with ceruse and paint, her breast spotted like a leopard, with paps swollen, and hanging downe like a pair of Bagpipes [...]; yet will these sottish fooles fancy out of these deformities, a Breast of snow, a Necke white as milk, a Bosom enriched with Pinkes and Violets[.][17]

The lovers fail to perceive what their beloved really looks like because their sensations are (mis)guided by melancholy. The senses are so much aroused by lust that they obscure reason. In another passage, Ferrand argues that 'it cannot be denied that those who are in Love have their imagination depraved, and their judgement corrupted'.[18] Following the theory of the humours in Galenic medicine, which was still prevalent at the time, Ferrand assumes that the melancholics suffer from an excess of black bile (also called melancholy), which creates vapours in the mind and thus numbs reason. Moreover, Ferrand's *Erotomania* testifies to the growing interest in the passions, so that the lovers' alienated senses provide a telling example of the dangerous influence of the passions on reason. The melancholics' external senses are too acute, as anything will entice them. Because it is in close contact with the external senses, the imagination goes wild, while reason is weakened.

Timothy Bright explicitly attributes such 'monstrous fictions' to the excess of black bile which overrules the senses:

> the spleane, and with his vapours anoyeth the harte and passing up to the brayne, counterfetteth terrible objects to the fantasie, and polluting both the substance, and spirits of the brayne, causeth it without external occasion, to forge monstrous fictions [...] For where that naturall and internall light is darkened, their fansies arise vayne, false, and voide of grounde, even as in the externall sensible darkenes, a false illusion will appeare unto our imagination, which the light being brought in is discerned to be an abuse of fancie: now the internall darknes affecting more nigh by our nature, then the outward, is cause of greater feares, and more molesteth us with terror, then that which taketh from us the fight of sensible thinges[.][19]

Bright's allusions to an 'internal' and to an 'outward darkness' testify to a conception of the senses that is derived from Aquinas's. Bright argues that the mistakes of the external senses can be solved if reason corrects the mistakes of all the other senses; but when the internal senses are troubled, nothing can be done to regain reason. Once induced, 'fictions' and 'illusions' can thus affect all the senses because of an excess of melancholy.

At first, these three authors do not seem to distinguish between the external and the internal senses when they evoke the alienating effect of love over the senses. For all three authors, love apparently affects both the external and the internal senses. However, when Ferrand refers to what the lovers 'fancy out of these deformities', he actually differentiates between the external and the internal senses. The lovers perceive their mistresses' ugliness through their external senses, but when these sensations are internalized, some sort of conversion takes place which transforms ugliness into perfect beauty. Imagination (which was also called fancy) takes over all the other, both external and internal senses. Thus, the alienation of the senses arises from a widening of the discrepancy, or even the creation of a conflict, between the external and the internal senses. This process corresponds to what Bright calls 'an abuse of fancie'. It is the connection between the external and the internal senses which is disturbed by love, more specifically by love melancholy, since what the reader witnesses in these examples is the effect of melancholy over the mind. Melancholy seems to affect the internal senses even more than it does the external senses, even if the line between the two is not always clear-cut.

Whether or not 'Physitians', such as the ones quoted above, were the most apt to define love was not, apparently, an issue for Robert Burton, although he acknowledged that love melancholy was 'too light for a Divine [such as himself], too Comicall a subject to speake of Love Symptomes, too phantasticall, & fit alone for a wanton Poet, a feeling young love-sicke gallant, an effeminate Courtier, or some such idle person'.[20] In early modern English poetry, we find rather different, and varied, experiences of love melancholy from that exemplified by Burton's *Anatomy*, and by other medical or philosophical treatises of the period. Among the vast body of early modern English literature that is devoted to love melancholy, Mary Wroth's works hold an almost unique status, in that they constantly favour the female perspective and experience of love melancholy.

Wroth wrote in a variety of textual genres, including prose romance, poetry and closet drama, exploring ideas of love melancholy in all of these forms. Her *Pamphilia to Amphilanthus*, a sonnet sequence, focuses on Pamphilia's emotional response to her lover's inconstancy. *The Countess of Montgomery's Urania* (1621), a prose romance, portrays an imagined community of victims of unrequited love.[21] Finally, in *Love's Victory*, a closet drama, Wroth also emphasizes the lovers' melancholy as they are thwarted by Venus and Cupid in their amorous pursuits. In a vast majority of cases, love is unhappy in Wroth's works, and can hardly be distinguished from melancholy. Love melancholy has notable effects over the characters' senses, as they fail to detect the signs of love in the beloved, or interpret those signs in the wrong way. Wroth's representation of love, then, often relies on a conflict between the senses, which often pits what the characters see against what they believe they see.

In both *Urania* and *Love's Victory*, Wroth uses the conflict of the senses to build up the plot, following a similar pattern in each. Lovers are deceived by their senses, and therefore feel disappointment, jealousy and despair. As they surrender to their emotions, they meet other characters who prompt them to tell their stories. This device accounts for the structure of *Urania*, which largely consists of a series of embedded narratives. The lovers' confidantes question the certainty of their perceptions. Thus, the narrators' perceptions are pitted against those of their lovers, who explain the reasons for their actions.

Wroth's sonnet sequence, *Pamphilia to Amphilanthus*, also emphasizes the lover/persona's senses. The sonnets focus on Pamphilia's emotions to the exclusion of her lover's, and follow the ups and downs of her feelings in the manner of Petrarch's *Rime*.[22] The acuteness of Pamphilia's senses – both external and internal – becomes a source of literary creation. *Urania* similarly contains many scenes in which the (mostly female) lovers give vent to their emotions through the writing of poems or the telling of stories. In both works, Wroth uses the conflict of the senses to represent the paradox of melancholy – that of a disease associated with creative genius.

There is no distinct biographical evidence regarding whether or not Wroth had read Aquinas, but as I have outlined above, it is clear that Aquinas had an important influence on early modern theories of mind and body. Wroth's interest in melancholy indicates that she is likely to have read at least some of the treatises on this topic that were popular in her time. Through those treatises, Wroth seems to have been indirectly influenced by Aquinas's vision of the senses. Mary Wroth's works often represent a conflict between the external senses and the internal senses, which contributes to or even generates the characters' melancholy.

At the beginning of *Urania*, one of the heroines, the eponymous Urania, enters a dark cave and discovers a man 'deprived of outward sense, as she thought, and of life, as at first did feare'.[23] The man presents the main symptoms of melancholy: he is lying on his back, crying and lamenting his situation. The fact that he could be confused with a dead man is also a characteristic sign of melancholy.[24] The phrase 'outward sense' alludes to Aquinas's notion of the external senses, which were also called 'outward senses' in some treatises, as, for instance, in Bright's text quoted above. Although Wroth does not refer to the 'inward senses' explicitly in *Urania*, there is a reference to the 'outward sense of sight' (p. 512), which confirms her at least partial knowledge of Aquinas's conception of the senses. The distinction between the external senses and the internal senses actually plays a part in the representation of love melancholy in the romance.

Among the five external senses, Wroth gives distinct precedence to sight. This preference may be explained in two ways. First, sight was considered to be the most noble sense. Aquinas notes that, 'the sight, which is without natural change either in its organ or in its object, is the most spiritual, the most perfect, and the most universal of all the senses'.[25] Likewise, du Laurens avers that, '[a]mongst all the sences, that of the sight, in the common judgement of all the Philosophers, hath been accounted the most noble, perfect, and admirable'.[26] Secondly, sight was associated with love, as the Neoplatonists believed that the eyes emitted beams which established a contact with the object, the latter being able to trigger feelings.[27] In Wroth's works, sight is at stake not only because it generates love, or because the lovers take pleasure in contemplating the beloved, but because the characters look for the confirmation of their feelings through sight. *Pamphilia* and *Urania* contain numerous references to a faithful lover's bitter disappointment when confronted with cold looks. Sight in itself does not deceive the characters, but they fail, rather, to interpret what they see.

The adventures of the shepherdess Liana, narrated by Urania, provide us with a particularly telling example of the tension between the senses. As Liana tries to escape from her father's guard in order to meet her lover Alanius, she discovers a strange scene and says:

> desire to see him, made me accuse myself of long tarrying, especially when I saw him there; but what saw I with that? death to my joye, and martirdome to my poore heart: for there I saw him in anothers armes, wronging my faith, and breaking his made vowes. I stood in amaze, not willing to believe mine eyes, accusing them that they would carry such light to my knowledge[.] (p. 252)

The passage reflects the ambivalent status of sight in the early modern period, as Jackie Watson explains in her chapter. Sight was valued as 'the most perfect sense', and its association with love in this extract ennobles it as well. It is because she loves Alanius that Liana longs to see him. The dynamic of sight as the origin of love has been reversed, paving the way for a more negative approach to sight. Sight, indeed, works as the instrument of deception – a deception which is twofold in this passage. Liana believes she is deceived both by her lover because she trusts her senses (mainly sight, but not only). As she learns later, however, her lover has not been unfaithful, which amounts to saying that Liana is deceived when she believes she is deceived. The scene is all the more confusing because hearing, which (as Watson points out) was also considered one of the more noble senses by André du Laurens, confirms the impressions received from Liana's sight. Liana then repeats what she heard her lover say:

> It its true; I lov'd Liana, or indeed her fortune, which made me seeke her; but in comparison to thee, that affection borne to her, was hate, and this onely love, rather esteeming my self happy in enjoying thee, and thy delights, then if endowed with this whole Iland. What is riches without love (which is in truth the only riches)? and that doe I now possesse in thee. (p. 252)

Such a long speech is little likely to have been mistaken because of the limitations of hearing. This type of speech, however, occurs frequently in *Urania*, and it is after all possible that Liana simply mistook her own name. In any case, her reaction testifies to her renewed belief in the reliability of her senses:

> These words turnd my amazednes to rage, crying out;
> 'O false and faithlesse creature, beast, and no man, why hast thou thus betrayd thy constant Liana?' (p. 252)

The issue of deceit has been transferred from the senses themselves to their object, which illustrates a move from the proper sense of 'false' (as 'erroneous, wrong') to the figurative sense of the word (as 'mendacious, deceitful, treacherous'), and we might add, in the context of a romance obsessed with male inconstancy, 'inconstant' (see *OED*). In addition, the move from proper to figurative usage indicates the transition from the external senses to the internal senses. The mistake actually occurs in the transition from the external to the internal senses, as the latter fail to interpret the sensations perceived by the former.

Shortly after, Alanius gets a say in the matter, explaining what Liana either failed to perceive or to understand:

> There liv'd a Shepherd then (and my companion he was) who bewitched with a young maydes love, that unluckily had plac'd her love on me, plotted to deceive her, and in my shape to winne, what his owne person wold not purchase him; wherefore that (in that) unlucky night, he came unto my lodging, and stole away my clothes, I usually on solemne dayes did weare; in these habits he went into the Grove, being so like in stature, speech, and favor, as he oftentimes was taken, even, for me. Knowing her walke in the evening, to be towards those woods, in the plaine he saw her, and followed her into the Grove, overtaking her, just in the same place appointed for our blisse; being a little darkish, she mistook him, and hoping it was I, was content to be blinded; but wherein I doe most accuse him, was, he used some words (to give her true assurance 'twas my selfe) concerning deare Liana. These unhappily shee heard, and these I must confesse, gave full assurance of my faulsest fault. (pp. 256–57)

As it turns out, Liana's external senses were right after all – if we take Alanius's word for it. She saw and heard the scene she thought she did: a shepherd declaring his love to a shepherdess and the end of his love for Liana. The problem here is one of mistaken identity, another shepherd having stolen Alanius's attire. To make things worse, the scene takes place at night, whose complex association with the senses is studied by Sue Wiseman in this collection. Interestingly, however, Alanius lays the blame on Liana's expectations, which have confused her senses: 'she mistook him, and hoping it was I, was content to be blinded'. The difficulty lies in the interplay between the external and the internal senses, and, one might add, with the emotions which blur the lines between them. Liana's melancholy stems from her idea that her lover deceived her, which derives from the confusion between her external senses and her internal senses.

As he begins to explain what happened, Alanius insists on the role of imagination, which is one of the internal senses:

> I will begin with the succession of that, and as I imagine where shee left, which was with her leaving mee in the plaine, or better to resolve you of the deceit, with the night before wee were to meet; she comming before me to the place appointed, saw (as she imagined) my selfe her lover, wronging my love, and her: well, and ill for me she might conceive of it so, but thus in truth it was. (p. 256)

Alanius uses the verb 'imagine' twice, to refer both to himself and to his beloved, but while his imaginings were right (conveniently for the narrative, as it thus avoids unnecessary repetitions), hers were wrong. Although 'imagine' can simply be understood as a synonym for 'think' or 'guess' in this passage, the focus on the senses invites us to read it as a possible allusion to Aquinas's understanding of imagination as one of the internal senses. Alanius does not challenge the acuteness of Liana's external senses, but rather lays the blame on the errors of the imagination, which were notably explored, a few decades later, by Blaise Pascal.[28]

If we use Aquinas's terminology, Liana perceives the 'sensible forms' correctly, but she fails to detect the 'intentions' behind those forms. Her mistake is due to an incorrect use of 'estimative power': 'for the apprehension of intentions which are not received through the senses, the estimative power is appointed'. More specifically, 'cogitative power', which is part of 'estimative power', comes into play:

> the power which in other animals is called the natural estimative, in man is called the cogitative, which by some sort of gathering together and comparisons discovers these intentions. Therefore it is also called the 'particular reason,' to which medical men assign a particular organ, namely, the middle part of the head; for it compares individual intentions, just as the intellectual reason compares universal intentions.[29]

Cogitative power differs from reason only in that it concerns individual intentions as opposed to universal ones; it is also 'preliminary to the intellect'. In *Urania*, Liana's faith in her external senses is coherent with a representation of a failure of cogitative power rather than a failure of reason.

Alanius, however, underlines the contrast between perception and understanding: '[she] saw (as she imagined)'; 'she might conceive of it so, but so in truth it was' (p. 256). In this passage, he demonstrates his ability to detect the intentions behind the forms he perceives. Alanius's superior knowledge of the situation as compared to Liana's, and the certainty of his own identity, obviously assist him in the correct use of his faculties. Simultaneously, however, he anticipates Liana's reactions, using cogitative power to 'compare [the] intentions' behind the actions perceived differently by himself and his beloved. The complementarity of the lovers' narratives – Alanius resuming the story just where Liana had left it – is of course designed by Wroth to avoid unnecessary repetition, but it is still indicative of the likely differences which may arise from the use of the external and the internal senses.

The confusion of identities through disguise is a *topos* of the pastoral romance, and reveals one of the main issues of the genre, namely the difficulty of distinguishing truth from illusion. In the artificial realm of Wroth's romance, both versions are valid: Liana and Alanius describe the same scene, which they witnessed through their external senses. They both rely on their supposedly correct use of estimative power to interpret what they have seen, but no material evidence can justify any of the versions. What aggravates this uncertainty is the fact that their story is re-told by Urania, who first listened to them. Her second-hand account is even more susceptible to mistakes than Liana's and Alanius's. Moreover, all three narrators are similarly unreliable as, being lovers, they are subject to their disturbed or 'alienated' senses, to use Coeffeteau's term.

As could be expected, Liana fully accepts Alanius's explanation, and the lovers are reconciled. The tension between the external senses and the internal senses is used as a structuring principle for the action and for the narration in this, as in other episodes as well.[30] Nevertheless, the resolution of the lovers' conflict is far from satisfactory for the reader. The validity of both versions of the same narrative re-enacts the questioning of truth and illusion which is developed throughout the romance. Alanius could be lying, but in any case, the end of the passage betrays a confusion between truth and illusion, as the words 'true' and 'false' are associated with their opposites: the usurper lied to 'give her true assurance 'twas [him]self', while the same words 'gave [Liana] full assurance of [his] faulsest fault'. Either Liana was right, and Alanius wronged her; or she was mistaken, and he does not deserve to be called 'false' (pp. 256–57). The passage thus ends with a deep epistemological uncertainty, which jars the happy note of the lovers' reconciliation.

Deceived senses are also the basis of Wroth's closet drama, *Love's Victory*. As in *Urania*, Wroth displays her concern with the reliability of sight. The concerns that this unreliability might raise become one of the central motifs in *Love's Victory*. In the play, Venus asks Cupid to set a number of ordeals for the shepherds who now scorn the powers of the gods. The plot revolves around two couples, Philisses and Musella (whose name evokes the muses), and Lissius and Simeana, who is Philisses's sister. The main line of action is driven by these characters' mistaken assumption that they are not loved in return. The first scene presents one of the main characters, Philisses – whose name is a tribute to Philisides, the melancholy shepherd and poet who functions as an image of the author in Philip Sidney's *Arcadia* – lamenting over his unrequited love:[31]

> Alas, poor shepherd, miserable me.
> Yet, fair Musella, love and worthy be;
> I blame thee not, but mine own misery.
> Live you still happy and enjoy your love,
> And let love's pain in me distressed move;
> For since it is my friend thou dost affect,
> Then wrong him once, myself I will neglect;
> And thus in secret will my passion hide,
> Till time or fortune doth my fear decide[.][32]

Although he perceives the signs of love in Musella's behaviour, Philisses imagines that they are addressed to his friend Lissius. As with Liana, sight is correct, but the character fails in his use of estimative power. Philisses's apparently unreciprocated feelings give rise to the topical representation of the melancholy lover, and more generally, of the malcontent ('I cannot perish more than I now do | Unless my death my miseries undo' (1.1)). The conflict of the senses thus contributes to characterization.

Musella, however, is aware of the misunderstanding. She confesses that she loves Philisses, but explains to Silvesta – a Diana-like figure who has vowed chastity but is in love with a character named Forester – that he thinks she is in love with Lissius:

> Then know, Silvesta, I Philisses love.
> But he, although, or that because, he loves,
> Doth me mistrust. Ah, can such mischief move
> As to mistrust her who such passion proves?
> But so he doth, and thinks I have Lissius made
> Master of my affections, which hath stayed
> Him ever yet from letting me it know
> By words, although he hides it not from show.
> Sometimes I fain would speak, then straight forbear,
> Knowing it most unfit; thus woe I bear.
> (3.1)

The action is structured so as to enable a reconciliation of the lovers through the explanation of their misunderstanding, that is, by setting up a successful equation between the external and the internal senses. Musella decides to tell Philisses the truth, but she faces the obstacle of the limits of the senses, as her lover is not ready to admit the mistake of his internal senses easily: 'Prove it, and I may live' (4.1).[33] Truth and illusion are not so easily distinguished. Once they have been struck by love, the shepherds are wary of their own senses, and appeal to some sort of material evidence which could be evaluated through reason. Significantly, Musella tentatively attributes Philisses's lack of faith in her to his love. Although the lines may refer to jealousy, they can also be interpreted as an allusion to the lover's troubled senses, which prevent him from gaining access to the truth.

In *Pamphilia to Amphilanthus*, Wroth uses the conflict of the senses to represent another facet of melancholy, namely its association with creative genius. The sonnet sequence, written from the perspective of Pamphilia, is centred on her own feelings, and more specifically on the acuteness of her senses, which is due to love melancholy. Many of the sonnets focus on Pamphilia's sight rather than on her beloved's eyes (as in *Astrophil and Stella*, for instance).[34] One of Pamphilia's concerns is that her eyes may grant people access to her interiority: 'Take heed mine eyes, how your lookes doe cast | Least they beetray my harts most secrett thought' (P39, ll. 1–2). Several sonnets in the sequence set up a dialogue between Pamphilia's external senses and either her reason (as is the case in the quote above) or her imagination:

> When I last saw thee, I did nott thee see,
> It was thine Image, which in my thoughts lay
> Soe lively figur'd, as noe times delay
> Could suffer mee in hart to parted bee;
> (P24, ll. 1–4)

The poem begins with the confusion of Pamphilia's actual sight and the 'inner eye' of her mind, for her imagination enables her to see her beloved even when he is absent. This stanza thus corresponds to Aquinas's already quoted definition of imagination as 'a storehouse of forms received through the senses'.[35] According to both Aquinas and Wroth, the internal sense of imagination is clearly superior to the external senses. In *Pamphilia*, however, Wroth resolves the conflict of the senses by choosing to suffer from melancholy so as to assert her identity as a writer.

The first known text establishing a connection between melancholy and creative genius is the pseudo-Aristotle's *Problem XXX* (now attributed to Theophrastus), which begins with the following question: 'Why is it that all those who have become eminent in philosophy or politics or poetry or the arts are clearly melancholics, and some of them to such an extent as to be affected by diseases caused by black bile?'.[36] The revival of interest in melancholy in the Renaissance brought medical and psychological treatises as well as literary works back to the same question.[37]

In one sonnet from *Pamphilia*, the eponymous speaker delights in solitude as it enables her to indulge in introspection, and consequently to write poetry:

> When every one to pleasing pastime hies
> Some hunt, some hauke, some play, while some delight
> In sweet discourse, and musique showes joyes might
> Yett I my thoughts doe farr above thes prise.
>
> The joy which I take, is that free from eyes
> I sitt, and wunder att his daylike night

Soe to dispose themselves, as voyd of right;
And leave true pleasure for poore vanities;

When others hunt, my thoughts I have in chase;
If hauke, my minde att wished end doth fly,
Discourse, I with my spiritt tauke, and cry
While others, musique choose as greatest grace.

O God, say I, can thes fond pleasures move?
Or musique bee butt in sweet thoughts of love?
(P26, ll. 1–14)

Although she does not explicitly mention melancholy in this sonnet, Wroth brings together two of the main attributes of the disease: solitude and creation. By depicting her isolation and her disdain for courtly pleasures as well as by self-consciously representing the actions of her mind, Pamphilia claims to be a melancholic genius. She distinctly though somewhat paradoxically finds 'true pleasure' in 'cry[ing]'. In contrast with many other sonnets which present the sufferings of the melancholy subject, Wroth draws a picture of what Burton calls 'sweet' melancholy.[38] While most of Wroth's sonnets depict Pamphilia as the victim of a melancholy caused by her beloved's inconstancy, this sonnet presents melancholy as a choice in which Pamphilia asserts her own identity and superiority through literary creation. As Lesel Dawson points out:

> For high-ranking women, melancholy provided a compelling discourse of interi-
> ority, through which they could express feelings of lovesickness, loneliness, or
> alienation. Often when such aristocratic women reveal their melancholy, they do
> so in a way that simultaneously advertises their learning and their understanding
> of elite cultural codes.[39]

Wroth's learning is apparent in the choice of the sonnet, an elaborate poetic genre which was prominent in court culture. The construction of a sonnet sequence invites a comparison with her literary predecessors, from Petrarch to her uncle Philip Sidney and her father Robert Sidney. The depiction of melancholy in Wroth's works is thus part of a general claim for the validity of her female authorship.

Wroth self-consciously represents her own writing practice and explores the interaction between melancholy and creation in another sonnet:

> Led by the powre of griefe, to waylings brought
> By faulse consiete of change fall'ne on my part,
> I seeke for some smal ease by lines, which bought
> Increase the paine; griefe is nott cur'd by art[.]
> (P9, ll. 1–4)

Wroth here challenges the notion of writing as a derivative of melancholy, which Burton notably draws upon: 'I write of melancholy, by being busy to avoid melancholy'.[40] In this sonnet, Pamphilia chooses to go on writing although it is detrimental for her psychological state (it 'increase[s] the paine'). The pain gives her the necessary incentive to write, which makes her unique:

> It makes mee now to shunn all shining light,
> And seeke for blackest clouds mee light to give,
> Which to all others, only darknes drive,
> They on mee shine, for sunne disdaines my sight.
> (P9, ll. 9–12)

This stanza expresses Pamphilia's preference for darkness, which was one of the most frequent symptoms of melancholy, but obscurity makes her shine above others, because she constructs her identity through melancholy and writing.[41]

Throughout her works, Wroth represents the conflict of the senses as both a source and a consequence of love melancholy. This conflict becomes part of her poetics, as it informs the plot, contributes to characterization, and most importantly, helps her build an image of the female writer in both *Urania* and *Pamphilia*. Although there is no distinct evidence showing that Wroth had read Aquinas, her works display not only an awareness of the debate around melancholy in the period, but also a desire to be a part of this conversation. Melancholy becomes a proof of Wroth's literary talent, and serves as a plea for women's writing.

Notes

1 Robert Burton, *The Anatomy of Melancholy*, ed. by Thomas C. Faulkner, Nicolas K. Kiessling and Rhonda L. Blair, 6 vols (Oxford: Clarendon Press, 1995 [1989]), III, 48–49.

2 In Burton's view, religious melancholy is akin to love melancholy, as it derives from the love of God (III, 330). Other causes of melancholy include 'love of gaming', 'imprisonment', 'poverty' and the 'death of friends' (I, 288–93, 341–44, 344–56, 356–72).

3 Jacques Ferrand also identifies love and melancholy: 'love is the ground and Principall cause of all our affections, and the Abstract of all the passions and perturbations of the mind. For when we desire and enjoy what we affect, [...] this we call covetousness, and Concupiscence. And being not able to compasse our desires, this we call Grief, and Despaire; when we enjoy the thing we desire, Love then takes upon it the Names of Pleasure and Delight. When we think we are able to effect our desires, 'tis then Hope: and Fearing to loose it, either wholy, or int part only; this we call Jealousie. By reason of these perturbations of the mind, the bloud becomes adust, earthy, and Melancholy.' *Erotomania, or A Treatise discoursing of the essence, causes, symptomes, prognosticks, and cure of love, or erotique melancholy* (1640), pp. 9–10. Whether love is reciprocated or not, 'enjoyed' or not, it always translates into melancholy. Nicolas Coeffeteau produces a similar explanation, in *A Table of Humane Passions*, trans. by Edward Grimeston (1621), pp. 170–71.

4 Burton, III, 57.

5 For the symptoms of love melancholy, see Burton (III, 139–96). They can be compared to the symptoms of melancholy (I, 381–96). For other descriptions of the symptoms of melancholy, see Thomas Elyot, *The Castel of Helth* (1539), p. 3; Timothy Bright, *A Treatise of Melancholie* (1586), pp. 123–24; Thomas Walkington, *The Optick Glass of Humors* (1607), pp. 67–68; Ferrand, pp. 7–10.

6 Burton repeatedly uses the phrases 'symptoms of the body' and 'symptoms of the mind'. See in particular III, 139.

7 Aristotle, *De Anima*, trans. by D.W. Hamlyn (Oxford: Clarendon Press, 1993 [1968]), p. 135 (429a). See also Thomas K. Johansen, *The Powers of Aristotle's Soul* (Oxford: Oxford University Press, 2012).

8 Thomas Aquinas, *Summa Theologica*, trans. by Fathers of the English Dominican Province, 2 vols (Chicago: Encyclopaedia Britannica, 1952), I, 411 (I.78.3).

9 Aquinas, I, 406–07 (I.78.1).

10 See Simon Kemp and Garth J.O. Fletcher, 'The Medieval Theory of the Inner Senses', *American Journal of Psychology*, 106 (1993), 559–76, and Carla di Martino, *Ratio particularis: la doctrine des sens internes d'Avicenne à Thomas d'Aquin* (Paris: Vrin, 2008).

11 For this example, and the whole definition of the internal senses, see Aquinas, I, 412-13 (I.78.4).

12 Du Laurens writes: 'for the sillie Sheepe having spied the Wolfe, getteth himselfe by and by out of his way, as from his enemie; this enmitie is not knowne by the sence, for it is no object of the sences, but it is the meere worke of imagination to know the same', *A Discourse of the Preservation of Sight*, trans. by Richard Surphlet (1599), pp. 74–75.

13 Lawrence Babb, *The Elizabethan Malady: A Study of Melancholia in English Literature from 1580 to 1642* (East Lansing, MI: Michigan College Press, 1951), pp. 1–5.

14 See Thomas Wright, *The Passions of the Mind in Generall* (1601), pp. 12–13; Coeffeteau, preface; du Laurens, pp. 72–76.

15 Bright, G3v. Burton refers to the 'five outward senses', which he identifies as hearing, sight, smell, taste and touch, and to which he adds the sixth sense of 'titillation', as Eschenbaum notes in her chapter. Burton also devotes one subsection to a presentation of the 'inward senses' or 'inner senses', namely 'Common Senses, Phantasie, Memorie' (I, 150–53). His presentation of the outer and the inner senses is therefore identical to Aquinas's.

16 Coeffeteau, pp. 169–70.

17 Ferrand, pp. 32–33.

18 Ferrand, p. 31.

19 Bright, p. 103. The use of terms such as 'internall light' and 'externall sensible' shows that Bright was influenced by Aquinas.

20 Burton, III, 1.

21 *Pamphilia* and *Urania* were published in a single volume in 1621, but the sonnet sequence seems to have been written several years earlier, around 1611–13, and circulated in manuscript form among Wroth's friends. See *The Poems of Lady Mary Wroth*, ed. by Josephine Roberts (Baton Rouge, LO: Louisiana State University

Press, 1983), pp. 61–62. 'Pamphilia to Amphilanthus' is quoted from this edition, with sonnet number and line numbers given in the text.

22 For Petrarch's influence over Wroth, see for instance Mary Moore, *Desiring Voices: Women Sonneteers and Petrarchism* (Carbondale, IL: SIU Press, 2000), pp. 125–50.

23 Mary Wroth, *The First Part of the Countess of Montgomery's Urania*, ed. by Josephine Roberts (Tempe, AZ: Arizona Center for Medieval and Renaissance Studies, 2005 [1995]), p. 3. Hereafter cited in the text.

24 See Walkington, p. 65.

25 Aquinas, I, 411 (I.78.3).

26 Du Laurens, p. 12.

27 See du Laurens, p. 12. See Jackie Watson's discussion of the workings of sight in her chapter and her analysis of the emission/intromission debate. See also Burton (III, 65, 77, 78), and Coeffeteau's definition of love (pp. 91–97).

28 Blaise Pascal, *Pensées*, trans. by Honor Levi (Oxford: Oxford University Press, 1995), pp. 16–20 (fragment 78).

29 Aquinas, I, 413 (I.78.4).

30 Four different narrators are required to tell this story: the unnamed narrator of the romance, Urania, Liana, and Alanius. See *Urania*, pp. 158–60, 196–98.

31 Philip Sidney, *The Old Arcadia*, ed. by Katherine Duncan-Jones (Oxford: Oxford University Press, 1985), p. 64 and pp. 140–42 in particular. On the identification of Philisides to Philip Sidney, see Dennis Moore, 'Philisides and Mira: Autobiographical Allegory in *The Old Arcadia*', *Spenser Studies*, 3 (1982), pp. 125–37.

32 Mary Wroth, 'Love's Victory', in *Early Modern Women's Writings. An Anthology 1560–1700*, ed. by Paul Salzman (Oxford: Oxford University Press, 2000), pp. 82–133, 1.1. Hereafter cited in the text.

33 The shepherdess Simeana similarly called for proof as her lover pledged love to her: 'How can I this believe?' (4.1).

34 Philip Sidney, 'Astrophil and Stella', in *The Major Works*, ed. by Katherine Duncan-Jones (Oxford: Oxford University Press, 2002), pp. 153–211 (pp. 155, 157).

35 Aquinas, I, 412–13. Du Laurens's definition of imagination is clearly indebted to Aquinas's: 'Thus, therefore, for the reception of sensible forms, the 'proper sense' and the 'common sense' are appointed [...]. But for the retention and preservation of these forms, the phantasy or imagination is appointed, which is as it were a storehouse of forms received through the senses' (du Laurens, pp. 73–75).

36 Quoted in Raymond Klibansky, Erwin Panofsky and Fritz Saxl, *Saturn and Melancholy*, trans. by E.S. Forster (Nendeln: Liechtenstein, 1979 [1964]), p. 18.

37 Montaigne thus affirms the link between melancholy and creation in his *Essays*: 'It is a melancholy humour, and consequently a hatefull enemy to my naturall complexion, bredde by the anxietie, and produced by the anguish of carking care, whereinto some yeares since I cast my selfe, that first put this humorous conceipt of writing into my head'. See Michel de Montaigne, *Essays*, trans. by John Florio (1613), p. 212.

38 Burton, 'The Author's Abstract of Melancholy', in *Anatomy of Melancholy*, I, lxix–lxx.

39 Lesel Dawson, *Lovesickness and Gender in Early Modern English Literature* (Oxford: Oxford University Press, 2008), p. 97.
40 'Democritus Junior to the Reader', in Burton, I, 6.
41 The impossibility of finding relief through writing is also explored in sonnet P68.

Part III

Aesthetic sensory experiences

9

'I see no instruments, nor hands that play': *Antony and Cleopatra* and visual musical experience

Simon Smith

In 1599, composer Richard Alison prefaced a book of four-part psalm settings with a particularly memorable sales pitch. Like the 1563 psalter frontispiece explored in our volume's introduction (Figure 1), Alison's dedicatory address imagines an ideal performance of psalms set to music. He foregrounds the breadth of sensory stimuli offered by such a performance as a clinching argument for the devotional and, of course, economic worth of his volume:

> And that our meditations in the Psalmes may not want their delight, we haue that excelle[n]t gift of God, the Art of Musick to accompany them: that our eyes beholding the words of Dauid, our fingers handling the Instruments of Musicke, our eares delighting in the swetenesse of the melody, and the heart obseruing the harmony of them: all these doe ioyne in an heauenly Consort, and God may bee glorified and our selues refreshed therewith.[1]

Stimulation of sense receptors in eye, finger, ear and heart are united in a bodily experience of 'heauenly Consort' that, fortuitously, both praises the Almighty and gives the performer a restorative boost. Through this experience, purchasers are included in the community of worshippers that Alison constructs with collective pronouns; all one need do is simply purchase the book, take it home and follow his directions. This passage is a work of art in itself, counterpoising expressions of genuine faith with business practicalities; musical experience theory with the textual authority of the Bible; pragmatic bodily benefits with points of theological principle. Yet this balancing act would not be possible if the idea at the centre of the passage – that musical performance should be experienced through a combination of different senses – did not have a similar centrality in widespread early modern understandings of music.

Many scholars argue that sensory experiences are encountered not in isolation, but in combination with one another. Michel Serres asks, 'How could we see the compact capacity of the senses if we separated them?', using the five chapters of his seminal work *The Five Senses* not to consider each sense in turn, but rather to explore how sensations become entangled in practice.[2] Recent studies of early modern performance, such as Janette Dillon's exploration of Elizabethan court spectatorship, have similarly acknowledged the co-functionality of the senses:

> The word 'spectator', linked as it is, through etymology, to sight, is inadequate to represent the nature of the engagement a subject makes with a spectacle (again a term that privileges sight). Perceiving a procession, as von Wedel's account [of Elizabeth I's Accession Day tournament at Whitehall on 17 November 1584] richly demonstrates, involves hearing, speech and motion, as well as deep roots in the order of power.[3]

Royal processions are not just experienced through sight, and likewise, musical experience is not limited to hearing alone. Accordingly, scholars have increasingly considered musical performance in relation to senses beyond hearing, seen in Richard Sennett's memorable account of the primacy of touch when playing the cello, and in Jennifer Nevile's recent exploration of dance as an important visual component of musical performance in fifteenth-century Italy.[4]

Early modern sources preserve many accounts of musical experience – both real and imagined – that constitute musical performance as a fundamentally multisensory phenomenon. Unsurprisingly, music was generally conceptualized in the early modern period as a primarily aural phenomenon, working upon the body and mind through the organs of hearing, yet this sensory process was not understood in isolation from the stimuli that music offered to the other senses. In particular, the sights of performance are overwhelmingly presented in early modern texts as integrated and critical to the experience of music. I wish to argue that this visual privileging is extremely significant for our understanding of early modern commercial drama, for this widespread expectation of seeing a musical performance underlay numerous dramatic uses of hidden music in commercial playhouses, in which an audience's interactions with key moments of a play were shaped through the distinctive responses that unseen music could draw. I offer two snapshots of this dramatic technique at work in Shakespeare's *Antony and Cleopatra*, in Act 4, Scene 10 and Act 4, Scene 3.[5]

Early modern expectations of visual musical experience are certainly evident in the wider textual record, with many sources preserving accounts both of visual engagement with music, and of responses to unseen music. But who exactly shared these expectations? Francis Bacon's irritation regarding the movement of ideas about music amongst non-specialists is helpful here. Published in 1627, his *Sylva Sylvarum* offers a detailed consideration of the processes of sound and hearing, including much attention to the experience of music. He complains that:

> Musicke in the Practise, hath bin well pursued; And in good Variety; but in the Theory, and especially in the Yeelding of the Causes of the Practique, very weakly; Being reduced into certaine Mysticall Subtilties, of no use, and not much Truth.[6]

For Bacon, making the case for the epistemological centrality of experimental empiricism, the circulation of rather broadly formed and untested ideas about music is a constant irritation.[7] Hot on the heels of this first remark comes a further observation:

> The *Cause* given of *Sound*, that it should be an *Elision* of the *Aire* (wherby, if they meane any thing, they meane a *Cutting*, or *Diuiding*, or else an *Attenuating* of the *Aire*) is but a Terme of Ignorance: And the Motion is but a Catch of the Wit upon a few Instances; As the Manner is in the *Philosophy* Receiued. And it is common with Men, that if they haue gotten a Pretty *Expression*, by a *Word* of *Art*, that *Expression*, goeth currant; though it be empty of *Matter*.[8]

Once again, the fact that an idea can hold vast cultural currency – it 'goeth currant' – without retaining its clear theoretical basis and empirical reference points is extremely problematic for Bacon.[9] Significantly, his emphasis on the movement of musical ideas in wider culture suggest that we should look broadly for references to visual musical experience, seeking a large and multifarious range of subjects who may have been familiar with the idea. Indeed, the notion of seeing music has a widespread presence in early modern texts, suggesting that this mode of sensory engagement is an idea about music, like Bacon's '*Elision* of the *Aire*', that 'goeth currant' in broad early modern culture, shaping engagements with practical musical performances for a wide range of subjects.

Sources describing visual musical experience range from works of music theory and the paratexts of printed music books, through to dramatic texts and the prefaces of popular psalm settings, like Richard Alison's 1599 publication.[10] This mode of engagement was thus rehearsed in a consistent form to subjects as diverse as professional musicians engaging with theoretical material, highly trained singers or instrumentalists with access to the latest publications by court composers, those with a rudimentary ability to read music and a desire to sing psalms, and anyone who could afford a ticket to a playhouse, regardless of whether they could read English – or musical notation – at all.[11] The necessity of seeing music appears consistently in these contrasting texts, indicating how far the visual permeated conceptions of musical experience for audiences well beyond any narrow group of professionals or specialists.

I first consider early modern accounts of the importance of visual musical experience, before examining accounts of musical response when music is hidden and unavailable for such engagement. These sources offer a clear picture of the reactions expected from contemporary subjects when faced either with visible or with unseen music. I then consider two particular responses to unseen music that, I suggest, were invited from playgoers at early performances of *Antony and Cleopatra*. As we have seen in Jackie Watson and Eleanor Decamp's chapters in this collection, our understandings of early playhouse engagements with drama can be usefully refined through close attention to the senses, for such attention can reveal distinctive early modern sensory expectations shaping

both dramatic performances and playhouse responses – in this case, expectations that music will be seen as well as heard.

Seeing music in early modern culture

Early modern sources consistently suggest that sight is by far the most necessary sense besides hearing for the experience of music.[12] Linda Phyllis Austern
has explored male accounts of the allure of early modern female-seeming
singers, arguing that an objectifying gaze was often as significant a part of men's
musical experience as the aural attention that they afforded a song.[13] However,
this visual draw of music in performance seems to have been just as strong
without alluring bodies to leer at. As I shall explore, accounts of performance
for high status audiences in England and elsewhere often relate uses of music
that rely upon the audience looking towards the source of the sounds in order
to achieve the desired dramatic or performative effect, without expectations of
the performer's physical appeal: in the seventeenth century, audiences wanted
their musical experience to consist of sight as well as sound.

Many scholars have examined the 'ocularcentrism' of twentieth- and twenty-
first-century culture, yet sensory engagement with music has seen a stubborn
trend not towards a privileging of sight, but rather towards aural emphasis in
the last 100 years.[14] Quite simply, unlike early modern subjects, we no longer
expect to watch musicians play as we listen to their performances. The reasons
for this shift have been explored by a number of commentators; William Forde
Thompson, Phil Graham and Frank A. Russo argue that '[a] significant event
in the current context is the invention of the radio and gramophone, which
isolated the audio mode of music, reinforcing the notion that musical experience was a solely aural phenomenon'.[15] Specific twentieth-century developments in recording technology have excised the visual experience of musicians
from everyday consumption of music, making commonplace a mode of
engagement with musical sound that was far more unusual before the advent
of recording technology. The musical culture of the last century or so has thus
seen the aural portion of music become increasingly divorced from the other
sensory stimuli of musical performance; whilst the sound of music is often
combined with other sensory stimuli – as cinematic underscore or videogame
accompaniment – it tends to be used as aural support for sights other than
that of the performing musician. Indeed, the influence of film scores on live
theatre music in the twentieth century illustrates this shift: modern theatrical
audiences might expect their music to be dramatically integrated and sympathetic to the context of the production, but in most cases, it remains very much
invisible.[16] In contrast, long before the isolation of 'the audio mode of music',
seventeenth-century subjects expected that music would be seen unless there
was a particular reason for it not to be, both in the theatre and elsewhere.

In accordance with this expectation of seeing music, early modern sources describing specialist musical performances to high status audiences are often particularly concerned with the visual presentation of music and musicians. Such a focus is evident in Thomas Campion's printed account of 'Lord Hay's Masque', performed on Twelfth Night 1607. He describes the layout of the hall meticulously, including the three groups of musicians used:

> The vpper part where the cloth & chaire of State were plac't, had scaffoldes and seates on eyther side continued to the skreene; right before it was made a partition for the dauncing place; on the right hand whereof were consorted ten Musitions, with Basse and Meane Lutes, a Bandora, a double Sack-bott, and an Harpsicord, with two treble Violins; on the other side somewhat neerer the skreene were plac't 9. Violins and three Lutes, and to answere both the Consorts (as it were in a triangle) six Cornets, and six Chappell voyces, were seated almost right against them, in a place raised higher in respect of the pearcing sound of those Instruments.[17]

His emphasis on the visible layout of the musicians 'as it were in a triangle', and their presence in front of the screen in the key line of sight from the 'chaire of State' confirms the common expectation of clear visual engagement as part of musical experience. Sight and sound are integrated in Campion's description of the set-up of the hall, just as they are in the underlying rationale that his comments reveal: six cornets and six singers are raised for aural reasons, as the former are 'pearcing', but the left, right and centre formation that these raised performers are slotted into – a spatial organization plotted, of course, to be seen in perfect perspective from the royal chair – reflects simultaneous interest in the sight of musical performance.[18]

Concern for the arrangement of musicians is even dramatized by John Fletcher and Philip Massinger in *The Custom of the Country* (King's Men, first performed 1619–20).[19] In Act 3, Scene 2, the frantic preparations for a banquet are staged. As a servant notes, the house expects 'some great person, | They would not make this hurry else'. As the playhouse audience watch the '*Banquet set forth*', it is clear that the characters are particularly determined to arrange the musicians in a visually appropriate performance formation. As the organizer Zabulon instructs the servants to 'Be quick, be quick', he demands 'where have you plas'd the musicke?' A servant shows him their position, indicating where 'they stand ready Sir', and he commends the placement, agreeing that ''Tis well'.[20] The actions of Zabulon and the servants demonstrate the absolute importance of the musician's visual arrangement to the experience of the banquet. This arrangement is one of the few aspects – including the pungency of the scent and the quality of the wine – that require his personal attention and approval. Fletcher and Massinger's scene of domestic organization indicates that visual musical experience was widely understood to be important: the playwrights expect concerns about seeing music to be just as comprehensible to their commercial playhouse audiences as they are central to Thomas Campion's understanding of private court entertainment at Whitehall Palace. It is clear, then, that those organizing musical performances anticipated visual engagement with music, requiring keen awareness of the physical appearance and spatial organization of musicians.

Further evidence for the importance of sight appears in a striking use of the term 'music' in several plays to indicate the physical performers themselves. Indeed, when Zabulon shows concern for visual layout in *The Custom of the Country*, he refers explicitly to musicians as 'the musicke', as 'they stand ready'. The 'music' he describes is not an isolated notion of invisible, purely aural harmony, but rather a specific performance, to be given by physical musicians, whose performing must be experienced with both eyes and ears. Similar uses of the term appear in *The Old Law* (1618–19). The text preserves stage directions including, '*Enter Musick one carrying a Bridecake,* | *the Clowne, the rest with them old Women*', and '*Enter* Clowne, *and* Wench, *the rest with the[m] old women,* | *The* Clownes *wife, Musick, and a Bride Cake to the wedding.*'[21] The 'music' here is sufficiently embodied to help carry a prop on stage, indicating once again that a physical, observed performer is a fundamental part of music. Likewise, in Fletcher and Massinger's *The Elder Brother* (King's Men, *c.* 1625), the 'music' is physical enough to require sustenance, for when Andrew asks the butler 'Is th' musicke come?', he learns that 'th'are here at breakfast'.[22] The everyday nature of these references to 'the music' indicates how ingrained multisensory musical experience was in early modern thought, with even the term that today refers specifically to aural harmony being used widely to encompass sight, sound and the physical bodies that perform.

Hiding music in early modern culture

Early modern sources are similarly clear about responses to unseen music. As I shall argue, it is through these responses that visual musical experience took on a particular significance for playgoers. Accounts of hidden musical performance appear in a range of dramatic and non-dramatic texts, with a brilliant and possibly unique dramatization occurring in Massinger and Nathan Field's *The Fatal Dowry* (King's Men, 1617–19). The play stages a delicate balancing act of hospitality and deceit, in which a domestic musical performance is presented by the host and singer Aymer to his guest Charalois. Aymer refuses to let his visitor see the accompanying musicians, in order to keep Charalois apart from his wife, Beaumelle, who is with male company 'within'. Charalois leaves absolutely no doubt that he considers musical experience partial without clear visual and aural access:

AYM. Begin the last new ayre.
CHA. Shall we not see them?

AYM. This little distance from the instruments
Will to your eares conuey the harmony
With more delight.
CHA. Ile not consent.
AYM. Y'are tedious,
By this meanes shall I with one banquet please
Two companies, those within and these Guls heere.
Song Aboue.
Musique and a Song, Beaumelle within — ha, ha, ha.
CHA. How's this? It is my Ladies laugh! Most certaine
When I first pleas'd her, in this merry language,
She gaue me thanks.[23]

Aymer is desperate to keep 'those within and these Guls heere' separate, to which end he makes his claim that the aural delight of music is heightened by visual sensory deprivation. Unsurprisingly, Charalois gives this argument short shrift, insisting that he will 'not consent' to such an incomplete experience of the ayre. In a neatly balanced moment of irony, despite Aymer's care to thwart Charalois's desire for a sight of the music in order to stop him seeing Beaumelle, Charalois still recognizes his wife aurally. Charalois's demand for visual stimulation typifies early modern expectations of complete musical experience, doing so in explicit and unequivocal terms.

Similar responses to hidden musical performance appear in textual accounts of court entertainment that circulated in print in early modern Europe. In Olivier de la Marche's late fifteenth-century French work, *Memoirs of the House of Burgundy*, a text that enjoyed multiple printings in the sixteenth and seventeenth centuries, the author describes a striking court entertainment:

A bit later four trumpets sounded a joyous and very loud fanfare. The trumpets were behind a green curtain hung over a large pedestal at one end of the hall. When the fanfare ended the curtain was suddenly drawn and a person playing the role of Jason, heavily armed, was spied on the pedestal.[24]

For this performance to succeed dramatically, the audience must be looking towards the sound, seeking sights of music, at the moment when the curtain is raised and the scene commences. Here, the gaze of the audience is drawn towards the sound because invisible, disembodied music would not constitute full musical experience for early modern spectators.

With this example, we are moving towards the dramaturgical use of a particular idea about music, just as we find in the early modern playhouse. The makers of the entertainment presuppose that their audience will seek a complete musical experience including both sight and sound, enabling them to draw visual attention towards a certain point by hiding music there. Writers and performers of commercial drama appear to have had similarly clear expectations of their audiences, for equally confident uses of hidden music are preserved in play-texts, suggesting that similar responses to unseen music occurred in London playhouses in the early seventeenth century.[25] In the rest of this chapter, I consider two such uses of unseen music in Shakespeare's *Antony and Cleopatra*. In one case, music conveys an unseen dramatic world to playgoers, reaching beyond the representation of the theatre's stage space. In the other, hidden music is used to evoke responses from playhouse attendees analogous with the responses of staged characters, thus inviting the audience to share the perspective of these characters for a moment.

Musical distraction in *Antony and Cleopatra*

In Act 4, Scene 10 of *Antony and Cleopatra* (King's Men, 1606–08), music's visual experience is suppressed in order to convey a dramatic world beyond the stage. This technique makes use of music performed offstage and out of sight, as a form of dramatic representation through sound. As David Lindley notes of early modern theatrical convention, 'instrumental music – whatever symbolic weight it might carry – is almost always assumed to be audible to the characters on stage' as well as to the audience, unless explicitly framed as otherwise.[26] When unseen music appeared, then, providing there was no suggestion that it was supernatural, disembodied and invisible, the audience's overwhelming understanding would be that the dramatic world extended beyond the playhouse's stage to the location of this hidden sound. Early modern playmakers exploited playgoers' desires to see the music in order to create this effect of musical narration. By removing the sight of music, playmakers encouraged their audience to fill in the gap imaginatively, mentally constructing the dramatic scene that the music aurally describes.

Musical narration allowed early modern commercial drama to reach beyond the inherent limits of a playhouse's physical dimensions, telling stories of the largest scale. There are many examples of this practice, in which scenes are constructed that would be too expansive to convey through stage action.[27] In these cases, playgoers experience music primarily as a narrative device – a theatrical language describing the dramatic world. This has been recognized in part by Frances Ann Shirley, who notes that 'musical sounds [...] create the illusion of marching armies off stage' in a number of Shakespeare's plays. She traces the particular meanings that certain musical and non-musical sounds can convey – how '[a] flourish, for example, adds an air of dignity and increases our excitement', or how 'the words of Caliban and Barnadine before they enter not only create anticipation in the audience, but also confirm the unflattering descriptions of each'. However, in accordance with what she sees as 'the necessity of classifying [...off-stage sounds...] according to some system', her work focuses on the nature, categories and meanings of sounds that occurred at the Globe and Blackfriars rather than on the dramatic effects and narratorial possibilities of hidden music.[28] In more recent work, Elizabeth Ketterer offers a sustained engagement with the dramaturgical possibilities of offstage music in a foundational study of music in the repertory of the Admiral's Men, giving a particularly rich account of a series of offstage 'musical military signals' in Christopher Marlowe's *The Massacre at Paris* (Strange's Men, 1593).[29]

In *Antony and Cleopatra*, unseen musical narration is used not just to create an offstage dramatic world, but also to interrupt the concurrent stage representation. Hidden sound punctuates a significant moment of stage action, making a competing bid for audience attention. In moments such as this, the stage business needs to be of particular significance to playgoers in order to create the desired tension between the demands of sight and sound. Few moments can be considered more dramatically key than the death of a central character in a tragedy, and so precisely this stage action is intruded upon by offstage music in *Antony and Cleopatra*, at the death of Enobarbus. This character plays a key role as a soldier and friend to Antony, his relentless observations combining choric and malcontent elements in a constant reflection upon the events that unfold, and upon Antony himself.

The musical narration of Act 4, Scene 10 is framed by the events that precede Enobarbus's death. He defects to Caesar early in the fourth act, but by Scene 6, upon receiving both his own treasure and Antony's 'bounty overplus' as a parting gesture from his former friend, he realizes the severity of his betrayal and is overcome with grief (4.6.21).[30] Absent from the stage for three scenes, Enobarbus eventually re-emerges in Scene 10, soliloquizing upon his guilt before he dies – apparently of a broken heart – calling 'O Antony! O Antony!' Three overhearing soldiers move in, hoping to ascertain whether he is returning to Antony, for such news 'May concern Caesar'. They attempt to wake him, offering the audience the possibility that he merely 'sleeps' rather than lies dead. This suggestion is significant, for by verbalizing the opinion that Enobarbus may recover, the characters raise expectations among the audience that they may yet hear more from him, directing attention towards his body. Uncertainty reigns until the Sentry concludes that 'The hand of death hath raught him' (4.10.22–29). At this point, playhouse attention would be focused on Enobarbus: the audience look and listen for any sign of life, just as the soldiers do.

When Enobarbus's death is confirmed, the focus of attention created by the preceding dialogue sets up audience expectations of reflection upon this complex character. Instead, the sound of '*Drums afar off*' immediately follows, signifying an army moving into action (l. 29.1). No consideration of Enobarbus is forthcoming, and the scene shifts abruptly to '*Antony and Scarus with their army*' (4.11.0.1). The principal effect of the '*Drums afar off*' is to extend the dramatic world beyond the stage, creating a tension in focus between the important stage business unfolding and the wider military context that the music creates offstage. These competing demands for attention are strong, with early modern playgoers' desires for visual musical experience foregrounding an unseen dramatic world, even as they are simultaneously concerned with Enobarbus. This would require subjects in the playhouse to consider which they found more important: the moral dilemmas and personal fate of a central and sympathetic character, or the global political meltdown unfolding beyond the stage.

The competing demands of the personal and the global are central concerns in *Antony and Cleopatra*. Jonathan Dollimore notes that 'heroism of Antony's kind can never be "entirely personal" [...] nor separated from either "heroic achievement" or the forces and relations of power which confer its meaning', for 'to kiss away kingdoms is to kiss away also the lives of thousands'.[31] Significantly, the suppression of visual musical experience at Enobarbus's death would have invited early modern audiences to live out this very tension in their response to the scene: even as they were encouraged to focus on the character taking centre stage, the music would make the competing demand that they should instead imagine the extended dramatic world beyond Enobarbus, a world of large scale military conflict. These concurrent demands for attention are thus an attempt to engage playhouse audiences in a direct and emotive way that is only possible with stage action and hidden music, distinct from the similarly unique engagements with drama in print that Hannah August traces in Chapter 11 of this collection. Here, a central tension of the play, a key development in the narrative, and the audience's own response to both of these would all be united in a single theatrical experience created through music. Michael Neill notes that this complex passage of stagecraft forms a 'semblance of a funeral march for Enobarbus' as the soldiers take the body offstage, but it is very much an inverted semblance.[32] The social function and related conventions of a funeral march are turned utterly inside out: the characters focus on themselves (the Sentry notes that 'Our hour | Is fully out'); they lack concern (the Second Watch casually remarks 'Come on, then. He may recover yet'); and, most significantly, the music describes the global conflict when it should be memorializing the deceased (4.10.29–33). The scene directly and confrontationally juxtaposes the hidden musical representation of military preparation with the stage presentation of death. This juxtaposition recalls a similar use of offstage music in another of Shakespeare's death sequences from the turn of the sixteenth century, in which Horiatio's eulogizing is famously concluded with the angry demand, 'Why does the drum come hither?' (*Hamlet*, 5.2.314).

Supernatural music in *Antony and Cleopatra*

Hidden music is also used with precise dramaturgical intentions in Act 4, Scene 3 of *Antony and Cleopatra*, this time in a supernatural context.[33] Here, playwright and playing company asked playgoers to respond to hidden, seemingly supernatural music in ways that were simultaneously echoed by the characters upon the stage, encouraging empathetic engagement with those characters. As we saw when trumpeters hid behind a green curtain, or when Charalois found himself excluded from the musical performance space, early modern responses to unseen music begin with an immediate, powerful desire to place the music visually.[34] In de la Marche's memoir and Massinger and Field's play, the musical performers were readily identifiable as human; significantly, however, when a hidden, earthly performer cannot easily be located, the desire to see music is typically followed with speedy resort to a supernatural explanation. This is dramatized in *The Costly Whore* (Revels Company, 1619–32). When a Duke hears music but can 'see no instruments, nor hands that play', he comes swiftly to the conclusion that 'Tis some celestiall rapture of the minde', and 'No earthlie harmonie'.[35] The Duke's immediate concern is to establish whether music is above him and thus heavenly, or below him and devilish: as Ferdinand asks in *The Tempest*, is this music 'I'th' air or th'earth?' (1.2.390).[36]

When playgoers heard unseen and unexplainable music, they were likely to display similar responses to those of the Duke and Ferdinand: visual desire; recourse to supernatural explanation; and, finally, attempts at further comprehension. Moreover, dramatic characters often responded ostentatiously to unseen playhouse music, seemingly to encourage playgoers to align themselves and their musical experience with the reactions – and the perspectives – of those characters. Shakespeare's dramatic use of hidden, supernatural music in *Antony and Cleopatra* occurs prior to Enobarbus's death, taking place as a group of soldiers stand guard at night in Act 4, Scene 3. Ideas of the mysterious and unexplained open the scene as two soldiers discuss an odd rumour that is circulating:

SECOND SOLDIER: Heard you of nothing strange about the streets?
FIRST SOLDIER: Nothing. What news?
SECOND SOLDIER: Belike 'tis but a rumour. Good night to you.
(4.3.3–5)

In these short lines, audience interest is piqued, and the possibility of a supernatural presence is hinted at. When the soldiers disperse shortly afterwards to stand guard, '*They place themselves in every corner of the stage*' (l. 7.1). This direction is critical for its striking visual impact, the stage space blocked out with soldiers presumably looking outward into the unknown 'night', preparing for unexpected sights. Their gaze draws attention to the very limits of the stage space as a mode of dramatic representation, quite literally looking beyond it for that which will remain unseen. This moment of stagecraft can be imagined just as persuasively at either of the playhouses in which *Antony and Cleopatra* is likely to have been performed; the vast crowd and openness of the Globe could convey the mysterious unknown just as aptly as the indistinct extremities of the indoor Blackfriars after 1609, where 'the sparkling audience – and actors –

will have emerged through a delicate haze; a confusion of smoke from candle and tobacco'.[37] Through the soldiers' opening dialogue and their subsequent stage movements, the audience are encouraged to expect the unexpected, and to give strong visual attention to the stage and its boundaries. The unexplained duly appears in aural form, when the '*Music of the hautboys is under the stage*' (l. 10.1). The audience's response to this unseen music would be heightened by the very fact that their visual attention has been demanded so directly by the preceding use of the stage space, as the soldiers look outward. The playgoers' unfulfilled desire to see and comprehend the hidden music would thus steer them towards an otherworldly explanation, supported by the music's continuing lack of embodiment.

It is significant that the hautboys (or shawms) play while generic soldiers stand watch, rather than alongside a previously characterized, noble personality. Instead of inviting empathetic engagement with a single, clearly defined character, the scene stages a group of marginal figures: the soldiers are outside of the small set of socially superior characters driving the tragedy, looking on and listening in. This is directly analogous to the audience's position; they are in close proximity to the events of the play, bound to the action in a collective theatrical experience, yet outside of the dramatic world in which the events unfold. As the soldiers describe their powerful response to the supernatural music, music that expresses the plight of a character central to the tragedy, the invitation is for the audience to do the same, emulating the soldiers' responses to the under stage hautboys. Playgoers are carefully steered towards an experience of the hautboy music as convincingly supernatural, at least within the dramatic world.

As the scene and the music continue, the soldiers make a series of remarks further suggesting a supernatural presence, and encouraging playgoers to continue aligning themselves with the soldiers. The soldiers listen carefully in an attempt to locate the music's source, and to establish – as always – whether it is 'Music i'th' air' or 'Under the earth' (l. 11). A more definite gloss is ultimately offered by the Second Soldier, who had initially displayed superior knowledge about the strange rumours at the start of the scene. He announces that ''Tis the God Hercules, whom Antony loved, | Now leaves him' (ll. 14–15). From this point, the audience have a specific reading of the music to take forward: this is supernatural music, and it does not bode well.

The presence of music is drawn directly from Plutarch's *Lives*, Shakespeare's major source for the play in Thomas North's translation.[38] However, rather than the subterranean hautboy music that is ascribed to Hercules by Shakespeare's soldier, Plutarch's text describes the sound of:

> A marvelous sweete harmonie of sundrie sortes of instrumentes of musicke, with the crie of a multitude of people, as they had bene dauncing, and had song as they use in *Bacchus* feastes, with movinges and turninges after the maner of the

Satyres: & it seemed that this daunce went through the city unto the gate that opened to the enemies.
(4P5^{r-v})

The most famous of Roman biographers is not describing Herculean revelry here, although the suggestion in Plutarch that 'it was the god vnto whom *Antonius* bare singular devotion to counterfeate and resemble him, that did forsake them' is echoed in Shakespeare's play (4P5^{v}). Plutarch remarks upon Antony's self-styled resemblance to both Hercules (4M6^{r-v}) and Bacchus (4N4^{v}), so in the context of revelry and satiric leapings, the 'god' intended here in the source text must be the latter.[39] Shakespeare's scene departs from Plutarch by changing the instrumentation, removing the procession, adopting a different style of music, and explicitly glossing the god in question as Hercules, rather than Bacchus.[40] This is certainly practical for the performers: rather than bringing a procession of dancers on stage, the unseen music is simple to implement and immediately conveys supernatural malevolence through choice of instrument. The substitution of deities is thus one part of a whole set of adjustments made in order to shape the scene into a powerfully engaging and appropriate moment of theatre. A spectacle of Bacchic dancers might have provided an entertaining diversion at this point, but the hidden hautboy music offers the audience an experience aligned with the concerns of the stage characters, making the scene a central part of their involvement in the play's global conflict.

Shakespeare adapts his source radically in the supernatural encounter that he dramatizes, and this departure would have gone some way towards normalizing different playgoers' understandings of what actually happens in the scene. Those who knew nothing of Antony's life beforehand would be seeking an explanation for the music until the moment that the Second Soldier speaks. Equally, those well versed in Plutarch would remain unsure whether the underground, devilish music of the hautboys is supposed to be a radical reworking of the Bacchae's procession, another supernatural presence, or something else entirely. Finally, it must not be forgotten that Plutarch only offers the Bacchic interpretation as what those 'in reason [...] thought' was the best explanation, rather than as a certain reading (4P5^{v}). Accordingly, a playgoer interested in the sources of the drama might be expecting an entirely new interpretation of the music in this narrative incarnation. It is extremely significant that the Second Soldier's explanation is held back until the final few lines, so that playgoers with a range of prior knowledge could all share the experience of seeking out understanding for most of the scene, aligning them with the soldiers. Whether they knew Plutarch or not, they would be hoping for further information – or better yet, sight of the music – that might clarify the signification of these hautboys. Until the mention of Hercules gives some degree of conclusion to the matter, the audience would have shared both the soldiers' uncertainty, and their desire for visual musical experience.

Shakespeare's scene ends as the soldiers give chase to the music, aiming to 'Follow the noise so far as we have quarter' (l. 19). There is a final gesture of inclusiveness to bring the audience directly into this moment, as the soldiers all speak simultaneously, declaring ''Tis strange' (l. 20). By closing the scene with a group of generic characters expressing themselves in chorus and in accordance with one another, the invitation is made one final time to the even larger crowd of playhouse witnesses to seek out the unseen music's source themselves, and thus imaginatively to enter the dramatic world.[41] Experience of hidden music would be central to the audience's experience of the supernatural here, central to their alignment with the stage characters and, ultimately, central to the stagecraft of this scene as it was produced on the early modern stage.

These unseen musical performances, in the tiring house and under the stage of a commercial playhouse, complete a picture of early modern sensory engagement with music that began with Richard Alison's devotional model of multi-sensory musical experience. Through textual evidence drawn from a diverse range of sources, I have argued for the significance of visual musical experience to early modern engagements with music in a range of contexts. These sources reveal an understanding of musical experience with particular relevance to the commercial playhouse, for the rich and interrelated accounts of sensory experience in these various sources shed new light on dramaturgical practices at the Globe and Blackfriars based on precise and sophisticated uses of unseen music. The traces of early performance practice in the Folio text of *Antony and Cleopatra* suggest playhouse music uses that were demonstrably shaped by the early modern expectation of visual – as well as aural – engagement with music.[42]

Notes

1 Richard Alison, *The Psalmes of Dauid in meter* (1599), A2r–v.

2 Michel Serres, *The Five Senses: A Philosophy of Mingled Bodies (I)*, trans. by Margaret Sankey and Peter Cowley (London: Continuum, 2008), p. 305 and *passim*.

3 Janette Dillon, 'Spectatorship at the Early Modern English Court', in *Spectatorship at the Elizabethan Court*, ed. by Daniel Dornhofer and Susanne Scholz, Special Issue of *Zeitsprünge: Forschungen zur Frühen Neuzeit*, 17 (Frankfurt: Klostermann, 2013), 9–21 (p. 21).

4 Richard Sennett, 'Resistance', in *The Auditory Culture Reader*, ed. by Michael Bull and Les Back (Oxford: Berg, 2003), pp. 481–84; Jennifer Nevile, 'A Measure of Moral Virtue: Women, Dancing and Public Performance in Fifteenth-century Italy', in *The Sounds and Sights of Performance in Early Music: Essays in Honour of Timothy J. McGee*, ed. by Maureen Epp and Brian E. Power (Farnham: Ashgate, 2009), pp. 197–210.

5 Similar uses appear in plays including: Anon., *The Costlie Whore* (1633), C3v; John Fletcher and Philip Massinger, 'The Double Marriage', in *Comedies and Tragedies Written by Francis Beavmont and Iohn Fletcher Gentlemen* (1647), 5D2v; Thomas Heywood, *The Wise-woman of Hogsdon. A Comedie* (1638), G1r; John Marston, *The*

Wonder of Women Or The Tragedie of Sophonisba (1606), F1v–F2r.

6 Francis Bacon, *Sylua syluarum: or A naturall historie* (1627), F1r.

7 William Rawley's preface to the volume explains that, 'true *Axiomes* must be drawne from plaine Experience, and not from doubtfull; And his Lordships course is, to make Wonders Plaine'. Bacon, A2r.

8 Bacon, F4r–v.

9 Christopher Marsh considers Bacon's remarks in the context of earlier music theory, in *Music and Society in Early Modern England* (Cambridge: Cambridge University Press, 2010), p. 40.

10 In addition to the examples considered below, see Anon., *Costlie Whore*, C3v; Michael East, *The fourth set of bookes, vvherein are anthemes for versus and chorus, madrigals, and songs of other kindes* (1618), A2r; John Fletcher, 'The Captaine', in *Comedies and Tragedies*, 2G4r; John Fletcher, 'The Chances', in *Comedies and Tragedies*, 3A4r–v; Fletcher and Massinger, 'The Double Marriage', 5D2v; Robert Jones, *Vltimvm Vale, with a triplicity of musicke* (1605), A2v; John Marston and John Webster, *The Malcontent [...] With the Additions played by the Kings Maiesties servants* (1604), B1r; Henry Shirley, *The Martyr'd Souldier* (1638), C2v; *Memoirs of Sir James Melville of Halhill, 1535–1617*, ed. by A. Francis Steuart (London: Routledge, 1929), pp. 96–97.

11 The question of who purchased and consumed the various music-related publications available in early modern England has been explored from a number of fruitful perspectives. Foundational work on the production and consumption of printed music books includes Donald Krummel, *English Music Printing, 1553–1700* (London: Bibliographical Society, 1975); *Music Printing and Publishing*, ed. by Donald Krummel and Stanley Sadie (Basingstoke: Macmillan, 1990). Linda Phyllis Austern's recent article exploring female domestic psalm-singing sheds light on a much-overlooked part of this picture: '"For musick is the handmaid of the Lord": Women, Psalms, and Domestic Music-making in Early Modern England', in *Psalms in the Early Modern World*, ed. by Linda Phyllis Austern, Kari Boyd McBride and David L. Orvis (Farnham: Ashgate, 2011), pp. 77–114. Christopher Marsh brings a cultural-historical perspective to this topic with extremely productive results: 'Recreational Musicians', in *Music and Society*, pp. 173–224.

12 See note 10.

13 Linda Phyllis Austern, '"Sing Againe Syren": The Female Musician and Sexual Enchantment in Elizabethan Life and Literature', *Renaissance Quarterly*, 42 (1989), 420–48; '"Alluring the Auditorie to Effeminacie": Music and the Idea of the Feminine in Early Modern England', *Music and Letters*, 74 (1993), 343–54; '"No Women Are Indeed": The Boy Actor as Vocal Seductress in Late Sixteenth- and Early Seventeenth-Century English Drama', in *Embodied Voices: Representing Female Vocality in Western Culture*, ed. by Leslie C. Dunn and Nancy A. Jones (Cambridge: Cambridge University Press, 1994), pp. 83–102.

14 Studies examining 'ocularcentrism' include Martin Jay, *Downcast Eyes: The Denigration of Vision in Twentieth-Century French Thought* (Berkeley, CA: University of California Press, 1993), pp. 45–90; 'The Rise of Hermeneutics and the Crisis of Ocularcentrism', *Poetics Today*, 9 (1988), 307–26; Constance Classen, *Worlds of Sense: Exploring the Senses in History and Across Cultures* (London: Routledge, 1993), pp. 6–7.

15 William Forde Thompson, Phil Graham and Frank A. Russo, 'Seeing Music Performance: Visual Influences on Perception and Experience', *Semiotica: Journal of the International Association for Semiotic Studies*, 156 (2005), 203–27 (p. 220).

16 As Claire van Kampen notes, 'Musicians are generally placed unseen in a music studio entirely disconnected from the stage action other than through a visual monitor and headphones, and their playing is "piped in" to the auditorium via a sound system.' This contrasts dramatically with the ostentatious display of musicians at the reconstructed Globe Theatre in London. 'Music and Aural Texture at Shakespeare's Globe', in *Shakespeare's Globe: A Theatrical Experiment*, ed. by Christie Carson and Farah Karim-Cooper (Cambridge: Cambridge University Press, 2008), pp. 79–89 (p. 82).

17 Thomas Campion, *The discription of a maske, presented before the Kinges Maiestie at White-Hall, on Twelfth Night last* (1607), A4r–v.

18 Particularly valuable scholarship exploring the relationships between performance space and royal spectatorship in court entertainment includes Janette Dillon, *The Language of Space in Court Performance, 1400–1625* (Cambridge: Cambridge University Press, 2010), pp. 103–28; Martin Butler, *The Stuart Court Masque and Political Culture* (Cambridge: Cambridge University Press, 2008), pp. 1–34; Helen Cooper, 'Location and Meaning in Masque, Morality and Royal Entertainment', in *The Court Masque*, ed. by David Lindley (Manchester: Manchester University Press, 1984), pp. 135–48.

19 Here and throughout, I give each play's posited dates of first performance and any associated playing company in parentheses, following *DEEP: Database of Early English Playbooks*, ed. by Alan B. Farmer and Zachary Lesser (2007) http://deep.sas.upenn.edu [accessed 12 July 2014].

20 John Fletcher and Philip Massinger, 'The Custome of the Countrey', in *Comedies and Tragedies* (1647), 2B1v.

21 Thomas Middleton, William Rowley and Thomas Heywood, *The Excellent Comedy, called The Old Law: or A new way to please you* (1656), K3r.

22 John Fletcher and Philip Massinger, *The Elder Brother a Comedie* (1637), E1v.

23 Philip Massinger and Nathan Field, *The Fatall Dowry: A Tragedy* (1632), I1r. Aymer performs a second song in a fruitless attempt to distract Charalois further; Tiffany Stern reveals the dramatic significance of this song in light of a missing verse that she has recovered. See *Documents of Performance in Early Modern England* (Cambridge: Cambridge University Press, 2009), p. 165.

24 This translation by Gary Tomlinson in *Source Readings in Music History*, ed. by Oliver Strunk, 2nd edn, rev. by Leo Treitler (New York: Norton, 1998), p. 314. Olivier de la Marche, *Les Mémoires De Messire Olivier De La Marche* (Lyon, 1561; repr. 1562; 1566; 1567; 1616; 1645).

25 See, for instance, John Fletcher, 'The Tragedie of Bonduca', in *Comedies and Tragedies* (1647), 4H1v; William Shakespeare, *Coriolanus*, 1.4–6; *Antony and Cleopatra*, 4.3 (considered below).

26 David Lindley, *Shakespeare and Music* (London: Thomson Learning, 2006), p. 112.

27 See note 25.

28 Frances Ann Shirley, *Shakespeare's Use of Off-Stage Sounds* (Lincoln, NE: University of Nebraska Press, 1963), pp. 51–55.

29 Elizabeth Ketterer, "'Govern'd by Stops, Aw'd by Dividing Notes": The Functions of Music in the Extant Repertory of the Admiral's Men, 1594–1621' (unpublished doctoral thesis, University of Birmingham, 2009), pp. 164–66.

30 The sole early textual witness to *Antony and Cleopatra* is the 1623 Folio, in which all the stage directions I consider are present.

31 Jonathan Dollimore, *Radical Tragedy* (Brighton: Harvester, 1984), pp. 206–15.

32 *Antony and Cleopatra*, ed. by Michael Neill, The Oxford Shakespeare (Oxford: Oxford University Press, 1994), p. 278n. See also Michael Neill, "'Exeunt with a Dead March": Funeral Pageantry on the Shakespearean Stage', in *Pageantry in the Shakespearean Theater* (Athens, GA: University of Georgia Press, 1985), pp. 153–93; *Issues of Death: Mortality and Identity in English Renaissance Tragedy* (Oxford: Clarendon Press, 1997).

33 The close links between music and the supernatural in early modern culture and drama have been widely explored; particularly significant studies include Gary Tomlinson, *Music in Renaissance Magic: Toward a Historiography of Others* (Chicago: University of Chicago Press, 1993); Amanda Eubanks Winkler, *O Let Us Howle Some Heavy Note: Music for Witches, the Melancholic, and the Mad on the Seventeenth-Century English Stage* (Bloomington, IN: Indiana University Press, 2006); Linda Phyllis Austern, "'Art to Enchant": Musical Magic and Its Practitioners in English Renaissance Drama', *Journal of the Royal Music Association*, 115 (1990), 191–206; Lindley, *Shakespeare and Music*, pp. 218–33.

34 De la Marche, in *Source Readings*, p. 314; Massinger and Field, *Fatall Dowry*, I1r.

35 *Costlie whore*, C3v. See similarly Fletcher and Massinger, 'Double Marriage', 5D2v; Robert Davenport, *A New Tricke to Cheat the Divell* (1639), F4r; Fletcher, 'The Chances', 3A4r–v.

36 Lindley's work on *The Tempest* is authoritative; for his discussion of Ferdinand's response to Ariel's invisible music (1.2.376–410), see *Shakespeare and Music*, pp. 1–3.

37 Tiffany Stern, 'Taking Part: Actors and Audience on the Stage at Blackfriars', in *Inside Shakespeare: Essays on the Blackfriars Stage*, ed. by Paul Menzer (Selinsgrove, PA: Susquehanna University Press, 2006), pp. 35–53 (p. 45). The play's 1608 entry in the Stationer's Register suggests that it was written for and first performed at the Globe, but given the King's Men's acquisition of the Blackfriars theatre by 1609, the play is likely to have seen later performance both indoors and outdoors (see *DEEP*).

38 Plutarch, *The liues of the noble Grecians and Romanes*, trans. by Thomas North (1579). All quotations are from this edition, hereafter cited in the text.

39 For accounts of the connections between Antony and Hercules, see Patricia R. Robertson, "'This Herculean Roman": Shakespeare's Antony and the Hercules Myth', *Publications of the Arkansas Philological Association*, 10 (1984), 65–75; Richard Hillman, 'Antony, Hercules, and Cleopatra: "The Bidding of the Gods" and "the Subtlest Maze of All"', *Shakespeare Quarterly*, 38 (1987), 442–51.

40 See Frank Kermode, *Renaissance Essays: Shakespeare, Spenser, Donne* (London: Fontana, 1973), pp. 98–99; John Coates, "'The Choice of Hercules" in *Antony and Cleopatra*', in *Shakespeare Survey Volume 31*, ed. by Kenneth Muir (Cambridge: Cambridge University Press, 1978), pp. 45–52.

41 Early modern plays often ask audiences to engage with narratives through imagination and fantasy; the *Henry V* Chorus speeches are merely the most famous and explicit examples of this (Prologue; 2.0; 3.0; 4.0; 5.0; Epilogue).

42 I am grateful to Hannah August, Anita Butler, Jackie Watson and Sue Wiseman for their comments on this material at various stages. I also wish to acknowledge the support of the Arts and Humanities Research Council, which enabled me to complete the research for this chapter.

10

'Gazing in hir glasse of vaineglorie': negotiating vanity

Faye Tudor

This chapter explores the problems that mirrors presented for women, at whom they were often directed, and discusses the potential for women to circumvent some of the mirror's negative associations. This essay will present three self-portraits by Sofonisba Anguissola and Artemisia Gentileschi which will reveal the different approaches of these women to the problem of representing themselves. These women seek out a new method of either sidestepping the issues of self-representation, often through a redirection of the gaze, or by presenting themselves as adhering to a particular set of societal conditions.

Herbert Grabes's seminal work *The Mutable Glass: Mirror-imagery in Titles and Texts of the Middle Ages and English Renaissance* explores comprehensively the multiple meanings applied to the mirror in the early modern period, covering a vast number of exemplary texts from the period. He notes that the 'various properties of mirrors' were 'frequently the chief stimulus for employing the mirror-metaphor', and includes the 'false or flatt'ring' glass, which makes the individual appear more attractive, the 'true' or 'pure' mirror, which is 'closely associated with [...] knowledge of the Divine', the tarnished or darkened mirror, which is 'an expression of a lack of moral integrity [...] relating to knowledge of the Divine', and the brittleness of the mirror, which was used to signal transience.[1] The mirror metaphor, however, has yet more uses and Grabes describes instances in which 'man, or specifically another human being' is reflected in the mirror, and examples are frequent in literature which 'can offer us a mirror-image of human existence'.[2]

William Rankins's *A Mirrovr of Monsters* (1587) is just such a text. Rankins's focus is on the *dangers* of 'show' and his text addresses the 'manifold vices' and 'spotted enormities' that are the result of the 'infectious sight of Playes'.[3] Rankins is particularly concerned with pride, and notes that players 'colour their vanitie with humanitie [...] because vnder colour of humanitie, they present nothing but prodigious vanitie'.[4] Rankins expands his thoughts on pride and 'lecherie', using the character of Luxuria:

> Amongst ye rest to make hir séeme more amiable to hir best beloued shée painted hir faire face w^t spots of shadowed modestie: not fro~ *Apelles* shop, whose colours

are cou~terfeit, nor yet from *Zeuxes* famous in portratures. But sent from *Proser-pina* wife to *Pluto*. A welwisher to this wedlocke: better coulours then *Psyches* carried to *Venus* quicklie decaied, but these last longer then they should. After shée had hanged at hir eares manie costlie fauours of follie farre set from the Indians of *Anglia*, [Note: Wherein is noted the pride that is caused by plaiers, the beholders framing themselues to their leude life.] she embroidered hir haire with embossed brouches of beastlie desire, then gazing in hir glasse of vaineglorie, shée concluded as fine as may be.[5]

Here Rankins draws upon the stories of Apelles and Zeuxes, Greek painters celebrated in antiquity for the illusion of realism in their works, to illuminate the themes of the 'counterfeit' and the fake, since the lady has to paint on the 'spots of shadowed modestie'. However, the implication is that her choice of 'colours' for painting her face is even worse than this, because they are compared in quality to those used by Venus, a goddess classically associated with eroticism and vanity. The theme of painting is apparent throughout the entire passage, with Rankins using terms such as 'shadowed', 'painted', 'portratures', 'coulours', 'beholders' and 'framing'. All of these words are set within a framework of sin, shame, vanity and pride, and associated with fakery and the counterfeit, placing the creative arts in a negative light, and Rankins concludes this section by noting that Luxuria 'seemed vnto hir selfe a second *Narcissus*'.[6] Female artists who represent themselves are hampered by the mirror's classic, symbolic associations with women which regularly portrays them in an unfavourable light.

'She held a mirrhour bright'

In *The Faerie Queene* Edmund Spenser addresses the traditional emblems of vanity – the mirror and the (often naked) young woman transfixed by it – to generate a negative exemplary mirror which serves to warn:

> So proud she shyned in her Princely state,
> Looking to heauen; for earth she did disdayne,
> And sitting high; for lowly she did hate:
> Lo vnderneath her scornefull feete, was layne
> A dreadfull Dragon with an hideous trayne,
> And in her hand she held a mirrhour bright,
> Wherein her face she often vewed fayne,
> And in her selfe-lou'd semblance tooke delight;
> For she was wondrous fair, as any liuing wight
> (I.IV.10)

In Lucifera's 'sinfull house of Pride', which contains all of the sins (in the form of Lucifera's advisers) – idleness, gluttony, lechery, avarice, envy and wrath – and where visual excess means that the 'mayden' Queen's 'bright beautie did assay | To dim the brightness of her glorious throne, | And enuying her self, that too exceeding shone' (I.IV.8), the bright mirror is emblematic of self-love and vanity. The use of the word 'wondrous' links to the Latin word for the mirror, 'mirari', which means to 'wonder at', yoking together the sense of wonder with the looking glass, while 'semblance' reminds the reader that the self reflected in the mirror is not a 'real' self, but a likeness. Lucifera is presented as a warning against pride and its associated sins.

The warnings we see in literature such as Spenser's *Faerie Queene* are replicated in the commonplace texts of the period – for example, Thomas Salter's *A mirrhor mete for all mothers, matrones, and maidens, intituled the Mirrhor of Modestie* (1579), Robert Greene's *Mamillia, A mirrour or looking-glasse for the ladies of Englande* (1583), *My ladies looking glasse* (1616) by Barnabe Riche, Richard Brathwaite's *The English Gentlewoman* (1631), *A looking-glasse for women, or, A spie for pride: shewing the unlawfulnesse of any outward adorning* by T.H. (1644) or *A looking-glasse for good vvomen, held forth by way of counsell and advice to such of that sex and quality* written in 1645 by John Brinsley. The majority of these texts offered guidance to young women on how best to dress themselves, fix their hair and make-up, and to conduct themselves in society. The typical 'mirror text' directed at a female readership used the mirror as a metaphor: the 'exemplary mirror' is the place where the woman will find her example, not her flawed real self. The mirror that is used to produce multiple images, or is angled to redirect the gaze, transformed from its associations with pride and vanity, simultaneously allowed women to circumvent the male gaze, which flowed freely upon them, and allowed them to gaze back. In the case of the exemplary mirror, it (and its message) was often directed specifically at women, with warnings against vanity and sinfulness.

The predominant themes in literature produced for women, then, were warning, instruction and direction. As Katherine Usher Henderson and Barbara F. McManus observe, from the 'pulpit and the printing press, Renaissance Englishwomen were enjoined to avoid contentious discourse and persuaded that silence enhanced their femininity'.[7] Not only was this a problem for women in everyday life as it limited virtually every aspect of their behaviour and modes of expression, but it problematized the nature of any work women chose to produce. Women often had no option but to create their art or literature within the constraints imposed by a patriarchal society. As we shall see, the works of female artists such as Sofonisba Anguissola, considered within this context, illustrate that 'what was a fundamental problem for the Renaissance female artist' was 'the differentiation of herself as artist (the subject position) from her self as trope and theme for the male artist (the object position)'.[8]

James Shirley's (1596–1666) short poem 'To a Lady Upon a Looking-Glass Sent' (1646) concentrates on the mirror's association with self-love and pride: its speaker advises the young lady on the appropriate use for the mirror that

10 Sofonisba Anguissola, *Self-Portrait* (1554), Kunsthistorisches Museum Vienna

has been gifted to her.[9] He tells her that the mirror will 'present your beauty to your eye' (l. 2), perhaps suggesting that until now she was unaware of her physical beauty. She is urged to consider this beauty as something that can be used to help her better herself and the speaker warns her against allowing the mirror to generate pride: 'think that face was meant | to dress another by' (l. 4). Instead, the mirror is a tool for comparison – the viewer must use the mirror to determine whether or not her 'inward beauty' matches with her 'outward grace'. She must endeavour to make herself 'fair in soule as well as face' (l. 10). Acknowledging the potential for vanity, the speaker points to the mirror's alternative uses: it is not just for gazing at one's own beauty but can be a practical tool for self-improvement. The mirror is not something to be feared but it is an object that can offer the woman assistance in finding her inner self and matching it to her external beauty. The mirror is the tool for showing the inward self so that the woman who gazes upon her soul can beautify herself to ensure that she is as inwardly perfect as she is outwardly so.

The didactic theme of Shirley's poem encompasses, in part, the sense of trepidation surrounding women and mirrors. The woman requires proper direction in order for her to make appropriate use of the mirror and thus avoid its potential pitfalls. Without this instruction, the woman will fall victim to the sins of vanity, pride and self-love. A woman's most intimate moment, alone with her mirror, is interrupted. She may not gaze on herself without guidance, and thus even her personal, private sphere is not her own. As Shirley's poem illustrates, the creation of self is particularly fraught with difficulties for women who must manage and negotiate a series of negative emblems and associations. The regularly developing and advancing mirror technology was not enough to push forward new meanings, metaphors and emblems. While technology allowed writers and artists new ways of exploring themselves and the world around them, the mirror metaphors they used rarely altered.

Sofonisba Anguissola, daughter of Amilcare Anguissola, was afforded the opportunity of 'training in humanist studies', alongside her five similarly talented sisters – they studied topics such as Latin, music and painting.[10] Anguissola's father paid for additional professional painting lessons with the Mannerist painter Bernadino Campi and Anguissola later produced a number of works for Philip II of Spain.[11] In the self-portrait the boundaries between subject and object naturally collapse: an early self-portrait by Anguissola, *Self-Portrait* of 1554, demonstrates these key issues (Figure 10).[12]

Anguissola presents herself, but if she is 'self-fashioning', her image is not created by means of objects, by presenting wealth or grandeur; rather the lack of adornment focuses the viewer's attention on Sofonisba herself, as the single most important aspect of the portrait. Her demure appearance shows a careful attempt not to seem showy – she looks 'pious and decorous' as society advises.[13] Her appearance is in accordance with the recommendations to be found in conduct texts such as *The English Gentlewoman* (1631) by Richard Brathwaite. Brathwaite argues that clothing is nothing more than a practical necessity, essential for the human being after Adam and Eve sinned and ate the fruit of the Tree of Knowledge. This sin left all humans subsequently vulnerable to the elements and therefore clothing became necessary but, 'to glory then in these necessities is to glory in sinne'.[14] For a woman to have pride in her appearance, in her clothes and in fashions, is to revel in the sins of Adam and Eve. Brathwaite picks at the flimsy fashions of contemporary society:

> Was apparell first intended for keeping in naturall heat and keeping out accidentall cold? How comes it then that you wear these thinne Cobweb attires which can neither preserve heat nor repell cold. Of what incurable cold would these Butterfly-habits possess, the wearer were pride sensible of her selfe? [...] No necessity, but mere vanity.[15]

Anguissola's self-portrait shows her dressed appropriately by Brathwaite's standards as she is covered against the elements to the neck and wrist in plain, practical clothing. Mary D. Garrard suggests, however, that this is not purely for the purposes of necessity, for appearing as a proper gentlewoman. Instead, Anguissola is making a deliberate effort to minimize her femininity, to seek a 'safe position between "not woman" and "like a man"', her black clothing, a colour more frequently worn by men, and her lack of adornment supporting this theory.[16] In this way, Anguissola manages her image, carefully negotiating herself a space in a society, in a working environment that did not readily admit women – Anguissola 'transformed the limitations imposed upon her as a woman into an opportunity'.[17] Anguissola's self-portrait demonstrates ways for a woman to express herself, but also illustrates that the woman who creates a portrait of herself must adhere to a number of societal rules which direct her in the appropriateness of her appearance. More than the simple creation and exploration of the self, the woman's self-portrait concerns wider issues of her position in society and of the female artist's place in the early modern environment. In presenting herself to be looked upon, the female artist who painted herself had to negotiate a male-dominated system of looking:

> The gaze, then a metaphor for worldliness and virility, made of Renaissance woman an object of public discourse, exposed to scrutiny and framed by the parameters of propriety, display and 'impression management'. Put simply, why else paint a woman except as an object of display within male discourse?[18]

As Cheney and colleagues remind us, 'humanism [...] was long in liberating the "man-feminine" from her subordinate status' and Anguissola uses the 'outward' to represent an appropriate 'inward'.[19] In her hand Anguissola holds a small book, the text of which reads, 'Sophonisba Angussola virgo seipsam fecit, 1554'.[20] Having presented herself in modest attire against a plain background, she uses the text of the book to declare her status as 'virgo' – maiden – which may be a 'conscious reference to the famous woman painter of antiquity called [...] Marcia by Boccaccio'.[21] Anguissola's overall image in her self-portrait is 'highly determined, constrained and serious, unadorned and stern' but she has a 'very impressive gaze [...] in which humility and self-confidence combine' to form 'a distinctive artistic-professional self-image'.[22]

In order to present this image of herself, Anguissola has negotiated a number of potential difficulties that the female will encounter in any interaction with the mirror. The mirror, in writings with mirror-titles, was alternately portrayed as an object of revilement and an object of (potential) glory. In *The Mirrhor of modestie* (1579) by Thomas Salter, the author instructs us that there are two types of mirror: one is a 'Christall Mirrhor [...] by whiche Maidens now adaies, dooe onely take delight daiely to tricke and trime their tresses' (the literal mirror), and the other is 'made of an other maner of matter, and is of muche more worthe then any Christall Mirrhor' (the metaphorical or exemplary mirror).[23] For the woman, the literal mirror is fraught with dangers, and is associated with sin and pride, whereas the metaphorical mirror, often exemplary in flavour and therefore safe, reflects not the individual woman but the ideal at which she should aim. It is the second mirror that is of interest to Salter and to his female reader: 'for as the one teacheth how to attire the outward bodie, so the other guideth to garnishe the inwarde mynde'.[24] The young woman must be taught how to be virtuous and pure or she will easily fall into pride and sinfulness.[25] Salter argues that a woman need not be taught to read for if she can 'reade and vnderstande the Christian Poetes' she will 'also reade the Lasciuious bookes of Ouide [...] and of their wicked adulteries and abhominable Fornications'.[26] Women were aligned with 'carnality, weakness and nature, with 'womanishness', while the male was associated with 'spirituality, strength, and mind or reason'.[27]

Phillip Stubbes also comments on the adornment of the female body: 'For what a dotage is it (saith hee) to chau~ge thy naturall face which God hath made thee, for a painted one which thou hast made thy self.'[28] One of the key ways for a woman to alter her appearance, through the 'dying and coulouring of faces with artificiall colours [...] is most offensiue to God', and clothing is similarly frowned upon since Stubbes proclaims that it is 'vnpossible to take away pride, except sumptuouse apparell be taken away'.[29] Stubbes categorizes pride and apparel as 'two collaterall Cosins, apparell, and Pride (the Mother and Daughter) which can 'hardlie be dyuorced from the other, without the distructio~ of them both'.[30] Hamlet pauses to address this situation with Ophelia, when he discusses truth, love and beauty with her saying, 'I have heard of your paintings, too, well enough, | God hath given you one face, and you make yourselves | another' (3.1.145–47). The distinction is drawn between the real and the forged but the suggestion, as with Stubbes, is that it is sinful for her to paint herself, to make herself more beautiful. Ultimately, Hamlet returns to his original point that "'tis not alone [his] inky cloak [...] that can denote [him] truly' (1.2.75–83), when he claims that the external cannot fully express the internal. The demoniacal portrayal of the adornment of the female via clothes, hairstyles and make-up, begins to hint at the problems facing the female artist; unable to express herself on a personal level, how could she begin to fashion herself on canvas?

The female body was, in particular, a site of deviance: 'If a good woman's essence was an obedient body, then the very sexuality of that body suggested possible means of deviant behaviour through the excessive demands of female sexuality.'[31] Anguissola, in choosing to represent herself, was forced to negotiate this dialogue of sin, reproach, fear and weakness, in order to place herself in society both as woman and artist. The mirror in her painting is implied, not shown, absent from the pictorial space but implicit in the self-portrait and, as such, has no bearing on the depiction. The mirror presents particular problems for the woman; problems which are due, at least in part, to its classical associations with the sins of pride and vanity, and with the figure of Venus. The woman's experience with her mirror therefore has certain limitations set upon it, as illustrated in Shirley's short poem – a woman must make use of the mirror to improve herself in deeper and more spiritual ways, *not* for fixing her hair or make-up. Anguissola's self-portrait demonstrates the ways in which a female artist can negotiate certain societal norms in order to produce an image of herself: she presents herself to be looked at, dressed appropriately, holding a prayer book, but she stares back, therefore returning and perhaps challenging the viewer's gaze on her.

Given the warnings detailing the dangers for women gazing at themselves in the mirror, such as those seen in Salter, the female self-portrait becomes yet more intriguing. I have thus far established some of the problems of the mirror for Renaissance women and the ways in which the exemplary mirror characterized gazing into the looking-glass as sinful, while the extracts from Salter and Stubbes in this essay have reinforced the fact that these issues prevent a woman gazing in the mirror freely. Anguissola had to negotiate a number of social expectations in order to create a self-portrait. Another example by Anguissola, *Bernadino Campi Painting the Portrait of Sofonisba* (1550), illustrates her approach to depicting the art of painting, her skill, and herself, in which she uses the social expectations as a tool in her self-imaging (Figure 11).

In this image, the mirror is again only implied: obvious from the fact that Anguissola has depicted herself, yet there is no trace of the object in the painting. In fact, Anguissola's painting at first appears not to be a self-portrait at all, since it includes a participant rather than focusing solely on the artist. Anguissola paints herself being painted by her master, Bernadino Campi: her image, as represented on the canvas on the easel, is considerably larger than

11 Sofonisba Anguissola, *Bernadino Campi Painting Sofonisba Anguissola* (1557–79), Pinacoteca Nazionale, Siena

Campi's, who paints her. It is Anguissola who fills much of the pictorial space, as her master stands by her side. The artist, then, pushes herself forward, foregrounding her abilities over those of her master and presenting herself through the trope of the painting that is in fact a self-portrait.[32] By presenting herself alongside a master, she aligns herself with the skills and talents of an artist, though by including Campi in her self-portrait, Anguissola 'seems self-effacing' and it 'has the effect of cancelling or concealing her own pride and ambition.[33] Garrard offers this interpretation as 'an elaborate deferential conceit' which Anguissola uses as a 'kind of disguise' in which she 'distinctly one-ups Campi'.[34] While this may be the case, it seems that the woman must carefully negotiate the area of self-portraiture: Anguissola did not directly portray herself but drew upon her relationship with Campi to offer herself as a female artist of skill. This style of portraiture allows Anguissola to displace the male gaze and subordinate its power over the female body: Campi looks at her for practical reasons in order to produce an accurate portrait. Anguissola stares out from the painting, 'rivet[ing] the viewer, making the outsider complicit in deconstructing the teacher–pupil relationship' and the 'inscribing of male authority on the body of the female'.[35] The self-portrait allows women painters more control over their appearance so that rarely do they depict themselves as objects of eroticism or lust.

As Felicity Edholm describes, there are problems of perception that a woman must overcome in order to portray herself:

> Women are [...] constructed, in part at least, by the gaze, by others. Women in Western culture are always aware of being looked at, they are the object of the look, and the look is essentially male. Women therefore experience their own bodies and faces from outside as well as from within – a woman must continually survey herself. A woman has, then a split relation to her body and her face; she is both inside and outside, both self and other'.[36]

This suggests that the very process involved in creating a self-portrait is problematic for the woman artist. In a period when the mirror is, for the woman, enmeshed in symbols of pride, vanity, excess and shame, the very act of looking at herself is sinful. It seems that, for the early modern woman, the examination of the self is bound up with particular problems. Such is the import of the imagery and symbolism surrounding the mirror that any woman holding a mirror is, to Stubbes, carrying with her, the 'deuills spectacles' which 'allure vs to pride, & co~sequently to distructio~ for euer'.[37] Certainly, the mirror is associated with Venus, whose negative associations make her a poor example for women: the women whose tables were 'littered with combs, perfume, and cosmetic vases and jars and "similar tools of Venus" [...] were in fact not ladies' and 'the association of the mirror with courtesans and with Venus has antique roots', claims Cathy Santore.[38] A woman holding a mirror had already established, negative connotations, and the female artist must negotiate these associations if she wishes to portray herself. It seems prudent, for example, to exclude the mirror altogether, as Anguissola does. The woman who makes a self-portrait must also steer a path through society's guidelines and expectations of women.

Artemisia Gentileschi, in *Self-Portrait as the Allegory of Painting* (1630), depicts herself allegorically, a trope that avoids her being directly associated with the idea of self-imaging (Figure 12).[39] Gentileschi was the daughter of Orazio Gentileschi, one of the Caravaggisti, and she was 'one of the first female Italian artist[s] determined to compete with the male artists of her time'.[40] Her paintings often draw on mythological and mythical themes and are characterized by 'Caravaggesque realism' and chiaroscuro, a technique which uses light and dark to create a particularly dramatic style.[41]

12 Artemisia Gentileschi, *Self-Portrait as the Allegory of Painting* (1630),
Royal Collection, Windsor

A lavishly dressed Gentileschi, adorned with pieces of jewellery, leans into the pictorial space, her low neck-line revealing an expanse of cleavage. Gentileschi presents herself in the midst of artistic creation, her hair flicking out of her haphazard bun and her sleeves bunched up around her elbows. Her hands are occupied with the tools of her trade, the brushes and palette, and her awkward pose shows her in the act of painting. As her intent gaze suggests, the purpose of this painting seems to be to focus on the act of creation, rather than the artist herself. Gentileschi, by presenting herself as in the midst of action, not looking at a mirror or at the viewer, avoids the male gaze and therefore its dominating force; Gentileschi, as the allegory of painting, is neither passive nor accepting of the gaze. Just as in Anguissola's portrait, Gentileschi presents herself indirectly, via the trope of allegory. In creating this side-view of herself, it is most likely that Gentileschi used 'two mirrors, placed at nearly right angles', a technique that would be more difficult to execute than a traditional frontal self-portrait, and this may have been a deliberate act on Gentileschi's part, offered to 'demonstrate her virtuosity in creating a complex picture'.[42]

Gentileschi, in choosing to paint herself as an allegory, thus elides the traditional issues, for women, of subject and object.[43] Judith W. Mann argues that it is obvious that 'Artemisia did think about her anomalous role as a female painter in a male profession' and that 'she would recognise a strictly female opportunity to fuse her own image and that of the profession of painting (traditionally portrayed as a female figure)'. R. Ward Bissell also considers that the *Allegory of Painting* 'presented Artemisia with an opportunity not afforded male painters: to feature her self, in all her recognisability, as the personifications, and to cement this connection with a full and prominent signature'.[44] However, Bissell feels that Gentileschi did not accomplish this – 'in type the female is more Polyhymnia than Artemisia, and the modest initials "A.G.F." on the right hand corner of the tabletop are threatened by shadow'. Instead, claims Bissell, 'what Gentileschi has done is to vitalize an abstract construct, and through a dazzling technique, to acclaim her mastery as *La Pittura's* sister'.[45] It seems, then, that Gentileschi's self-portrait is successful in allowing her to avoid the typical restraints imposed upon women, and avoiding the themes often associated with women, mirrors and self-imaging. However, the painting's success is limited in that it fails to truly move beyond the expectations and constraints that women face. Anguissola and Gentileschi both create images of themselves, they both use tropes to escape the fact of their self-imaging, but they both do so within the boundaries set for them. For example, Anguissola's first image portrays her demurely dressed holding a prayer book, signifiers that meet with social expectation; while the image of herself painting her master, and Gentileschi's allegorical self-portrait both play with notions of self-representation but do so in a way that does not threaten social order.

While the technologies of the mirror and theories of vision developed rapidly throughout this period, the images of Anguissola and Gentileschi, combined with the discussion of Shirley's 'To A Lady Upon a Looking-Glass Sent', illustrate that the mirror is still being used in its traditional context of sin, pride and vanity, and blended with Platonic theories of vision to fall in line with the Pauline directive in I Corinthians, 'For now we see through a glasse darkely: but then shal we se face to face. Now I knowe in parte: but then shal I knowe euen as I am knowen.'[46] Mirrors are implicated in the struggles for definition and power, particularly as they relate to women, who are at the centre of representation in their self-portraits but who are short of institutional and formal power. In the development of ways of seeing, the mirror appears as a tool of self-improvement, as a means of gazing into the truth of the soul, or what the soul ought to be, and as a motif for true self worth. The mirror and its reflection both expands and limits the possibilities of the gaze, whether by offering the woman an opportunity to redirect the gaze that falls upon her, thus securing her privacy, or by inhibiting the content and composition of the female self-portrait.

Notes

1 Herbert Grabes, *The Mutable Glass: Mirror-imagery in Titles and Texts of the Middle Ages and English Renaissance* (Cambridge: Cambridge University Press, 1982), pp. 104–05.

2 Grabes, p. 116.

3 William Rankins, *A Mirrovr of Monsters*, (1587), A1r; Janet Clare, 'Marlowe's Theatre of Cruelty', in *Constructing Christopher Marlowe*, ed. by James Allan Downie (Cambridge: Cambridge University Press, 2000) pp. 74–88 (p. 86).

4 Rankins, fol. 2r.

5 Rankins, fol. 4r.

6 Rankins, fol. 4v.

7 Katherine Usher Henderson and Barbara F. McManus, *Half Humankind: Contexts and Texts of the Controversy about Women in England 1540-1640* (Urbana and Chicago: University of Illinois Press, 1985), p. 54.

8 *Self-Portraits by Women Painters*, ed. by Liana De Girolami Cheney, Alicia Craig Faxon and Kathleen Lucey Russo (Aldershot: Ashgate, 2000), p. 556.

9 James Shirley, 'To A Lady Upon a Looking-Glass Sent', in *Ben Jonson and the Cavalier Poets*, ed. by Hugh Maclean (New York: Norton, 1974), p. 193.

10 Jo Eldridge Carney, *Renaissance and Reformation 1500–1620* (Westport, CT: Greenwood Press, 2001), p. 14.

11 Carney, pp. 14–15. Julia K. Dabbs describes Anguissola as 'undoubtedly the most documented and celebrated woman artist of the early modern period' and notes that 'her fame was first proclaimed by Giorgio Vasari in his 1568 edition of *Le Vite de' più eccellenti pittori* even though [...her...] career was in its early stages' (Julia

K. Dabbs, *Life Stories of Women Artists, 1550–1800* (Aldershot: Ashgate, 2009), p. 107).

12 Sofonisba Anguissola, *Self-Portrait* (1554), Kunsthistorisches Museum, Vienna, *Web Gallery of Art* www.wga.hu/index1.html [accessed 22 May 2009].

13 Fredrika H. Jacobs notes that the 'prescriptives for the ideal *gentil-donna* [were] set forth in an ever-increasing number of sixteenth century texts' including Giovan Giorgio Trissino's *I Ritratti* (1524), Lodovico Dolce's *Della institution delle donne* (1554), and Domenico Bruni's *Difesi delle donne* (1559). 'Woman's Capacity to Create: The Unusual Case of Sofonisba Anguissola', *Renaissance Quarterly*, 47 (1994), 74–101 (p. 75).

14 Richard Brathwaite, *The English Gentlewoman* (1631), p. 3.

15 Brathwaite, pp. 3–4.

16 Mary D. Garrard, 'Here's Looking at Me: Sofonisba Anguissola and the Problem of the Woman Artist', *Renaissance Quarterly*, 47 (1994), 556–622 (p. 586).

17 Carney, p. 15.

18 Patricia Simons, 'Women in Frames: The Gaze, the Eye, the Profile in Renaissance Portraiture', *History Workshop*, 25 (1988), 4–30 (p. 8).

19 Cheney and others (eds), p. 28.

20 Sylvia Ferino-Pagden and Maria Kusche, *Sofonisba Anguissola: Renaissance Woman* (Washington, DC: National Museum of Women in the Arts, 1995), p. 19.

21 Ferino-Pagden and Kusche, p. 18.

22 Ferino-Pagden and Kusche, p. 18.

23 Thomas Salter, *The Mirrhor of modestie* (1579), A6r–v.

24 Salter, A6v.

25 Kate Aughterson finds that 'most of the texts were not actually addressed to women, but to men who had responsibility for women, whether as fathers, husbands or brothers' and that 'conduct literature … had a booming market share in early modern England' (p. 67). However, Aughterson argues that 'even if filtered through the reading of men', most conduct literature is 'addressed ultimately to women' (p. 67). She finds that conduct literature is 'exhortative, claiming certain rules for the public and private behaviour of women' and that 'the content of the exhortation is structured around certain characteristics, described as ideal feminine virtues: chastity, obedience, humility and silence' (p. 67). However, while 'it is safe to argue that conduct literature shows us how and what women were asked to be, it does not … tell us what they were' (p. 68). Aughterson finds two images of women emerging – the 'picture of women in need of counselling, instructing and leading' and 'accounts of active and successful women struggling with both this ideology and other economic, social and political troubles' (p. 69). See *Renaissance Woman: A Sourcebook: Constructions of Femininity in England*, ed. by Kate Aughterson (London: Routledge, 1995). Particularly, see the introduction to Chapter 3, 'Conduct', pp. 67–69.

26 Salter, B7v.

27 Marina Warner, *Monuments and Maidens: The Allegory of the Female Form* (London: Pan Books, 1985) p. 63.

28 Phillip Stubbes, *The anatomie of abuses* (1583), F1v.

29 Stubbes, F2r.

30 Stubbes, D2r. It is worth noting that the writings of authors like Stubbes and Salter, in which women are advised to be uninterested in appearance, sumptuous clothing and accessories, appear to conflict with ideas of rank, which would suggest that higher ranking women should have expensive, well-made lavish clothing.

31 Irene Burgess, '"The Wreck of Order" in Early Modern Women's Drama', *Early Modern Literary Studies*, 6 (2001), 6.1–24 http://extra.shu.ac.uk/emls/06-3/burgwrec.htm [accessed 1 October 2010].

32 John T. Paoletti and Gary M. Radke argue that this painting is a 'wry commentary on the very structures of artistic production (a story within the story, so to speak, that points to male construction of female form), as well as a witty reference to the standard imagery of St. Luke painting the Virgin' – *Art in Renaissance Italy*, ed. by John T. Paoletti and Gary M. Radke (London: Laurence King, 1997), p. 16.

33 Garrard, p. 560.

34 Garrard, pp. 561–62.

35 Paoletti and Radke, p. 16.

36 Felicity Edholm, 'Beyond the Mirror: Women's Self-Portraits', in *Imagining Women: Cultural Representations and Gender*, ed. by Francis Bonner and others (Cambridge: Polity Press, 1995), p. 135.

37 Stubbes, G1v.

38 Cathy Santore, 'The tools of Venus', *Renaissance Studies*, 11 (1997), 179–207 (p. 179).

39 Artemisia Gentileschi, *Self-Portrait as the Allegory of Painting* (1630), Royal Collection, Windsor, *Web Gallery of Art* www.wga.hu/frames-e.html?/html/g/gentiles/artemisi [accessed 22 May 2009].

40 Carney, p. 159.

41 Carney, p. 159.

42 Judith W. Mann, 'The Myth of Artemisia as Chameleon: A New Look at the London *Allegory of Painting*', in *Artemisia Gentileschi: Taking Stock*, ed. by Judith W. Mann (Turnhout: Brepols, 2005), pp. 51–77 (p. 57).

43 See Mann, pp. 51–77 (p. 55).

44 R. Ward Bissell, *Artemisia Gentileschi and the Authority of Art* (University Park, PA: Pennsylvania State University Press, 1999), pp. 65–69.

45 Bissell, pp. 65–69.

46 *The Geneva Bible: A Facsimile of the 1560 Edition* (Peabody, MA: Hendrickson, 1969), I Corinthians, 13:12, p. 81. [Note at 'now we see' which reads 'the mysteries of God' – now we see (the mysteries of God) through a glasse, darkly.] St Paul's words are considered particularly difficult to translate. The use of 'through' has often led critics to suppose that the 'glass' St Paul invokes is a clear pane of glass, a window. For example, Debora Shuger argues that 'one looks through rather than at' some mirrors, including the Pauline mirror, which is treated as a window rather than as a mirror – see Debora Shuger, 'The "I" of the Beholder: Renaissance Mirrors and the Reflexive Mind', in *Renaissance Culture and the Everyday*, ed. by Patricia Fumerton and Simon Hunt (Philadelphia: University of Pennsylvania Press, 1999), pp. 21–41 (pp. 30–31). However, in I Corinthians in the Vulgate, the word 'speculum' is used, that is, a mirror –'Videmus nunc per speculum in ænigmate : tunc autem facie ad faciem. Nunc cognosco ex parte : tunc autem

cognoscam sicut et cognitus sum'. *Biblia Sacra juxta Vulgatam Clementinam 1598*, ed. by Michael Tweedale (2005) http://vulsearch.sf.net/html [accessed 24 March 2008]. The glass is a mirror and the use of 'through' indicates that the mirror is the medium by which the individual must analyse the religious self.

11

'Tickling the senses with sinful delight': the pleasure of reading comedies in early modern England

Hannah August

In the introduction to *Shakespearean Sensations* (2013), Katharine A. Craik and Tanya Pollard foreground the degree to which early modern antitheatricalists' anxieties about the theatre are couched in descriptions of sensory affect. They cite Stephen Gosson's complaint that plays' 'straunge consortes of melody [...] tickle the ear', the actors' 'costly apparel [...] flatter[s] the sight', while their 'effeminate gesture[s] [...] ravish the sence' and their 'wanton speache [...] whet[s] desire too inordinate lust'.[1] The final item on Gosson's list of sensory dangers, and its consequence, exemplifies what Craik and Pollard go on to demonstrate through further examples from the corpus of antitheatrical writing: namely, that '[a]ntitheatricalists' concerns about plays' physical and emotional consequences centred especially on their potentially aphrodisiac effects'.[2]

These are, crucially, plays in performance. Although Craik and Pollard state that their volume's 'particular aim [...] is to consider together the sensations aroused by reading and playgoing', neither they nor their contributors consider the sensations that might be aroused by encountering plays on the page.[3] It is my aim in this chapter to do precisely that, with particular focus on printed comedies: the genre of which, as Philip Stubbes points out a year after Gosson, 'the matter and ground is love', meaning that they are most likely to produce the same aphrodisiac effects that the antitheatricalists fear in performance.[4] Where performed comedies supposedly produce a titillating pleasure that relies on the stimulus of the external senses, printed comedies offer a pleasure that relies on the workings of what was, in the period, conceived of as an 'internal sense' – the imagination.[5]

Antitheatricalists routinely argued that printed drama was less sensually overpowering and therefore less dangerous than performed drama; what I hope to demonstrate is that, on the contrary, the material contexts of playreading and the role played by the imagination may have enabled a fuller submission to the 'sinful lusts of the flesh' than did the playhouse.[6] Furthermore, I argue, a variety of dramatic paratexts appear to both create and respond to a market desire for printed comedies as repositories of the type of erotic pleasure that antitheatricalists feared audiences would experience in the theatre. That such a motivation for playreading existed is confirmed by the early seventeenth-century manuscript commonplace book of William Drummond of Hawthornden, which I discuss in my conclusion. Craik and Pollard point out that 'early modern writers who discussed how it felt to experience [plays and poetry] shared a conceptual and discursive vocabulary' but fail to consider the experience of readers who encountered plays *as* poetry (rather than performance).[7] In this chapter, I place pressure on the way in which the crossover between playgoing and playreading markets established by scholarship may go hand in hand with a similar crossover in the motivations and responses of sixteenth- and seventeenth-century English playgoers and playreaders encountering comedies on stage and on the page.[8]

When Gosson considers the relative demerits of comedy and tragedy, he finds comedy particularly perturbing because its sensory affect inheres in the provision of pleasure, and pleasure is what leads to moral incontinence. As he puts it, '[c]omedies so tickle our senses with a pleasanter vaine [than tragedies] that they make us lovers of laughter, and pleasure, without any meane, both foes to temperance' (C6r). The quality of this pleasure, and the quality of the moral incontinence, can be inferred from Stubbes's description of the genre's recurring subject matter. It is not simply love that forms the 'matter and ground' of comedies, but sex ('bawdrie, [...] whordome, adulterie', as Stubbes puts it), and the genre's stock characters are those in search of it: 'whores, queanes, bawdes, scullions, Knaves, Curtezans, lecherous old men, amorous yong men, with such like of infinit varietie' (L7r). Despite the fact that he is writing before the heyday of the early modern professional theatre, Gosson's description remains superficially apt well into the seventeenth century, which sees the London stage peopled with Dutch courtesans, honest whores and cunning lovers, engaged in losing both labour and maidenheads in the pursuit of love.[9]

As Craik and Pollard correctly identify, the concern for the antitheatricalists is that the erotic subject matter of comedies will have an aphrodisiac effect upon audiences. William Prynne in his 1633 *Histrio-mastix* describes 'those enchanting, powerfull, overcomming sollicitations unto lewdnesse' that occur when 'the Bawdes, the Panders, the Lovers, the Wooers, the Adulterers, the Womans, or Love-sicke persons parts are lively represented' on the public stage (Y3v), and Gosson warns that 'vice is learned with beholding, sense is tickled, desire pricked, and those impressions of mind are secretly conveyed over to the gazers, which the plaiers do counterfeit on the stage' (G4r). The amorous emotional states of the embodied characters can be involuntarily adopted by the spectators over the course of a performance: it is unsurprising that the antitheatricalists repeatedly stress the fact that playhouses and brothels share a common clientele.[10] Much of what Gosson calls the 'sinfull delight' (G2ʳ) of seeing a comedy performed, it is clear, is imagined as stemming from its bawdy or amorous scenes' provision of a pleasurable titillation to the audience.

Despite the fact that in certain formulations of early modern sense theory 'titillation' could constitute a sense in and of itself, for both playwrights and antitheatricalists this pleasure was conceived of as being created largely by the visual and aural stimuli of performance.[11] The epilogue to Phineas Fletcher's *Sicelides*, performed in 1615 at King's College, Cambridge, confirms the dual importance of engaging the senses of sight and hearing, beginning:

> As in a Feast, so in a Comedy,
> Two Sences must be pleas'd, in both the Eye.
> In Feasts, the Eye and Taste must be invited,
> In Comedies, the Eye and Eare delighted:
> And he that onely seekes to please but either,
> While both he doth not please, he pleaseth neither[.][12]

The pleasure of attending a performance of a comedy – which, as I have argued above, was often construed as an erotic pleasure – inhered in the stimulation of the senses of sight and hearing. This stimulation is naturally described in antitheatrical rhetoric as a dangerous enticement to sin. Gosson, for instance, portrays the effect of hearing metrical verse thus:

> Because the sweete numbers of Poetrie flowing in verse, do wonderfully tickle the hearers eares, the devill hath tyed this to most of our playes, that whatsoever he would have sticke fast to our soules, might slippe downe in suger by this intisement, for that which delighteth never troubleth our swallow[.] (D8ᵛ)

It is worth noting that even though Gosson is describing the effect on an audience of the aural stimulus of verse, he cannot help dressing his point in figurative language that evokes two further senses, those of touch (the verse 'tickle[s] the hearers eares') and taste (the devil's words are swallowed with as much delight as sugar). The depiction of performance becomes one of sensory overload, in which the combination of stimuli is such that the audience is 'ravish[ed] [...] with varietie of pleasure' (E1ʳ). Elsewhere antitheatrical rhetoric fixates on the dangers of what is *seen*: John Rainolds, for instance, in his 1599 *Overthrow of Stage-Plays*, refuses to allow for the remove of mimesis, and expressly condemns the cross-dressing of boy players for the emotions it has the ability to incite. Rainolds asks his correspondent, William Gager, if he can 'accuse [himself] [...] of anie wanton thought stirred up in [him] by looking on a beautifull Woman? If you can; then ought you beware of beautifull boyes transformed into women by putting on their raiment, their feature, lookes and facions.'[13] It is the *sight* of the boy players impersonating women that is a spur to wanton thoughts: in the theatre, as in other areas of early modern discourse, sight is at the top of the hierarchy of the senses.[14] This is why the printer's address to the 1620 quarto of J.C.'s *The Two Merry Milkmaids* can claim that the comedy 'was made more for the Eye, then the Eare; lesse for the Hand, then eyther'.[15] The sensual pleasures inherent in this 'Pleasant Comedie' lay, according to the printer, in seeing and, to a lesser extent, hearing it performed – the printed book which the reader holds in his or her hand is not the play's intended incarnation.

The absence of sensory stimulation inherent in silent, solitary reading is precisely what causes Prynne to find printed plays a more acceptable evil than performed plays. '[W]hen a man reads a Play', he states:

> he ever wants that *viva vox*, that flexanimous rhetoricall Stage-elocution, that lively action and representation of the Players themselves which put life and vigor into these their Enterludes, and make them pierce more deeply into the Specta-tors eyes, their eares and lewde affections, precipitating them on to lust: yea, the eyes, the eares of Play-readers want all those lust-enraging objects, which [...] Spectators meet with in the Play-house[.] (6C2^v–6C3^r)

For Prynne, the lack of speech and action is the printed play's main asset: when a playtext no longer posseses the 'life and vigor' that actors give to it, it can no longer affect the senses that are most susceptible in the playhouse, and is far less likely to 'precipitat[e] [its readers] on to lust'. Yet Prynne reckons without the power of the imagination, understood by early modern writers such as Robert Burton to be itself a sense, albeit an 'inward' one.[16] Because the imagination functions through the translation of signals received by the external senses, the imaginary acts required in reading are often described using the vocabulary of external sensory affect.[17] In the subsequent section, I argue that the identity of the language used to describe response to 'lively represented' mimetic action and to that printed on the page invokes an identity of sensory experience – and that the material context of the reader's engagement with the play may in fact involve a more complete abdication of self in the pursuit of erotic pleasure than does the spectator's.

In 1655, the scholar and divine Meric Casaubon published his *Treatise Concerning Enthusiasm*, in which he discusses the pleasure of reading. For Casaubon, this pleasure is sensory. It rests largely in the type of figurative language central to much dramatic writing, which creates what he calls 'paper pictures'; crucially, in Casaubon's account, these have the same visual sensory appeal when they consist of words on the page, as when the things they describe are visibly present.[18] Quoting Cicero to support his argument, Casaubon remarks that 'every Metaphor (and so of the rest [of the rhetorical figures]) that is proper and natural, exposeth the things that are spoken of to the senses; especially to that of the eyes' (N3^r). Regardless of whether the things are 'spoken of' or encoun-tered through silent reading, the sense which they affect is predominantly that of sight. This is because, as Casaubon puts it, 'a man may see inwardly, as well as outwardly': describing his experiences of reading the vivid figurative language of the classical authors, he notes, 'I do not only phansy to my self, that I see those things that they describe; but also find in my self (as I phansy) the very *same* content and pleasure that I should, if my eyes beheld them' (N4ʳ; my emphasis). This equivalence of sensory pleasure created by imagining the things described with one's 'inward eye' is also invoked by certain dramatic paratexts. Robert Chamberlain's commendatory verse which prefaces Richard Brome's 1640 comedy *The Antipodes* describes the power of reading to 'transport' the reader:

> thy Book, being in my hand,
> Hurried my Soule to th'Antipodian strand,
> Where I did feast my Fancy, and mine Eyes
> With such variety of Rarities
> That I perceive thy Muse frequents some shade,
> Might be a Grove for a Pierian Maide.[19]

Chamberlain goes still further than Casaubon: deploying a metaphor of taste which serves to highlight the sensory experience of playreading, he removes the contingent 'if', and declares simply that both his imagination *and* his eyes are feasted by his reading of Brome's play. His eyes do not feast on the letters printed on the page, but on the 'variety of Rarities' made present through the creation of 'paper pictures'.

The power of printed plays to influence the senses to the same degree that they do in performance is asserted by the couplet entitled 'The Stationer to Dramatophilus' that appears on the title page of the 1631 edition of Francis Beaumont and John Fletcher's *A King and no King*. Punning on the play's title, it declares 'A Play and no Play, who this Booke shall read, | Will judge, and weepe, as if 'twere done indeed'.[20] The 'Booke' is 'no play' (as the century progresses, the word is used more and more to denote performance only, while 'work' or 'poem' describes a print incarnation), and yet it is, because the text's ability to affect the reader intellectually and emotionally will cause him or her to respond with judgement and grief, just as at a performance with the full range of sensory stimuli identified by the antitheatricalists. The written word's influence on the imagination is stressed still further by John Ford in his contribution to the commendatory verses that preface Philip Massinger's 1629 *The Roman Actor*. Ford's praise of Massinger inheres in his claim that the actions of Paris:

> meerly were related
> Without a Soule, Untill thy abler Pen
> Spoke them, and made them speake, nay Act agen
> In such a height, that Heere to know their Deeds
> Hee may become an Actor that but Reades.[21]

While Ford begins by lauding the play in performance, by the final line he is making a claim not for the equivalence but the *superiority* of reading to spectatorship. What Ford asserts is that Massinger's play is of such a quality that it will enable the reader not merely to identify with Paris (the 'Actor' of the final line and the play's title), but, for the duration of the reading, to *become* him. This is more than assuming the 'impressions of mind' of the characters that one watches onstage, as Gosson feared audiences would do: this is a total abandonment of self enabled by complete engagement with the dramatic narrative, something that is, paradoxically, only enabled by the *lack* of an actor to personate Paris on stage. How can the spectator imagine *himself* Paris when confronted by an actor who is, for the duration of the performance, clearly the embodiment of the character? Only when reading the play can his imagination fully take hold and enable him to identify himself not *with* Paris, but *as* Paris.

That such an immersive dramatic reading experience was conceived of as furnishing at least one category of readers with an erotic pleasure which surpassed that of spectatorship is indicated by Richard Brathwaite's 1638 conduct book, *A Nursery for Gentry*. One of Prynne's reasons for preferring playbooks over performance is that the former 'may be read without using or beholding any effeminate amorous, lustfull gestures, complements, kisses, dalliances, or embracements; [...] any lively representations of Venery, whoredome, adultery, and the like, which are apt to enrage mens lusts' (6C2ᵛ). Yet as Casaubon and the dramatic paratexts discussed above aver, readers are just as capable of 'beholding' the amorous scenes of a play in their imaginations, despite the absence of the titillating 'lively representation' of performance. What Brathwaite implies in the following description of young men reading 'Idle pamphlets' (which almost certainly include plays) is that these readers are also imaginatively 'using' the 'lustfull gestures, complements, kisses, [and] embracements' about which they read.[22] Brathwaite describes the reading preferences of 'voluptuous' young gentlemen, who are

> altogether for Stories of Love; where every line workes such moving impressions in their unsteady fancies: as they reduce every period of Loves discourse, to a Sceane of Action; wherein they wish themselves Prime-actors, to close in a personal re-greet, with so light and sensuall a Relation.[23]

'Stories of Love', as Stubbes has identified, are the dominant subject matter of comedies, and the likelihood that the young men's reading material includes drama is further implied by Brathwaite's deployment of a theatrical metaphor: the power exerted by the written word upon the young men's 'unsteady fancies' enables the transformation of the textually encountered 'period[s] of Loves discourse' into 'Sceane[s] of Action', in which, as in the verse by Ford quoted above, the readers can imagine themselves 'Prime-actors'. Lacking a concrete visual referent in the body of the actor, playreading enables what playgoing does not: the opportunity not to vicariously experience the amorous emotions enacted by those on stage, but to imaginatively 'close in a *personal* re-greet' with the characters depicted in scenes of love-making, to 'feel', as Craik puts it in her discussion of Brathwaite's *Nursery*, 'as though they are participating in them as central protagonists'.[24]

As Brathwaite points out, even a silently read textual 'Relation' of a 'Story of Love' can be 'sensuall'. That the erotic pleasure produced by this sensuality can in fact be amplified by the context of private reading is testified by seventeenth-century descriptions of the role of the imagination in the pathology of love-sickness. Lesel Dawson in her work on the subject notes that while writers in the early modern period 'held erotic obsession to be a real and virulent disease', they also acknowledged that the lover's 'agonies are simultaneously experienced as extreme pleasure'.[25] This pleasure most often inheres in imagining the object of one's desire, an activity that is facilitated by privacy. The section of André du Laurens's 1599 *Discourse of the Preservation of the Sight* that deals with 'melancholie which commeth by the extremitie of loue' notes that the love-sick 'lov[e] solitarines, the better to feed & follow [their] foolish imaginations'.[26] They also love reading plays: Burton in the *Anatomy of Melancholy* lists 'play-bookes' among the reading material of 'Inamoratoes', and when Richard West declares in the commendatory verse which prefaces the 1640 edition of Jacques Ferrand's *Erotomania* that 'Playes are the Sores of Love, this Book the Cure', it is clear from the context that the plays he is referring to are printed, not performed.[27] The internal sense of the imagination, crucial to the creation of pleasure in both activities, is activated to its fullest extent when the reader/lover is alone, his or her fixation on the text unimpeded by external distractions. Thus when Prynne notes that 'Stage-playes may be privately read over without any danger of infection by ill company [...] without giving any ill example, without any incouraging or maintaining of Players in their ungodly profession, or without participating with them in their sinnes' (6C2ᵛ), his observation is countered by contemporary writing that holds that it is precisely the solitary nature of the readerly encounter with the amorous playbook that enables the imagination to take full flight.[28]

Participation in the pleasurable 'sinnes' depicted by actors of comedies did not have to take place in the playhouse: as the clergyman Anthony Burgess warned the 'Christian reader' of his 1658 treatise on original sin, 'many times sinne is acted by the Imagination with delight and content, without any relation at all to the external Actings of sinne.' The 'conceits of [...] lust' that were the offerings of many early modern comedies and which Burgess ordered his reader to shun were, according to contemporary discourses on the imagination and erotic pleasure, just as likely to 'defile' solitary playreaders as they were playgoers – if not more so.[29] The seventeenth-century physician Thomas Fienus explicitly states that 'the imagination is fitted by nature to move the appetite and excite the emotions': in the next section of this chapter, I want to consider some of the paratextual rhetoric in pre-Restoration quartos of commercial comedies which seems to imply that publishers and playwrights acknowledged this fact, marketing printed comedies as repositories of erotic pleasure, an emotion created by the sensory power of the imagination.[30]

When Thomas Nabbes dedicates his 1638 *Tottenham Court: A Pleasant Comedie* to William Mills, he writes that if Mills will 'vouchsafe the reading of it, [he] will find (after the light title) a light subiect, more gravely drest then the vulgar perhaps expected'.[31] As it is hardly the purely descriptive 'Tottenham Court' that constitutes the 'light title', it is clear that the expectations of 'the vulgar' are created by the conventional phrase 'A Pleasant Comedie', which appears on numerous title pages of commercial comedies printed prior to the Restoration. The adjective 'pleasant' is rarely appended to other dramatic genres, and an examination of the sensual connotations of the verb 'please' as it occurs in other comedies' paratexts helps to clarify what exactly it was that 'the vulgar' may have hoped for when their expectations were confounded by the 'grave dress' of *Tottenham Court*.

In the epistle that prefaces Edward Sharpham's 1607 comedy *The Fleer*, the printer casts the play as a book 'to make you laugh and lie downe too, if you please'.[32] 'Laugh and lie down' is proverbial, and often has sexual connotations: it is used, for instance, in the bawdy exchange between the female 'Merry Beggars' and their suitors in Richard Brome's 1652 *A Jovial Crew*, in which a passage of innuendo culminates with the women being told that they will 'laugh and lye down | When [their] bellies are full'.[33] In the epistle to *The Fleer*, the normally formulaic 'if you please', when used in conjunction with the first half of the sentence, seems to be advertising a pleasure that is to do with erotic stimulation: if the reader is pleased by the comedy's titillating subject matter, he will need to 'lie down'. Fienus held that the emotions created by the sense of the imagination could have a physical effect upon the body, and in hinting at the sexual quality of the pleasure that may arise from reading, the epistle implies that the physical alteration in the reader's body may be that typically produced by sexual arousal.[34]

Given that it is most noticeably male bodies that exhibit physical alteration as a result of imaginatively produced erotic pleasure, it is unsurprising that one of the most common ways of advertising playbooks as repositories of such pleasure is to metaphorically construct them as female.[35] Such a strategy can be found in the anonymous epistle to Thomas Middleton's 1608 *The Family of Love*. Lamenting the time that has elapsed between the play's first performance and its subsequent publication (a lag of perhaps five years), the epistle's writer explains his concern in these terms: 'For Plaies in this Citie are like wenches new falne to the trade, onelie desired of your neatest gallants, whiles the'are fresh: when they grow stale they must be vented by Termers and Cuntrie chapmen.'[36]

In equating playbooks with prostitutes, the epistle explicitly invokes a sexual desire for the printed play, the link reinforced by the orthographical pun in 'Cuntrie'. Thus when the writer declares in the sentence that follows, 'I know not how this labor will *please*', the type of reading pleasure invoked – as in the epistle to *The Fleer* – is rhetorically linked with the sexual desire of the preceding simile. The verb 'please' when deployed in proximity to other sexual metaphors assumes its erotic connotations, and the ways in which a 'pleasant comedy' is conceived of as pleasing its readers may have more to do with the provision of a titillating erotic pleasure created by the sensual stimulation of the imagination than the conventional phrase seems to imply.[37] This is particularly the case if 'comedy' is a generic index of a bawdy subject matter, as Stubbes, for instance, holds it is, and as playwrights such as Middleton openly affirmed: see, for example, his titling of the epistle to the 1611 *The Roaring Girl*, 'To the Comicke Play-readers: Venery, and Laughter', which promotes sex over humour as the most immediately obvious attribute of the comic genre.[38]

The paratextual sexualization of printed comedies is most evident in the prefatory materials of plays whose titles name their female protagonists. Thus 'F.T.' in his contribution to the commendatory verses prefacing Richard Brome's 1632 *The Northern Lass* further develops the image of the playbook as prostitute when he begins his verse to Brome by exclaiming, 'What! wilt thou prostitute thy *Mistresse* (Friend) | And make so rich a Beauty common[?]' He continues: 'What end | Do'st thou propose? Shee was thine owne, but now | All will enioy her free', before concluding that Brome must have 'tri'd her, found her chast, | And fear'st not that Shee'll lewdly be embrac't'.[39] The verse's conclusion does not quite contain the common anxiety about the ungovernable circulation of a multiplicity of print copies in the public sphere, which is akin to the period's pervasive anxiety about women's chastity, and despite the assertion that *The Northern Lass* will not be subjected to 'lewd embraces', the commendatory verse that follows it, by 'St. Br.', casts the play not just as an object of desire but of *incestuous* desire, 'St. Br.' addressing Brome thus: 'Although I call you by a Brothers name, | I must confesse (nor doe I feare the shame) | I am in love with your faire Daughter, this.'[40]

In another eponymously female play, John Fletcher's 1610 *The Faithful Shepherdess*, Fletcher takes pains to stress that his rationale for publishing the play is *not* to 'ravish kinde Atturnies, | in their journies'.[41] This assumes that other printed comedies – perhaps most often those with female titles – intend to do exactly that, and implies that the rhetorical construction of playbooks as erotically desirable intersects with an understanding of them as objects that offer to their male readers a pleasurable 'ravishment', defined by the OED as 'the transportation of [the] mind with the strength of some emotion; the filling with ecstasy, intense delight, or sensuous pleasure; the entrancement, captivation, or enrapturing'. In Gosson's conceit, it is 'effeminate gesture' that 'ravish[es] the sence' in performance, but in Fletcher's, it is the playreading lawyers' imaginative engagement with less lofty comedies than *The Faithful Shepherdess* that provides them with such 'sensuous pleasure'.

As Craik reminds us, 'pornography', certainly in the early modern period, is 'a matter not so much of textual content but readerly approach'.[42] Although the dramatic paratexts discussed above seem to imply an expectation that reading printed comedies could, through engaging the internal sense of the imagination, produce an emotion that equated to an erotic pleasure, they do not prove that early modern readers actually approached them in this way. In the final section of this chapter I want to consider the example of an early seventeenth-century reader who appears to have treated printed comedies as precisely the locations of sensually stimulated erotic pleasure that their paratexts took pains to construct them as.

One of the aspects of playreading that makes it preferable, in Prynne's opinion, to attending a performance, is that 'he that reades a Stage-play may passe by all obscene or amorous passages, all prophane or scurrill Iests, all heathenish oathes and execrations even with detestation' (6C2ᵛ). This type of selective skim-reading is a bowdlerizing inversion of the utilitarian method of reading taught in English grammar schools well into the seventeenth century, a hangover from humanism that involved privileging focus on a text's noteworthy parts over interpretation of its whole.[43] Gosson asserts that 'whatsoever such Playes as conteine good matter, are set out in print, may be read with profite' ('but cannot be playd, without a manifest breach of Gods commaundement'): the 'good matter' that inheres in printed plays can be 'read with profit', even picked out in the same way that readers were encouraged to pick out worthy *sententiae* in their non-dramatic reading, while that which is objectionable can be passed over (E6ʳ).[44] Numerous readers' marks in extant early modern playbooks demonstrate readers pausing at rhetorically striking or aphoristic passages that are 'of some speciall excellency, or use, worthy the noting', as the pedagogical theorist John Brinsley encouraged students to do in his popular *Ludus Literarius, or The Grammar Schoole* (1612).[45] However, just as often, marginal marks accompany precisely the types of 'obscene and amorous passages' which Prynne believed playreaders could and should pass by.[46] Using these marks to extrapolate reader preference or motivation can be problematic: it is often impossible to know who made them, or when, or why. However, when the passages they accompany are transcribed by a named reader into a roughly dateable commonplace book, they form part of a new textual creation that reflects more clearly the generic similarities between the passages that have appealed sufficiently to the reader to render them worthy of extracting and revisiting. The accumulated dramatic extracts in the manuscript commonplace book of the Scots poet William Drummond of Hawthornden demonstrate quite clearly that the scenes and passages in the printed comedies he read that appealed to him most were those of a bawdy, titillating nature, and his transcription of them into a location that facilitated repeated revisiting hints at the sensory effect they may have held for him.

Drummond was born in 1585, and died in 1649. Throughout his life he read widely and voraciously, accumulating a large library, much of which is still intact and housed by the University of Edinburgh – including his marked-up quartos of *Romeo and Juliet* and *Love's Labour's Lost.*[47] The manuscript lists he compiled of the books he owned and read demonstrate that he had a predilection for drama that extended well into adulthood: what is striking about his reading from his younger years, however, is his clear preference for comedy over other dramatic genres, which may intersect with Brathwaite's view that 'Stories of Love' (and thus comedies) are the preferred reading material of youths.[48]

Of the 12 plays from which Drummond copies extracts into his common-place book (MS 2059 in the National Library of Scotland), 10 are comedies.[49] Seemingly transcribed in the years 1609–10, lines and passages and sometimes entire abridged scenes cover 23 folios of his commonplace book, scrawled in a large untidy secretary hand.[50] Many of them are accompanied by a residual marker of a humanist pedagogical training, the marginal gloss or keyword. The glosses thus give away Drummond's favourite theme: of those that are legible (some recede into the book's binding so as to be unreadable), the only one that is repeated is 'women', which appears at least eight times.[51] Considered in conjunction with the frequency of glosses such as 'madenhead', 'adulterie', 'courses of Loue' and 'cupids laws', Drummond's playreading priorities become clear.[52]

Drummond exhibits a prurient interest in scenes or metaphors of an overtly erotic nature. He repeatedly pauses over passages that mention maidenheads: in the section of extracts from John Day's *Law Tricks*, the lines 'upon her finger wore her Madenhead' and 'Arbors with sweet violet Beds | that hath beene prest to death w^t madenheads' are overlined for emphasis; in the section of transcriptions from Middleton's *A Mad World My Masters*, the gloss 'maden-head' accompanies the line 'fouls then ar maides to locke from mē y^t treasure | wich death wil plucke & neuer yeeld thē pleasure' (although interestingly, these two lines are scored through with a diagonal line, as though Drummond at a later date no longer approved of their sentiment).[53] In the section containing extracts from Day's *The Isle of Gulls*, he transcribes almost the entirety of the interaction between the characters of Violetta and Hippolita in which they speculate about what the experience of losing their virginity will be like.[54] In this innuendo-heavy scene, Violetta recounts a dream she has had of the stages of her wedding, from courtship to occupation of the marital bed, and her annoyance at awakening from the dream just prior to the marriage's consum-mation: 'Lord how it chaft me that I wakt so soone, | One minuts dreaming longer, I had tride, | The difference twixt a virgin and a bride.' The scene deliberately builds to a titillating climax which it then fails to deliver, and it is hard to resist the temptation to read a note of sexual frustration in the firmly scored vertical line in the margin next to the passage quoted above, which is conflated in Drummond's rendering with Hippolita's response, 'Otwould ha' vext a Saint, my blood would burne | To be so neere, and misse so good a turne' – perhaps a moment when the sensually stimulated erotic pleasure of playreading was interrupted.[55]

When he transcribes a passage such as the character of Fuller's lengthy speech from Thomas Heywood's 1602 *How a Man May Choose a Good Wife From a Bad* in which he describes his courtship and eventual conquest of a former lover, it is impossible to know whether Drummond's reading of the speech – which ends with an image of the lovers lying on the woman's 'wanton bed' – involves the erotic pleasure of imagining himself a 'Prime-actor' in the scene.[56] The speech's final couplet is, '"Now sweeting kisse me, having time and place" | So clings me too her with a sweet imbrace': it can only be guessed at whether deploying the internal sense of the imagination created for the young Drummond a pleasurably titllating 'Sceane of Action' in which he himself enacted the 'lustfull gestures [...] kisses, [and] embracements' described by the dramatic dialogue. I have suggested that the proliferation of such passages in Drummond's commonplace book – rendering it an anthology of dramatic writing that certainly could, in Craik's formulation, be read pornographically – imply that he did. By juxtaposing manuscript evidence of reader response with the printed discourses that theorize and construct this response, conclusions that might be drawn through separate consideration of both types of evidence are strengthened.

Drummond, I argue, seems to read comedies in the way certain dramatic paratexts offered them up to be read, which seems to correspond to the way Brathwaite and other writers assumed they would be read, which seems to involve the sensory stimulation, via the imagination, of an erotic pleasure equal or greater to that which the antitheatricalists believed was experienced in the playhouse. When the printer of *The Two Merry Milkmaids* complains that the sensory affect of the printed play – which technically involves only the sense of touch as the reader turns its pages – will be inferior to the visually and aurally stimulating experience of performance, he underestimates the potential sensuality of 'paper pictures' and the potency of the internal sense of the imagination in the creation of an erotically pleasurable comic playreading.

Notes

1 *The schoole of abuse* (1579), B6v.

2 Katharine A. Craik and Tanya Pollard, 'Introduction: Imagining Audiences', in *Shakespearean Sensations: Experiencing Literature in Early Modern England*, ed. by Craik and Pollard (Cambridge: Cambridge University Press, 2013), pp. 1–25 (p. 14).

3 Craik and Pollard, p. 8. In a growing corpus of criticism on early modern reading and physiological affect, plays remain a largely unexamined genre, although Lucy Munro does consider briefly the ability of printed comedy to move its readers to laughter in 'Reading Printed Comedy: Edward Sharpham's *The Fleer*', in *The Book of the Play: Playwrights, Stationers, and Readers in Early Modern England*, ed. by Marta Straznicky (Amherst, MA: University of Massachusetts Press, 2006), pp. 39–58 (p. 42). Recent work that focuses more broadly on early modern reading and physiological affect includes Craik's *Reading Sensations in Early Modern England* (Basingstoke: Palgrave Macmillan, 2007); Helen Smith's '"More swete vnto the eare | than holsome for ye mynde": Embodying Early Modern Women's Reading', *Huntington Library Quarterly*, 73 (2010), 413–32; and, providing an overview of the topic, Adrian Johns's chapter 'The Physiology of Reading: Print and the Passions', in *The Nature of the Book: Print and Knowledge in the Making* (Chicago: University of Chicago Press, 1998), pp. 380–443.

4 *The Anatomie of Abuses* (1583), L7r; hereafter cited in the text.

5 See Chapter 8 of this volume, where Aurélie Griffin gives an account of the distinction between the external and internal senses, as articulated by Thomas Aquinas.

6 It is William Prynne in his 1633 *Histrio-mastix: The Players Scourge* who says that of 'all the sinfull lusts of the flesh [...] Stage-Playes are the chiefe' (B2r). Prynne holds that, while it would be preferable not to read plays at all, to 'read a Play-booke' is nevertheless not as dangerously corrupting as to 'compose, or act, or see a Stage-play' (6C2r). *Histrio-mastix* is hereafter cited in the text. Gosson, too, had asserted in his 1582 *Playes Confuted in Five Actions* that 'whatsoever such Playes as conteine good matter, are set out in print, may be read with profite, but cannot be playd, without a manifest breach of Gods commaundement' (E6r); hereafter references to Gosson's work are to the *Playes Confuted* rather than *The Schoole of Abuse*, and are cited in the text.

7 Craik and Pollard, p. 8. For a discussion of the paratextual elevation of commercial playbooks to the more esteemed genre of 'poetry', see Wayne Chandler, *Commendatory Verse and Authorship in the English Renaissance* (Lewiston, NY: The Edwin Mellen Press, 2003), pp. 112–15.

8 On the crossover between playgoing and playreading markets, see Zachary Lesser, *Renaissance Drama and the Politics of Publication: Readings in the English Book Trade* (Cambridge: Cambridge University Press, 2004), p. 52.

9 John Marston's *The Dutch Courtesan* was first performed in 1605; Thomas Dekker and Thomas Middleton's *1 The Honest Whore* in 1604; Alexander Brome's *The Cunning Lovers* in 1638; William Shakespeare's *Love's Labour's Lost* in 1595; and Thomas Heywood's *A Maidenhead Well Lost* in 1633. Dates and author attributions follow *DEEP*.

10 See, for instance, Stubbes, who complains that as often as men 'goe to those howses where Players frequent, thei go to Venus pallace' (L7v).

11 See Natalie Eschenbaum's discussion, in Chapter 6 of this volume, of both Robert Burton and Francis Bacon's acknowledgment of Joseph Scaliger's designation of titillation as the 'sixth [external] sense'.

12 *Sicelides* (1631), L4v.

13 *The Overthrow of Stage-Playes* (1599), E3v.

14 Robert Burton's 1621 *Anatomy of Melancholy*, for instance, points out that of the 'fiue outward senses [...] Sight is held to bee most pretious, and the best' (C1r).

15 'The Printer to the Reader', in *A pleasant comedie, called the two merry milke-maids; or, the best words weare the garland*, by J.C. [John Cumber?] (1620), A2r.

16 The three 'inward senses' identified by Burton are common sense, 'phantasie' or imagination, and memory (C1r).

17 A discussion of the 'standard beliefs' regarding the way the function of the imagination relies on the external senses can be found in L.J. Rather, 'Thomas Fienus' (1567–1631) Dialectical Investigation of the Imagination as Cause and Cure of Bodily Disease', *Bulletin of the History of Medicine*, 41 (1967), 349–67 (pp. 352–53).

18 Meric Casaubon, *A treatise concerning enthusiasme, as it is an effect of nature, but is mistaken by many for either divine inspiration, or diabolical possession* (1655), N4v; hereafter cited in the text.

19 'To the Author on his Comedy, *The Antipodes*', in *The Antipodes*, by Richard Brome (1640), A4r.

20 'The Stationer to Dramatophilus', in *A King, and no King*, by Francis Beaumont and John Fletcher (1631), A2r.

21 'Upon Mr. Massinger His *Roman Actor*', in *The Roman Actor*, by Philip Massinger (1629), A4r.

22 Peter Stallybrass argues that early modern play quartos belong among the slim, ephemeral publications termed 'pamphlets': see 'What Is a Book?' (plenary paper, Centre for Material Texts Inaugural Conference, University of Cambridge, 2010).

23 *A suruey of history: or, a nursery for gentry* (1638), T2r–v; 2Y1v.

24 Craik, p. 116 (my emphasis); and further on Brathwaite's discussion of reading in the *Nursery*, pp. 115–34.

25 *Lovesickness and Gender in Early Modern English Literature* (Oxford: Oxford University Press, 2008), pp. 2, 7.

26 *A discourse of the preseruation of the sight* (1599), R3r.

27 Burton, Z2r; West, 'On this Learned Treatise Love-Melancholy', in *Erotomania*, by Jacques Ferrand (1640), b3r–c1v (b3v).

28 For a discussion of the physical and material conditions of 'private' reading in early modern England, see Sasha Roberts, 'Shakespeare "creepes into the womens closets about bedtime": Women Reading in a Room of Their Own', in *Renaissance Configurations: Voices/Bodies/Spaces, 1580–1690*, ed. by Gordon McMullan (Basingstoke: Macmillan, 1998), pp. 30–63.

29 *A Treatise of Original Sin* (1658), A3r; 2Z4v; 3A1r.

30 Fienus quoted in Rather, p. 356.

31 'To the Worshipfull William Mills, Esquire', in *Totenham Court: A pleasant comedie* (1638), A3r.

32 'To the Reader and Hearer', in *The Fleire* (1607), A3r.

33 The full exchange involves the men declaring that they are 'Merry and lusty', 'can hold out no longer' and that '[t]his night' they will 'lye togither' with their lovers (*A Jovial Crew; or, The Merry Beggars* (1652), G3v). Although the line about filling their bellies is literal given the subsequent conversation about food, it also recalls Celia's taunting accusation in *As You Like It* that Rosalind wishes to know who is writing her love poetry 'so [she] may put a man in [her] belly' (3.2.200).

34 See Rather, p. 353.

35 Wendy Wall discusses the early modern publishing industry's gendering of texts as female and the rhetorical sexualization of book-buying and reading in *The Imprint of Gender: Authorship and Publication in the English Renaissance* (Ithaca, NY: Cornell University Press, 1993).

36 'To the Reader', *The famelie of loue* (1608), A2r. The date of the first performance is taken from *DEEP*.

37 Fred Schurink, in his discussion of the use of the root 'pleas-' and its cognates on the title page of John Lyly's *Euphues: The Anatomy of Wit* (1578; reprinted multiple times into the 1630s), also notes that it suggests an 'intimate relationship between the pleasure of love and the pleasure of reading', and implies that 'reading is almost a substitute for love'. See 'The Intimacy of Manuscript and the Pleasure of Print: Literary Culture from *The Schoolmaster* to *Euphues*', in *The Oxford Handbook of Tudor Literature, 1485–1603*, ed. by Mike Pincombe and Cathy Shrank (Oxford: Oxford University Press, 2009), pp. 671–86 (p. 681).

38 *The Roaring Girle* (1611), A3r. I have repunctuated the epistle's title for sense: it reads in the 1611 quarto, 'To the Comicke, Play-readers, Venery, and Laughter.'

39 'To his approved Friend M. Richard Brome on his *Northern Lasse*', in *The Northern Lass* (1632), A3r.

40 St. Br., 'To his ingenious Brother M. Rich. Brome, upon this witty issue of his Brayne, the *Northern Lasse*', in *The Northern Lasse*, A3v. Julie Sanders notes in her modern edition that 'St. Br.' is unlikely to be a blood relative (an otherwise unlocatable 'Stephen Brome'), and may instead be the physician Stephen Bradwell, a friend of Thomas Heywood. The incestuous desire for the playbook invoked by the verse is thus a deliberate rhetorical construction. See 'Preliminary and paratextual materials to the 1632 quarto', in Richard Brome, *The Northern Lass*, Modern Text, ed. by Julie Sanders, *Richard Brome Online* www.hrionline.ac.uk/brome [accessed 2 August 2012].

41 'To the inheritour of all worthines, Sir William Scipwith', in *The Faithful Shepherdess* (1610), ¶1v.

42 Craik, p. 117.

43 For an overview of the contexts and extant evidence of this type of reading, see William H. Sherman's introduction to *Used Books: Marking Readers in Renaissance England* (Philadelphia, PA: University of Pennsylvania Press, 2008), pp. 3–24.

44 The most famous advocate of the noting of 'commonplaces and maxims' as one reads is Desiderius Erasmus in his 1512 treatise on rhetoric, *De duplici copia verborum ac rerum commentarii duo*. See 'Copia: Foundations of the Abundant Style (De duplici copia verborum ac rerum commentarii duo)', trans. and annotated by Betty I. Knott, in *Collected Works of Erasmus*, ed. by Craig R. Thompson, 79 vols

(Toronto: University of Toronto Press, 1974–), XXIV, 279–659 (p. 638).

45 *Ludus Literarius, or The Grammar Schoole* (1612), G3v.

46 See, as an example, the number of overtly bawdy lines picked out by an early reader of Edward Sharpham's *Cupid's Whirligig* (1611) in a British Library copy of the play (BL 643c10).

47 On Drummond's life and library, see *The Library of Drummond of Hawthornden*, ed. with an introduction by Robert H. MacDonald (Edinburgh: Edinburgh University Press, 1971).

48 These lists, dated by Drummond himself, are to be found in Hawthornden MSS 2059 (fols. 359–67) and 2060 (fols. 122–23) held in the National Library of Scotland, Edinburgh.

49 They are *How a Man May Choose a Good Wife From a Bad* (attributed to Thomas Heywood); Thomas Dekker and Thomas Middleton's *1 The Honest Whore*; George Chapman's *All Fools* and *Sir Giles Goosecap*; John Marston's *Parasitaster*; John Day's *The Isle of Gulls* and *Law Tricks*; Dekker and John Webster's *Westward Ho*; and Middleton's *A Mad World, My Masters* and *Your Five Gallants*. If Drummond's dating of his reading lists is taken at face value, it is most likely that the editions from which he transcribes were all printed prior to 1611.

50 These dates can be inferred from the appearance of the excerpted plays in the manuscript lists Drummond compiled of the books he read in the years 1606–14 (see Hawthornden MS 2059).

51 On fols. 209r; 214r; 219r; 220v; 221v; 223v; 346v; 347v of Hawthornden MS 2059.

52 For example on fols. 221v; 345v; 348v of Hawthornden MS 2059.

53 Hawthornden MS 2059, fols. 210v; 221v. The originals of these lines are found at C3r; C4v of *Law-trickes or, Who would haue thought it*, and D2v of *A mad world, my masters* (both 1608).

54 Hawthornden MS 2059, fols. 223v–224r. The interaction between Violetta and Hippolita is at D2v–D3v of the 1606 edition of *The Ile of Guls*.

55 Quotations are taken from *The Ile of Guls* (1606), D3v.

56 *A Pleasant conceited Comedie, wherein is shewed how a man may chuse a good Wife from a bad* (1602), B4r.

Afterword

Farah Karim-Cooper

In 1620, Richard Brathwaite worried that the five senses, which had the capacity to convey 'morall or diuine discourse to the imagination', could instead be abused and therefore make the body vulnerable to vice and corruption. Here, Brathwaite demonstrates the tension that existed within the medical and moral discourses on sense perception in the early modern period: the senses were gateways to knowledge and God, but they were bodily channels susceptible to Satan's devastating influences too.[1] Early modern discussions of the senses were fraught with anxiety, contradiction and absolutes. Some writers, as contributors have pointed out here, were certain that there was a clear hierarchy of the senses, with sight at the top. This ordering of the senses occurs as early as Aristotle, but is later reimagined within a Christian framework through the Middle Ages and early modern periods. Other writers, such as Brathwaite, were troubled by the double nature of the senses and sense organs. For example, Jackie Watson shows us in Chapter 2 to what extent theories of vision were in flux and how the eyes were seen both as the '"most noble, perfect and admirable" of the senses', while being burdened with the notion of 'visual deception' (p. 42). As a result of this dichotomy, the ability of sense perception to enlighten or harm an individual meant that people were constantly reminded to be vigilant, guarded and to regulate their sensory activities. Our senses are often taken for granted in everyday life, but to early moderns, ignoring the sensations of the world upon the body would have been unthinkable.

In addition to hierarchies and dichotomies, the senses are beset by conflict, vulnerable to deception and held hostage to the emotions. Aurélie Griffin shows in her contribution, for instance, how this is noted by early modern writers who were concerned about the effects of love melancholy upon the eyes. Griffin also highlights an important point that medievalists tend to pay more attention to than those of us working with later texts, and that is the notion that there are five external and three internal senses. As scholars of early modern texts, we need to be aware of the ways in which sensory theory changed or evolved from one epoch to another. Refreshingly, this awareness is heightened throughout the chapters in this volume.

As the editors point out in their introduction, being able to recreate the early modern sensory environment or replicate the early modern subject's sensory experience would be impossible and in many ways misses the point of why we should historicize the senses. As David Howes suggests in *Empire of the Senses: The Sensual Culture Reader*, culture mediates the senses and vice versa. To understand a culture, we must uncover its ways of perceiving and acquiring knowledge, and in doing so, identify what that culture understood about its ways of perceiving and knowing. This volume of essays is timely, then, as scholars and critics of early modern literature and culture are turning their attention from the fashioning of the body to its processes, and what this study provides is a way of assessing how those processes, in particular sense perception, affected, mediated and influenced the reception of art, literature and theatre in this period. In examining the role of the senses in the reception of art and the experience of intense emotion, the chapters in this volume have uncovered the origins of sensory theory. The vast range of texts – classical, medieval, religious and medical – shows how far into the past we must glance in order to identify the many facets of the history of sensory theory that developed and shaped the way art was interpreted and literature was read during the early modern period.

Scholars in a range of disciplines are beginning to ask how early moderns perceived phenomena and how artists and writers interpreted and represented the sensory worlds they encountered. Art historian François Quiviger, for example, explores the 'presence, nature, function and meaning of sensation in Renaissance art as productive of space and meaning', opening up new avenues for a profound engagement with not only visual components of art but how it reflected sound, taste, touch and smell.[2] The editors of this volume take up the question of how a theory of early modern sense perception can aid our own interpretation of art work and its reception in its moment as well as ours. Although we cannot necessarily recover the specific sensations of the early modern period, an examination of how writers and artists accounted for those sensations can help us to structure our own encounters with the texts and artefacts left behind. In particular, taking into consideration how early modern subjects describe their experiences of love, pain and death through a lexicon of the senses forces us to take note of the inextricable links between language, emotion and the physiology of sense perception in this period. The synaesthetic effect of desire, for example, is discussed in this collection by Natalie Eschenbaum in her chapter on Robert Herrick. Herrick suggests that 'to sensually engage with things or people is usually to infuse with them, to melt into them, to liquefy' (p. 115); here the double nature of the senses seems to be invoked deliberately by Herrick in order to express the nature of desire. Equally, the process of sense perception is bound up with the humoral condition of an individual subject. Some of the chapters in this volume are right, therefore, to address the ways in which the passions, humours and senses merge within the complex physiology of the human body.

To understand ourselves and our own sensory engagement with the world is one justification for a cultural history of the senses. But we may ask ourselves why this book and others like it (as there are more studies on the senses in early modern England on the way) are particularly important and why they are important at the moment. In October 2011, Globe Education launched a series of lectures, staged readings and conferences on Shakespeare and the Senses to explore early modern sensory theory, to reveal the number of works in the period that are preoccupied with themes and language of the senses and to challenge the idea that Shakespeare's first audiences went only to 'hear' plays or that they were either auditors or spectators. We wanted to suggest that early modern theatrical performance was a multisensory phenomenon and that audiences/spectators/congregators/assemblies responded to performance with the entirety of their bodies.

Reconstructed early modern playhouses, such as the Globe Theatre, the Blackfriars in Staunton, Virginia and the newly built Sam Wanamaker Playhouse (at Shakespeare's Globe) provide extraordinarily fertile testing grounds to measure the ways in which all the senses are called to attention simultaneously through performance. As we learn more about attending to plays in those old playhouses through these reconstructed playhouses, we are learning more about the early modern sensorium and how language, the body and theatre architecture function together when attending to plays. Juxtaposing studies of sensory performance, such as Simon Smith's chapter on visual musical experience in Shakespeare's playhouse, with studies of performance in reconstructed venues can lead us to important discoveries about the development of performance practices through time. However, the chapters here do more than that; they provide a sustained analysis of the ways in which art, literature and theatre pushed into the body and how the senses heighten, transform and induce melancholy or a wide range of humorally inflected passions in response – suggesting that a dialogic, fully embodied engagement with aesthetic phenomena was contingent upon these five crucial portals to the body.

Notes

1 Richard Brathwaite, *Essaies Vpon the Fiue Senses with a Pithie One Vpon Detraction* (1620), p. 19.

2 François Quiviger, *The Sensory World of Italian Renaissance Art* (London: Reaktion Books, 2010), p. 7.

Select bibliography

Pre-1700[1]

Anon., *The costlie whore* (1633)

—— 'A Merry New Catch of All Trades' (*c.* 1620), a ballad

—— 'The Northern Ladd' (1670–1696), a ballad

—— *A Pleasant Conceited Comedie, Wherein is Shewed, How a Man may Chuse a Good Wife From a Bad* (1602)

—— 'The Rimers New Trimming' (*c.* 1614), a ballad

—— *A Treatise of daunses wherin it is shewed, that they are as it were accessories and depe[n]dants (or thinges annexed) to whoredome, where also by the way is touched and proued, that playes are ioyned and knit togeather in a rancke or rowe with them* (1581)

—— *The Whole Psalmes in Foure Partes* (1563)

Adams, Thomas, *The Happiness of the Church* (1619)

Alison, Richard, *The Psalmes of Dauid in meter* (1599)

Arbeau, Thoinot (Jehan Tabourot), *Orchesographie* (Langres, 1589)

—— *Orchesographie*, 2nd edn (Langres, 1596)

Ariosto, Ludovico, *Orlando Furioso*, trans. by John Harington (1591)

Bacon, Francis, *Sylua syluarum: or A naturall historie* (1627)

Becon, Thomas, *Pomander of Prayer* (1563)

Bold, Henry, *Latine Songs With their English* (1685)

Brathwaite, Richard, *Essaies Vpon the Fiue Senses with a Pithie One Vpon Detraction* (1620)

—— *A suruey of history: or, a nursery for gentry* (1638)

Bright, Timothy, *A Treatise of Melancholie* (1586)

Brinsley, John, *Ludus Literarius, or The Grammar Schoole* (1612)

Brome, Richard, *The Love-Sick Court in Five New Playes* (1659)

Bulwer, John, *Chirologia* (1644)

Burgess, Anthony, *A Treatise of Original Sin* (1658)

Burton, Robert, *Anatomy of Melancholy* (1621)

Campion, Thomas, *The discription of a maske, presented before the Kinges Maiestie at White-Hall, on Twelfth Night last* (1607)

Casaubon, Meric, *A treatise concerning enthusiasme, as it is an effect of nature, but is mistaken by many for either divine inspiration, or diabolical possession* (1655)

Chandos, Grey Brydges, *A Discourse Against Flatterie* (1611)

Chapman, George, *The Shadow of Night* (1594)

Charleton, Walter, *Natural History of Nutrition, Life, and Voluntary Motion* (1659)

Coeffeteau, Nicolas, *A Table of Humane Passions*, trans. by Edward Grimeston (1621)

---

1 All pre-1700 material is published in London, unless stated otherwise

Coryate, Thomas, *Coryats Crudities* (1611)

Crooke, Helkiah, *Mikrokosmographia* (1615)

Davenport, Robert, *A New Tricke to Cheat the Divell* (1639)

Davies, John, *Orchestra, or a Poeme of Dauncing Iudicially proouing the true obseruation of time and measure, in the authenticall and laudable vse of dauncing* (1596)

de la Marche, Olivier, *Les Mémoires De Messire Olivier De La Marche* (Lyon, 1561)

de la Primaudaye, Pierre, *The French Academie* (1618)

Dekker, Thomas, *Blurt Master-Constable* (1602)

—— *The Noble Souldier* (1634)

Dekker, Thomas and Philip Massinger, *The Virgin Martyr* (1620)

Della Casa, Giovanni, *Galateo*, trans. by Robert Peterson of Lincoln's Inn (1576)

Dryden, John, *The Annual miscellany* (1694)

du Laurens, André, *A Discourse of the Preservation of Sight*, trans. by Richard Surphlet (1599)

Dupleix, Scipion, *The Resolver* (1635)

East, Michael, *The fourth set of bookes, vvherein are anthemes for versus and chorus, madrigals, and songs of other kindes* (1618)

Edwards, Richard, *Damon and Pithias* (1571)

Egerton, Stephen, *The Boring of the Eare* (1623)

Eliot, John, *Ortho-epia Gallica* (1593)

Elyot, Thomas, *The Castel of Helth* (1539)

Erasmus, Desiderius, *De duplici copia verborum ac rerum commentarii duo* (1512)

Evelyn, John, *An essay on the first book of T. Lucretius* (1656)

Ferrand, Jacques, *Erotomania, or A Treatise discoursing of the essence, causes, symptomes, prognosticks, and cure of love, or erotique melancholy* (1640)

Fetherston, Christopher, *A Dialogue against lewd and lascivious dancing wherein are refuted all those reason which the common people use to bring in defence thereof* (1582)

Fletcher, John, 'The Captaine', in *Comedies and Tragedies* (1647)

—— 'The Chances', in *Comedies and Tragedies* (1647)

—— 'The Tragedie of Bonduca', in *Comedies and Tragedies* (1647)

Fletcher, John and Philip Massinger, *The Elder Brother a Comedie* (1637)

—— 'The Custome of the Countrey', in *Comedies and Tragedies* (1647)

—— 'The Double Marriage', in *Comedies and Tragedies Written by Francis Beavmont and Iohn Fletcher Gentlemen* (1647)

Fletcher, Phineas, *Sicelides* (1631)

Ford, John, *The Fancies, Chast and Noble* (1638)

Gosson, Stephen, *The schoole of abuse* (1579)

—— *Playes Confuted in Five Actions* (1582)

Greene, Robert, *A Quip for an Upstart Courtier* (1592)

Harrison, William, *The Difference of Hearers* (1614)

Heywood, Thomas, *The Wise-woman of Hogsdon. A Comedie* (1638)

Holme, Randle, *Academy of Armory* (Chester, [1688])

Hoole, Charles, *An Easie Entrance to the Latine Tongue* (1649)

Jones, Robert, *Vltimvm Vale, with a triplicity of musicke* (1605)

Leigh, Edward, *Three Diatribes* (1671)

Lichfield[?], Richard, *Trimming of Thomas Nashe* (1597)

Lyly, John, *Euphues: The Anatomy of Wit* (1578)

—— *Sixe Court Comedies* (1632)

Markham, Gervase, and William Sampson, *Herod and Antipater* (1622)

Marson, George, 'The Nymphs and Shepherds Danced', in *The Triumph of Oriana*, compiled by Thomas Morley (1601)

Marston, John, *The Wonder of Women Or The Tragedie of Sophonisba* (1606)

Marston, John and John Webster, *The Malcontent [...] With the Additions played by the Kings Maiesties servants* (1604)

Massinger, Philip and Nathan Field, *The Fatall Dowry: A Tragedy* (1632)

Middleton, Thomas, William Rowley and Thomas Heywood, *The Excellent Comedy, called The Old Law: or A new way to please you* (1656)

Montaigne, Michel de, *Essays*, trans. by John Florio (1613)

Munday, Anthony, *A second and third blast of retrait from plaies and Theaters* (1580)

Nashe, Thomas, *Have With You to Saffron-Walden* (1596)

Norden, John, *A Good Companion for a Christian Directing Him in the Way to God* (1632)

Northbrooke, John, *A treatise wherein Dicing, Dauncing, Vaine plaies [...] are reproved* (1579)

Overbury, Thomas, *Characters* (1616)

Paré, Ambroise, *The Workes*, trans. Th[omas] Johnson (1634)

Peele, George, *The Old Wives Tale* (1595)

Plutarch, *The liues of the noble Grecians and Romanes*, trans. by Thomas North (1579)

—— *The Philosophie*, trans. by Philemon Holland (1603)

Primaudaye, *The Second Part of the French Acadamie* (1594)

Prynne, William, *Histrio-mastix: The Players Scourge* (1633)

Rainolds, John, *The Overthrow of Stage-Playes* (1599)

Randolph, Thomas, *Poems with The Muses Looking-Glasse: and Amyntas* (Oxford, 1638)

Rudyerd, Benjamin, *Le Prince D'Amour* (1660)

S., W., *The True Chronicle Historie of the whole life and death of Thomas Lord Cromwell* (1602)

Scaliger, Julius Caesar, *Exotericarvm Exercitationvm* (Paris, 1557)

Shirley, Henry, *The Martyr'd Souldier* (1638)

Shirley, James, *The Humorous Courtier* (1640)

—— *St Patrick for Ireland. The First Part* (1640)

Stubbes, Philip, *The anatomie of abuses* (1583)

Suckling, John, *Aglaura* (1638)

Taylor, Jeremy, *XXV Sermons Preached at Golden-Grover* (1653)

Taylor, Thomas, *Peter his Repentance Shewing* (1653)

Tomkis, Thomas, *Lingua, or The combat of the tongue, and the fiue senses for superiority* (1607)

Tusser, Thomas, *Five Hundred Points of Good Husbandry* (1570)

Walkington, Thomas, *The Optick Glass of Humors* (1607)

Walton, Isaac, *The Lives of Dr. John Donne, Sir Henry Wotton, Mr. Richard Hooker, and Mr. George Herbert* (1670)

Whitford, Richard, *Pomander of Prayer* (1531)

Wilkinson, Robert, *A Jewell for the Eare* (1610)

Woodall, John, *The Surgions Mate* (1617)

Wright, Thomas, *The Passions of the Mind in Generall* (1601)

Post-1700

Ainsworth, Maryan and Joshua Vaterman, *German Paintings in the Metropolitan Museum of Art, 1350–1600* (New York: Metropolitan Museum of Art, 2013)

Allen, Don Cameron, *Doubt's Boundless Sea* (New York: Arno Press, 1979)

Aquinas, Thomas, *Summa Theologica*, trans. by Fathers of the English Dominican Province, 2 vols (Chicago: Encyclopaedia Britannica, 1952)

Arbeau, Thoinot, *Orchesography*, trans. by Mary S. Evans, with introduction and notes by Julia Sutton and Laban notation by M. Becker and J. Sutton. (New York: Dover Publications, 1967)

Arena, Antonius, 'Rules of Dancing', trans. by John Guthrie and Marino Zorzi, *Dance Research*, 4.2 (1986), 3–53

Aristotle, *Parva Naturalia,* revised text with introduction and commentary by David Ross (Oxford: Clarendon Press, 1955)

—— *De anima* (*On the Soul*), trans. intro. and notes H. Lawson-Tancred (Harmondsworth: Penguin, 1986)

—— *De Anima*, trans. by D.W. Hamlyn (Oxford: Clarendon Press, 1993 [1968])

Arnold, Ken, *Cabinets for the Curious: Looking Back at Early English Museu*ms (Aldershot: Ashgate, 2006)

Austern, Linda Phyllis, '"Sing Againe Syren": The Female Musician and Sexual Enchantment in Elizabethan Life and Literature', *Renaissance Quarterly*, 42 (1989), 420–48

—— '"Art to Enchant": Musical Magic and Its Practitioners in English Renaissance Drama', *Journal of the Royal Music Association*, 115 (1990), 191–206

—— '"Alluring the Auditorie to Effeminacie": Music and the Idea of the Feminine in Early Modern England', *Music and Letters*, 74 (1993), 343–54

—— '"No Women Are Indeed": The Boy Actor as Vocal Seductress in Late Sixteenth- and Early Seventeenth-Century English Drama', in *Embodied Voices: Representing Female Vocality in Western Culture*, ed. by Leslie C. Dunn and Nancy A. Jones (Cambridge: Cambridge University Press, 1994), pp. 83–102

—— '"For musick is the handmaid of the Lord": Women, Psalms, and Domestic Music-making in Early Modern England', in *Psalms in the Early Modern World*, ed. by Linda Phyllis Austern, Kari Boyd McBride and David L. Orvis (Farnham: Ashgate, 2011), pp. 77–114

Babb, Lawrence, *The Elizabethan Malady: A Study of Melancholia in English Literature from 1580 to 1642* (East Lansing, MI: Michigan College Press, 1951)

Bald, R.C., *John Donne: A Life* (Oxford: Oxford University Press, 1970)

Beattie, John, *Policing and Punishment in London 1660–1750: Urban Policing and the Limits of Terror* (Oxford: Oxford University Press, 2001)

Beaumont, Francis, *The Knight of the Burning Pestle*, ed. by Michael Hattaway, 2nd edn, New Mermaids (London: A & C Black, 2002)

Bell, Ilona, 'The Role of the Lady in Donne's Songs and Sonnets', *Studies in English Literature, 1500–1900*, 23 (1983), 113–29

Berendt, Joachim-Ernst, *The Third Ear: On Listening to the World*, trans. by Tim Nevill (Shaftesbury: Element, 1988)

Berger, John, *Ways of Seeing* (London: Penguin, 1972)

Bloom, Gina, *Voice in Motion* (Philadelphia, PA: University of Pennsylvania Press, 2007)

Boon, George C., 'Tonsor Humanus', *Britannia*, 22 (1991), 21–32

Botelho, Keith M., *Renaissance Earwitnesses* (New York: Palgrave Macmillan, 2009)

Bowers, Fredon (gen. ed.), *The Dramatic Works in the Beaumont and Fletcher Canon*, 10 vols (Cambridge: Cambridge University Press, 1966–96)

Bradbrook, M.C., *Themes and Conventions of Elizabethan Tragedy*, 2nd edn (Cambridge: Cambridge University Press, 1980)

Britland, Karen, 'Circe's Cup: Wine and Women in Early Modern Drama', in *A Pleasing Sinne: Drink and Conviviality in Seventeenth-Century England*, ed. by Adam Smyth (Woodbridge: Brewer, 2004), pp. 109–25

Brooks, Douglas A., 'Inky Kin: Reading in the Age of Gutenberg Paternity', in *The Book of the Play: Playwrights, Stationers, and Readers in Early Modern England*, ed. by Marta Straznicky (Amherst, MA: University of Massachusetts Press, 2006), pp. 203–28

Brown, Jonathan, *Velázquez: Painter and Courtier* (New Haven, CT: Yale University Press, 1986)

Brown, Peter, *The Body and Society: Men, Women, and Sexual Renunciation in Early Christianity* (New York: Columbia University Press, 1988)

Bull, Michael and Les Back (eds), *The Auditory Culture Reader*, Sensory Formations (Oxford: Berg, 2003)

Burgess, Irene, '"The Wreck of Order" in Early Modern Women's Drama', *Early Modern Literary Studies*, 6 (2001), 6.1–24

Burton, Robert, *The Anatomy of Melancholy*, ed. by Thomas C. Faulkner and others, 6 vols (Oxford: Clarendon Press, 1995 [1989])

Butler, Martin, *The Stuart Court Masque and Political Culture* (Cambridge: Cambridge University Press, 2008)

Cahill, Patricia, 'Take Five: Renaissance Literature and the Study of the Senses', *Literature Compass*, 6 (2009), 1014–30

Carney, Jo Eldridge, *Renaissance and Reformation 1500–1620* (Westport, CT: Greenwood Press, 2001)

Cavell, Stanley, '"Who Does the Wolf Love?": Reading *Coriolanus*', *Representations*, 3 (1983), 1–20

Chandler, Wayne, *Commendatory Verse and Authorship in the English Renaissance* (Lewiston, NY: Edwin Mellen Press, 2003)

Cheney, Liana De Girolami, Alicia Craig Faxon and Kathleen Lucey Russo (eds), *Self-Portraits by Women Painters* (Aldershot: Ashgate, 2000)

Christensen, Ann C., 'Settling House in Middleton's *Women Beware Women*', *Comparative Drama*, 29 (1995–6), 493–506

Cicero, *De Oratore*, trans. by E.W. Sutton (London: Heinemann, 1967)

Clark, Stuart, *Vanities of the Eye: Vision in Early Modern European Culture* (Oxford: Oxford University Press, 2007)

Classen, Constance, *Worlds of Sense: Exploring the Senses in History and Across Cultures* (London: Routledge, 1993)

—— (ed.), *The Book of Touch*, Sensory Formations (Oxford: Berg, 2005)

Classen, Constance and David Howes, 'The Museum as Sensescape: Western Sensibilities and Indigenous Artifacts', in *Sensible Objects: Colonialism, Museums, and Material Culture*, ed. by Elizabeth Edwards, Chris Gosden and Ruth Phillips (Oxford: Berg, 2002), pp. 199–222

Coates, John, '"The Choice of Hercules" in *Antony and Cleopatra*', in *Shakespeare Survey Volume 31*, ed. by Kenneth Muir (Cambridge: Cambridge University Press, 1978), pp. 45–52

Cockayne, Emily, 'Cacophony, or Vile Scrapers on Vile Instruments', *Urban History*, 29 (2002), 35–47

—— 'Experiences of the Deaf in Early Modern England', *The Historical Journal*, 46 (2003), 493–510

—— *Hubbub* (New Haven, CT: Yale University Press, 2007)

Coffin, Charles, *John Donne and the New Philosophy* (New York: Columbia University Press, 1937)

Cole, J.A., 'Sunday Dinner and Thursday Suppers: Social and Moral Contexts of the Food Imagery in *Women Beware Women*', in *Jacobean Drama Studies: Jacobean Miscellany 4*, ed. by James Hogg (Salzburg: Institut für Anglistik und Amerikanistik, Universität Salzburg, 1984), pp. 86–98

Cooper, Helen, 'Location and Meaning in Masque, Morality and Royal Entertainment', in *The Court Masque*, ed. by David Lindley (Manchester: Manchester University Press, 1984), pp. 135–48

Corbin, Alain, *Time, Desire and Horror: Towards a History of the Senses*, trans. by Jean Birrell (Cambridge: Polity Press, 1995)

Craik, Katherine A., *Reading Sensations in Early Modern England* (Basingstoke: Palgrave Macmillan, 2007)

Craik, Katharine A. and Tanya Pollard (eds), *Shakespearean Sensations: Experiencing Literature in Early Modern England* (Cambridge: Cambridge University Press, 2013)

Crockett, Bryan, '"Holy Cozenage" and the Renaissance Cult of the Ear', *The Sixteenth Century Journal*, 24 (1993), 47–65

—— *The Play of Paradox* (Philadelphia, PA: University of Pennsylvania Press, 1995)

Dabbs, Julia K., *Life Stories of Women Artists, 1550–1800* (Aldershot: Ashgate, 2009)

Dawson, Lesel, *Lovesickness and Gender in Early Modern English Literature* (Oxford: Oxford University Press, 2008)

Decamp, Eleanor, 'Performing Barbers, Surgeons and Barber-Surgeons' (unpublished doctoral thesis, University of Oxford, 2012)

Degenhardt, Jane Hwang, 'Catholic Martyrdom in Dekker and Massinger's *The Virgin Martir* and the Early Modern Threat of "Turning Turk"', *English Literary History*, 73 (2006), 83–117

Dekker, Thomas, *The Dramatic Works of Thomas Dekker*, ed. by Fredson Bowers, 4 vols (Cambridge: Cambridge University Press, 1953–61)

Descartes, Rene, *Discourse on Method, Optics, Geometry, and Meteorology*, trans. by Paul J. Olscamp (Indianapolis, IN: Hackett, 2001)

Deutermann, Allison K., '"Caviare to the general": Taste, Hearing, and Genre in *Hamlet*', *Shakespeare Quarterly*, 62 (2011), 230–55

di Martino, Carla, *Ratio particularis: la doctrine des sens internes d'Avicenne à Thomas d'Aquin* (Paris: Vrin, 2008)

Dillon, Janette, *Drama, Court and City, 1595–1610: Drama and Social Space in London* (Cambridge: Cambridge University Press, 2000)

—— *The Language of Space in Court Performance, 1400–1625* (Cambridge: Cambridge University Press, 2010)

—— 'Spectatorship at the Early Modern English Court', in *Spectatorship at the Elizabethan Court*, ed. by Daniel Dornhofer and Susanne Scholz, Special Issue of *Zeitsprünge: Forschungen zur Frühen Neuzeit*, 17 (Frankfurt: Klostermann, 2013), 9–21

Dixon, Peggy, *Dances from the Courts of Europe*, 8 vols (London: Nonsuch, 1986–93)

Dollimore, Jonathan, *Radical Tragedy* (Brighton: Harvester, 1984)

Donkin, R.A., *Dragon's Brain Perfume: An Historical Geography of Camphor* (Leiden: Brill, 1999)

Donne, John, *The Complete English Poems*, ed. by A.J. Smith (London: Penguin, 1996)

Drobnick, Jim (ed.), *The Smell Culture Reader*, Sensory Formations (Oxford: Berg, 2006)

Dugan, Holly, 'Shakespeare and the Senses', *Literature Compass*, 6 (2009), 726–40

—— *The Ephemeral History of Perfume: Scent and Sense in Early Modern England* (Baltimore, MD: Johns Hopkins University Press, 2011)

Edholm, Felicity, 'Beyond the Mirror: Women's Self-Portraits', in *Imagining Women: Cultural Representations and Gender* ed. by Francis Bonner and others (Cambridge: Polity Press, 1995)

Edwards, Elizabeth and Kaushik Bhaumik (eds), *Visual Sense: A Cultural Reader*, Sensory Formations (Oxford: Berg, 2008)

Elias, Norbert, *The Civilizing Process: The History of Manners* (New York: Urizen Books, 1978)

Elyot, Sir Thomas, *The Book Named the Governor*, ed. by S.E. Lehmberg, Everyman's Library, 227 (London: Dent, 1962)

Erasmus, Desiderius, 'On the Freedom of the Will', translated by E. Gordon Rupp, in *Luther and Erasmus: Free Will and Salvation* (Philadelphia, PA: Westminster Press, 1969)

—— 'Copia: Foundations of the Abundant Style (De duplici copia verborum ac rerum commentarii duo)', trans. and annotated by Betty I. Knott, in *Collected Works of Erasmus*, ed. by Craig R. Thompson, 79 vols (Toronto: University of Toronto Press, 1974–), XXIV, 279–659

Evelyn, John, *Diary of John Evelyn, Esq.*, ed. by William Bray (London: Bickers, 1906)

Farmer, Alan B., 'Print Culture and Reading Practices', in *Ben Jonson in Context*, ed. by Julie Sanders (Cambridge: Cambridge University Press, 2010), pp. 192–200

Fisher, Will, 'Staging the Beard', in *Staged Properties in Early Modern English Drama*, ed. Jonathan Gil Harris and Natasha Korda (Cambridge: Cambridge University Press, 2002), pp. 230–57

Fitzpatrick, Joan, 'Reading Early Modern Food: A Review Article', *Literature Compass*, 8 (2011), 118–29

Flachmann, Michael, '*Epicoene*: A Comic Hell for a Comic Sinner', *MaRDiE*, 1 (1984), 131–42

Folkerth, Wes, *The Sound of Shakespeare* (London: Routledge, 2002)

Foote Crow, Martha (ed.), *Elizabethan Sonnet-Cycles* (Chicago: McClurg, 1897)

Forscher Weiss, Susan, 'The Singing Hand', in *Writing on Hands: Memory and Knowledge in Early Modern Europe*, ed. by Claire Richter Sherman (Carlisle, PA: Trout Gallery and Folger Shakespeare Library, 2000), pp. 35–45

Gallagher, Lowell and Shankar Raman (eds), *Knowing Shakespeare: Senses, Embodiment and Cognition* (Basingstoke: Palgrave, 2010)

Garber, Marjorie and Nancy J. Vickers (eds), *The Medusa Reader* (New York and London: Routledge, 2003)

Garrard, Mary D., 'Here's Looking at Me: Sofonisba Anguissola and the Problem of the Woman Artist', *Renaissance Quarterly*, 47 (1994), 556–622

Garrioch, David, 'Sounds of the City: The Soundscape of Early Modern European Towns', *Urban History*, 30 (2003), 5–25

Gelfand, Laura, 'Sense and Simulacra: Manipulation of the Senses in Medieval Copies of Jerusalem', *Postmedieval*, 3 (2012), 407–22

Ghiberti, Lorenzo, *I Commentari*, ed. by O. Morisani (Naples: Riccardo Ricciardi, 1947)

Gigante, Denise, *Taste: A Literary History* (New Haven, CT: Yale University Press, 2005)

Goldstein, David, 'Shakespeare and Food: A Review Essay', *Literature Compass*, 6 (2009), 153–74

Grabes, Herbert, *The Mutable Glass: Mirror Imagery in Titles and Texts of the Middle Ages and the English Renaissance*, trans. by Gordon Collier (Cambridge: Cambridge University Press, 1982)

Gras, Henk K., 'Direct Evidence and Audience Response to *Twelfth Night*: The Case of John Manningham of the Middle Temple', *Shakespeare Studies*, 21 (1995), 109–54

Griffin, Benjamin, 'Nashe's Dedicatees', *Notes and Queries*, 44 (1997), 47–49

Guazzo, Stefano, *La Civile Conversation of M. Steeven Guazzo*, trans. by George Pettie (books 1–3, 1581) in *The Tudor Translations*, 2 vols. (Constable, 1925)

Hallahan, Hudson D., 'Silence, Eloquence, and Chatter in Jonson's *Epicoene*', *Huntington Library Quarterly*, 40 (1977), 117–27

Hansen, Miriam, 'Benjamin's Aura,' *Critical Inquiry*, 34 (2008), 336–76

Harvey, Elizabeth (ed.), *Sensible Flesh: On Touch in Early Modern Culture* (Philadelphia, PA: Pennsylvania University Press, 2003)

Heinemann, Margot, *Puritanism and Theatre: Thomas Middleton and Opposition Drama Under the Early Stuarts* (Cambridge: Cambridge University Press, 1980)

Herrick, Robert, *The Complete Poetry of Robert Herrick*, ed. by J. Max Patrick, rev. edn (New York: Norton, 1968)

Herz, Rachel, *Scent of Desire: Discovering our Enigmatic Sense of Smell* (New York: Harper Perennial, 2007)

Hillman, Richard, 'Antony, Hercules, and Cleopatra: "The Bidding of the Gods" and "the Subtlest Maze of All"', *Shakespeare Quarterly*, 38 (1987), 442–51

Hooke, Robert, *Posthumous Works of Robert Hooke*, ed. by Richard Westfall (New York: Johnson Reprint Corp, 1969)

Hope-Nicolson, Marjorie, 'Kepler, The *Somnium*, and John Donne', *Journal of the History of Ideas*, 1 (1940), 259–80

Howes, David, *Sensual Relations: Engaging the Senses in Culture and Social Theory* (Ann Arbor, MI: University of Michigan Press, 2003)

—— (ed.), *Empire of the Senses: The Sensual Culture Reader*, Sensory Formations (Oxford: Berg, 2005)

—— 'Hearing Scents, Tasting Sights: Toward a Cross-Cultural Multi-Modal Theory of Aesthetics', in *Art and the Senses*, ed. by Francesca Bacci and David Melcher (Oxford: Oxford University Press, 2011), pp. 161–81

Husserl, Edmund, 'A Phenomenology of Reason', in *General Introduction to a Pure Phenomenology* (The Hague: M. Nijhof, 1982)

Ichikawa, Mariko, '"*Maluolio Within*": Acting on the Threshold Between Onstage and Offstage Spaces', *Medieval and Renaissance Drama in England*, 18 (2005), 123–45

Jaeckle, Daniel, 'The Sixth Sense in Cleveland's "The Hecatomb to his Mistresse"', *Notes and Queries*, 54 (2007), 411–12

Jay, Martin, 'The Rise of Hermeneutics and the Crisis of Ocularcentrism', *Poetics Today*, 9 (1988), 307–26

—— *Downcast Eyes: The Denigration of Vision in Twentieth-Century French Thought* (Berkeley, CA: University of California Press, 1993)

Johansen, Thomas K., *The Powers of Aristotle's Soul* (Oxford: Oxford University Press, 2012)

Johnson, Bruce, '*Hamlet*: Voice, Music, Sound', *Popular Music*, 24 (2005), 257–67

Johnson, Geraldine A., 'Touch, Tactility, and the Reception of Sculpture in Early Modern Italy', in *A Companion to Art Theory*, ed. by Paul Smith and Carolyn Wilde (Oxford: Blackwell, 2002), pp. 61–75

Jonson, Ben, *Epicoene*, ed. by Richard Dutton, The Revels Plays (Manchester: Manchester University Press, 2003)

—— *Epicoene*, ed. by Roger Holdsworth, New Mermaids (London: A & C Black, 2005)

—— *The Cambridge Edition of the Plays of Ben Jonson*, general editors David Bevington, Martin Butler and Ian Donaldson, 6 vols (Cambridge: Cambridge University Press, 2012)

—— *The Works of Ben Jonson*, ed. by C.H. Herford and Percy Simpson (Oxford: Clarendon Press, 1925–52)

Kahn, Victoria, *Rhetoric, Prudence and Skepticism* (Ithaca, NY: Cornell University Press, 1985)

Karim-Cooper, Farah, *Cosmetics in Shakespearean and Renaissance Drama* (Edinburgh: Edinburgh University Press, 2006)

Keeble, N.H., 'To "Build in Sonnets Pretty Rooms?": Donne and the Renaissance Love Lyric", in *Donne and the Resources of Kind*, ed. by A.D Cousins and Damian Grace (Madison, NJ: Fairleigh Dickinson University Press, 2002), pp. 71–86

Kemp, Simon and Garth J.O. Fletcher, 'The Medieval Theory of the Inner Senses', *American Journal of Psychology*, 106 (1993), 559–76

Kermode, Frank, *Renaissance Essays: Shakespeare, Spenser, Donne* (London: Fontana, 1973)

Kerwin, William, *Beyond the Body* (Amherst and Boston: University of Massachusetts Press, 2005)

Ketterer, Elizabeth, '"Govern'd by Stops, Aw'd by Dividing Notes": The Functions of Music in the Extant Repertory of the Admiral's Men, 1594–1621' (unpublished doctoral thesis, University of Birmingham, 2009)

King, Anya, 'Tibetan Musk and Medieval Arab Perfumery', in *Islam and Tibet: Cultural Interactions Along the Musk Route*, ed. by Anna Akasoy, Charles S. Burnett and Ronit Yoeli-Tlalim (Aldershot: Ashgate, 2011), pp. 145–62

Klibansky, Raymond, Erwin Panofsky and Fritz Saxl, *Saturn and Melancholy*, trans. by E.S. Forster (Nendeln: Liechtenstein, 1979 [1964])

Korsmeyer, Carolyn (ed.), *The Taste Culture Reader: Experiencing Food and Drink*, Sensory Formations (Oxford: Berg, 2005)

Koslofsky, Craig, *Evening's Empire: A History of the Night in Early Modern Europe* (Cambridge: Cambridge University Press, 2011)

Krummel, Donald, *English Music Printing, 1553–1700* (London: Bibliographical Society, 1975)

Krummel, Donald and Stanley Sadie (eds), *Music Printing and Publishing* (Basingstoke: Macmillan, 1990)

Launert, Edmund, *Perfume and Pomanders: Scent and Scent Bottles* (Munich: Potterton, 1987)

Lesser, Zachary, *Renaissance Drama and the Politics of Publication: Readings in the English Book Trade* (Cambridge: Cambridge University Press, 2004)

Lindberg, David C., *Theories of Vision from Al-Kindi to Kepler* (Chicago: University of Chicago Press, 1976)

Lindley, David, *Shakespeare and Music* (London: Thomson, 2006)

Loades, D.M. (ed.), *Chronicles of the Tudor Kings* (Godalming: Bramley Books, 1996)

Lucretius, *On the Nature of the Universe*, trans. by R.E. Latham, rev. edn (London: Penguin, 1994)

—— *The Nature of Things*, trans. by A.E. Stallings (London: Penguin, 2007)

Lyly, John, 'Midas', in *Galatea/Midas*, ed. by George K. Hunter and David M. Bevington, The Revels Plays (Manchester: Manchester University Press, 2000)

MacDonald, Robert H. (ed.), *The Library of Drummond of Hawthornden* (Edinburgh: Edinburgh University Press, 1971)

Maclean, Hugh (ed.), *Ben Jonson and the Cavalier Poets* (New York: Norton, 1974)

Maguire, Laurie, 'Cultural Control in *The Taming of the Shrew*', *Renaissance Drama*, 26 (1995), 83–104

—— 'Petruccio and the Barber's Shop', *Studies in Bibliography*, 51 (1998), 117–26

—— 'Audience-Actor Boundaries and *Othello*', in *Proceedings of the British Academy – 181, 2010–11 Lectures* (Oxford: Oxford University Press for the British Academy, 2012)

Manningham, John, *Diary of John Manningham of the Middle Temple and of Bradbourne, Kent, Barrister-at-Law, 1602–3*, ed. John Bruce, Esq. (London: J.B. Nichols and Sons, 1868)

Marsh, Christopher, *Music and Society in Early Modern England* (Cambridge: Cambridge University Press, 2010)

Marston, John, *Antonio and Mellida*, ed. by G.K. Hunter (London: Edward Arnold, 1965)

—— *The Dutch Courtesan*, ed. by David Crane (London: A&C Black, 1997)

Massinger, Philip, *The Roman Actor*, ed. by Martin White (Manchester: Manchester University Press, 2007)

Masten, Jeffrey, 'Toward a Queer Address: The Taste of Letters and Early Modern Male Friendship', *GLQ: A Journal of Lesbian and Gay Studies*, 10 (2004), 367–84

Mazzeo, Tilar, *The Secret of Chanel No. 5: The Intimate History of the World's Most Famous Fragrance* (New York: Harper Collins, 2010)

McDermott, Jennifer Rae, '"The Melodie of Heaven": Sermonizing the Open Ear in Early Modern England', *Religion and the Senses in Early Modern Europe*, ed. by Wietse de Boer and Christine Göttler (Leiden: Brill, 2013), pp. 177–97

McGowan, Margaret M., *Dance in the Renaissance* (New Haven, CT: Yale University Press, 2008)

Melchior-Bonnet, Sabine, *The Mirror: A History*, trans. by Katherine H. Jewett (New York and London: Routledge, 2002)

Melville, James, *Memoirs of Sir James Melville of Halhill, 1535–1617*, ed. by A. Francis Steuart (London: Routledge, 1929)

Middleton, Thomas, *The Collected Works*, general editors Gary Taylor and John Lavagnino (Oxford: Clarendon Press, 2007)

Miller, William Ian, *The Anatomy of Disgust* (Cambridge, MA: Harvard University Press, 1997)

Moore, Dennis, 'Philisides and Mira: Autobiographical Allegory in *The Old Arcadia*', *Spenser Studies*, 3 (1982), 125–37

Moore, Mary, *Desiring Voices: Women Sonneteers and Petrarchism* (Carbondale, IL: Southern Illinois University Press, 2000)

Morris, Pam, *The Bakhtin Reader* (London: Arnold, 1994)

Moulton, Ian Frederick, *Before Pornography: Erotic Writing in Early Modern England* (Oxford: Oxford University Press, 2000)

Neill, Michael, '"Exeunt with a Dead March": Funeral Pageantry on the Shakespearean Stage', in *Pageantry in the Shakespearean Theater*, ed. by David M. Bergeron (Athens, GA: University of Georgia Press, 1985), pp. 153–93

—— *Issues of Death: Mortality and Identity in English Renaissance Tragedy* (Oxford: Clarendon Press, 1997)

Nevile, Jennifer, *The Eloquent Body: Dance and Humanist Culture in Fifteenth-century Italy* (Bloomington, IN: Indiana University Press, 2004)

Nicholl, Charles, *A Cup Of News* (London: Routledge and Kegan Paul, 1984)

Nordenfalk, Carl, 'The Five Senses in Late Medieval and Renaissance Art', *Journal of the Warburg and Courtauld Institutes*, 28 (1985), 1–22

Novarr, David, '"Amor Vincit Omnia": Donne and the Limits of Ambiguity', *The Modern Language Review*, 82 (1987), 286–92

O'Callaghan, Michelle, *The English Wits: Literature and Sociability in Early Modern England* (Cambridge: Cambridge University Press, 2007)

Paoletti, John T. and Gary M. Radke (eds), *Art in Renaissance Italy* (London: Laurence King, 1997)

Parker, Patricia, 'Barbers and Barbary', *Renaissance Drama*, 33 (2005), 201–44

Pascal, Blaise, *Pensées*, trans. by Honor Levi (Oxford: Oxford University Press, 1995)

Pawlisch, Hans S., *Sir John Davies and the Conquest of Ireland* (Cambridge: Cambridge University Press, 1985)

Pheby, Helen, 'Contemporary Art', in *Museum Materialities: Objects, Engagements, Interpretations*, ed. by Sandra Dudley (New York: Routledge, 2010), pp. 71–88

Pickett, Holly Crawford, 'Dramatic Nostalgia and Spectacular Conversion in Dekker and Massinger's *The Virgin Martyr*', *Studies in English Literature*, 49 (2009), 437–62

Plato, *Timaeus and Critas*, trans. by Desmond Lee (Harmondsworth: Penguin, 1965 [1977])

Prater, Andreas, *Venus at her Mirror: Velázquez and the Art of Nude Painting* (London and New York: Prestel, 2002)

Quiviger, François, *The Sensory World of Italian Renaissance Art* (London: Reaktion Books, 2010)

Rather, L.J., 'Thomas Fienus' (1567–1631) Dialectical Investigation of the Imagination as Cause and Cure of Bodily Disease', *Bulletin of the History of Medicine*, 41 (1967), 349–67

Ricks, Christopher, 'Wordplay in Middleton's *Women Beware Women*', *Review of English Studies*, 12 (1961), 238–50

Roberts, Sasha, 'Shakespeare "creepes into the womens closets about bedtime": Women Reading in a Room of Their Own', in *Renaissance Configurations: Voices/Bodies/ Spaces, 1580–1690*, ed. by Gordon McMullan (Basingstoke: Macmillan, 1998), pp. 30–63

Robertson, Patricia R., '"This Herculean Roman": Shakespeare's Antony and the Hercules Myth', *Publications of the Arkansas Philological Association*, 10 (1984), 65–75

Ronchi, Vasco, *Optics: The Science of Vision*, trans. by Edward Rosen (New York: Dover, [1957] 1991)

Ryken, Lelan, *Worldly Saints: The Puritans as They Really Were* (Grand Rapids, MI: Zondervan, 1986)

Sanger, Alice and Siv Tove Kulbrandstad Walker (eds), *Sense and the Senses in Early Modern Art and Cultural Practice* (Farnham: Ashgate, 2012)

Santore, Cathy, 'The Tools of Venus', *Renaissance Studies*, 11 (1997), 179–207

Schafer, R. Murray, *The Soundscape* (Rochester, VT: Destiny Books, 1994)

Schanfield, Lillian, '"Tickled with Desire": A View of Eroticism in Herrick's Poetry', *Literature & Psychology*, 39 (1993), 63–83

Schoenfeldt, Michael, *Bodies and Selves in Early Modern England* (Cambridge: Cambridge University Press, 1999)

Searle, John R., '"Las Meninas" and the Paradoxes of Pictorial Representation', *Critical Inquiry*, 6 (1980), 477–88

Secular Lyrics of the XIVth and XVth Centuries, ed. by Rossell Hope Robbins (Oxford: Oxford University Press, 1955)

Sennett, Richard, 'Resistance', in *The Auditory Culture Reader*, ed. by Michael Bull and Les Back, Sensory Formations (Oxford: Berg, 2003), pp. 481–84

Serres, Michel, *The Five Senses: A Philosophy of Mingled Bodies (I)*, trans. by Margaret Sankey and Peter Cowley (London: Continuum, 2008)

Shakespeare, William, *A Midsummer Night's Dream*, ed. by Harold Brooks, The Arden Shakespeare Second Series (London: Methuen, 1979)

—— *Antony and Cleopatra*, ed. by Michael Neill, The Oxford Shakespeare (Oxford: Oxford University Press, 1994)

—— *The Complete Works*, ed. by Stanley Wells and Gary Taylor, 2nd edn (Oxford: Clarendon Press, 2005)

—— *The Taming of the Shrew*, ed. by Barbara Hodgdon, The Arden Shakespeare Third Series (London: A & C Black, 2010)

Shannon, Laurie, *The Accommodated Animal: Cosmopolity in Shakespearean Locales* (Chicago: University of Chicago Press, 2013)

Shearman, John, *Only Connect: Art and the Spectator in the Italian Renaissance* (Washington DC: Princeton University Press, 1998)

Sherman, William H., 'What Did Renaissance Readers Write in Their Books?', in *Books and Readers in Early Modern England: Material Studies*, ed. by Jennifer Andersen and Elizabeth Sauer (Philadelphia, PA: University of Pennsylvania Press, 2002), pp. 119–37

—— *Used Books: Marking Readers in Renaissance England* (Philadelphia, PA: University of Pennsylvania Press, 2008)

Shirley, Frances Ann, *Shakespeare's Use of Off-Stage Sounds* (Lincoln, NE: University of Nebraska Press, 1963)

Shuger, Debora, 'The "I" of the Beholder: Renaissance Mirrors and the Reflexive Mind', in *Renaissance Culture and the Everyday*, ed. by Patricia Fumerton and Simon Hunt (Philadelphia, PA: University of Pennsylvania Press, 1999)

Sidney, Philip, 'Astrophil and Stella', in *The Major Works*, ed. by Katherine Duncan-Jones (Oxford: Oxford University Press, 2002), pp. 153–211

—— *The Old Arcadia*, ed. by Katherine Duncan-Jones (Oxford: Oxford University Press, 1985)

Siebers, Tobin, *The Mirror of Medusa* (New Zealand: Cyber Editions, 2000)

Skiles, Howard, *The Politics of Courtly Dancing in Early Modern England* (Amherst, MA: University of Massachusetts Press, 1998)

Smith, Bruce R., *The Acoustic World of Early Modern England: Attending to the O-Factor* (Chicago: University of Chicago Press, 1999)

—— *The Key of Green: Passion and Perception in Renaissance Culture* (Chicago: University of Chicago Press, 2009)

Smith, Helen, '"More swete vnto the eare | than holsome for ye mynde": Embodying Early Modern Women's Reading', *Huntington Library Quarterly*, 73 (2010), 413–32

Stallybrass, Peter, 'Reading the Body: *The Revenger's Tragedy* and the Jacobean Theater of Consumption', *Renaissance Drama*, 18 (1987), 121–48

Stern, Tiffany, 'Taking Part: Actors and Audience on the Stage at Blackfriars', in *Inside Shakespeare: Essays on the Blackfriars Stage*, ed. by Paul Menzer (Selinsgrove, PA: Susquehanna University Press, 2006), pp. 35–53

—— *Documents of Performance in Early Modern England* (Cambridge: Cambridge University Press, 2009)

Stewart, Susan, *Poetry and the Fate of the Senses* (Chicago: University of Chicago Press, 2002)

Stoichita, Victor I., *A Short History of the Shadow* (London: Reaktion Books, 1997)

Straznicky, Marta, 'Reading through the Body: Women and Printed Drama', in *The Book of the Play: Playwrights, Stationers, and Readers in Early Modern England*, ed. by Marta Straznicky (Amherst, MA: University of Massachusetts Press, 2006), pp. 59–79

Strunk, Oliver (ed.), *Source Readings in Music History*, 2nd edn, rev. by Leo Treitler (New York: Norton, 1998)

Targoff, Ramie, *John Donne, Body and Soul* (Chicago: University of Chicago Press, 2008)

Thompson, William Forde, Phil Graham and Frank A. Russo, 'Seeing Music Performance: Visual Influences on Perception and Experience', *Semiotica: Journal of the International Association for Semiotic Studies*, 156 (2005), 203–27

Tomlinson, Gary, *Music in Renaissance Magic: Toward a Historiography of Others* (Chicago: University of Chicago Press, 1993)

Vale, Marcia, *The Gentleman's Recreations* (Cambridge: Brewer, 1977)

van Kampen, Claire, 'Music and Aural Texture at Shakespeare's Globe', in *Shakespeare's Globe: A Theatrical Experiment*, ed. by Christie Carson and Farah Karim-Cooper (Cambridge: Cambridge University Press, 2008), pp. 79–89

Vinge, Louise, *The Five Senses: Studies in a Literary Tradition* (Lund: LiberLäromedel, 1975)

Walker, Julia M., *Medusa's Mirrors: Spenser, Shakespeare, Milton, and the Metamorphosis of the Female Self* (London: Associated University Presses, 1998)

Wall, Wendy, *The Imprint of Gender: Authorship and Publication in the English Renaissance* (Ithaca, NY: Cornell University Press, 1993)

—— 'Circulating Texts in Early Modern England', in *Teaching Tudor and Stuart Women Writers* (New York: Modern Language Association of America, 2000), pp. 35–51

Ward, John M., 'Apropos "The Oulde Measures"', *Records of Early English Drama*, 18 (1993), 2–21

Watson, Jacqueline, '"He writes, he railes, he jests, he courts, what not,/ And all from out his huge long scraped stock/ Of well penn'd playes": Learning the Performance of Courtiership at the Early Modern Inns of Court', in *Spectatorship at the Elizabethan Court*, ed. by Susanne Scholz and Daniel Dornhofer, special issue of *Zeitspruenge. Forschungen zur Fruehen Neuzeit*, 17 (2013), 63–83

Whigham, Frank, *Ambition and Privilege: The Social Tropes of Elizabethan Courtesy Theory* (Berkeley, CA: University of California Press, 1984)

Whitney, Charles, *Early Responses to Renaissance Drama* (Cambridge: Cambridge University Press, 2006)

Wilcox, Helen, 'New Directions: *Women Beware Women* and the Arts of Looking and Listening', in *Women Beware Women: A Critical Guide*, ed. by Andrew Hiscock (London: Continuum, 2011), pp. 121–38

Williams, Nevile, *The Life and Times of Elizabeth I* (London: Weidenfeld & Nicolson, 1992)

Wilson, D.R., *The Basse Dance Handbook* (New York: Pendragon Press, 2012)

—— 'Dancing in the Inns of Court', *Historical Dance*, 2.5 (1986–7), 3–16

Wilson, Jr, G.R., 'The Interplay of Perception and Reflection: Mirror Imagery in Donne's Poetry', *Studies in English Literature, 1500–1900*, 9 (1969), 107–21

Winkler, Amanda Eubanks, *O Let Us Howle Some Heavy Note: Music for Witches, the Melancholic, and the Mad on the Seventeenth-Century English Stage* (Bloomington, IN: Indiana University Press, 2006)

Woolgar, C.M., *The Senses in Late Medieval England* (New Haven, CT: Yale University Press, 2006)

Wroth, Mary, *The Poems of Lady Mary Wroth*, ed. by Josephine Roberts (Baton Rouge, LO: Louisiana State University Press, 1983)

—— 'Love's Victory', in *Early Modern Women's Writings. An Anthology 1560–1700*, ed. by Paul Salzman (Oxford: Oxford University Press, 2000), pp. 82–133

—— *The First Part of the Countess of Montgomery's Urania*, ed. by Josephine Roberts (Tempe, AZ: Arizona Center for Medieval and Renaissance Studies, 2005 [1995])

Yates, Frances, *Occult Philosophy in the Elizabethan Age* (London: Routledge, 2001)

Yglesias, Caren, 'Seeing Air', in *Visuality/Materiality: Images, Objects, and Practices*, ed. by Gillian Rose and Divya P. Tolia-Kelly (Farnham: Ashgate, 2012), pp. 85–108

Index

Page numbers in italics signify an illustration